The Climber's Guide

to the High Sierra

A Sierra Club Totebook®

The Climber's Guide to the High Sierra

by Steve Roper

Sierra Club Books San Francisco

1976

Roper, Steve.
    The climber's guide to the High Sierra.

    (A Sierra Club Totebook)
    Includes index.
    1. Sierra Nevada Mountains—Description and travel—
Guide-books. 2. Rock climbing—Sierra Nevada Mountains.
I. Title.
F868.S5R59   917.94'4'045   75-45108
ISBN 0-87156-147-6

Frontispiece: Summit spire of Mt. Darwin. Drawing by Carol Ingram.

Production by Charlsen + Johansen & Others
Manufactured in the United States of America

Contents

Acknowledgments

From the early 1930s various people have carefully collected records of ascents in the High Sierra. When the first climber's guide was published in 1954, it was the work of numerous authors. To these authors I owe an enormous debt, for it was these unpaid, unheralded climbers who wrote the definitive source work for all future Sierra guidebook authors. Although the actual words of these writers have not been perpetuated in this book, their research and labor are not forgotten—this guide is largely an update of the old material, with the exception of the addition of many new technical rockclimbing routes. The following persons had a hand in writing and final production of the original guidebook: Al Baxter, George Bloom, Dave Brower, Bill Dunmire, Louis Elliott, Alan Hedden, Mildred Jentsch, Fred Jones, Jim Koontz, Dick Leonard, John Mendenhall, Ruth Mendenhall, Dave Nelson, Art Reyman, Ed Robbins, Mr. and Mrs. William Shand and William Shand, Jr., Bob Smith, Walter Starr, Bob Swift, Ray Van Aken, and Hervey Voge.

The next two guidebooks, published in 1965 and 1972, respectively, were essentially the same as their progenitor; a few road and trail changes and a handful of new routes were added. Hervey Voge, editor of the original book, was again responsible for the 1965 book, while Andrew Smatko was in charge of the 1972 edition.

This guide has been totally rewritten and contains a large number of new technical routes. Much of the recent information was gleaned from the *American Alpine Journal* and *Ascent*, the Sierra Club's mountaineering journal. Other information was obtained from individuals. Tom Gerughty was for several years the custodian of Tuolumne Meadows rockclimbing lore and was generous in his help. Vern Clevenger and Tom Higgins, among others, were also important sources for this region, which is rapidly becoming known as one of the country's finest climbing areas.

Information for the many new technical routes in the Palisades was supplied by the late Don Jensen, who gave me excellent descriptions gained from years of familiarity with the region.

For the multitude of new climbs in the Whitney area, Galen Rowell and Fred Beckey were invaluable sources. Rowell is unfortunate enough to live within a mile of my house and so was bombarded with hundreds of petty questions which he answered accurately and with little outward show of impatience. Beckey sent me scores of letters scrawled on a bizarre assortment of stationary, telling of his many new routes and giving me names and clues for further research.

Others who helped in various ways are: Roger Breedlove, Greg Donaldson, Don Lauria, Mike Loughman, Andy Smatko, and Walt Vennum.

The maps were produced by Allen Steck, and the sketches were drawn by Carol Ingram.

I am extremely grateful to Kathy Larson and Chuck Pratt for editorial assistance. The book has been much improved by their suggestions.

The *Sierra Club Bulletin*, "that model of all mountaineering publications," was a source I studied every day for months. Almost all of the quoted material in the historical sections comes from this journal, and the reader interested in further information about certain eras and climbs will have an enjoyable time perusing back issues of the *Bulletin*.

The topographical maps opposite the chapter openings are used with permission of the United States Geological Survey. The scale is an inch to a mile.

Introduction

Bordered by a great agricultural area on one side and an inhospitable desert on the other, California's Sierra Nevada is the highest mountain range in the contiguous United States, and some say it is the most beautiful. It has almost everything a mountaineer desires: rugged peaks, glaciers, and splendid, isolated chunks of granite. And these attractions are set in a lovely locale of lake basins, streams, and high meadows. The rock is generally good, the weather during the summer months excellent, and the access is easy. What more could a climber want? If there is any disadvantage, it lies in the hordes of people who have recently found the range to their liking. The John Muir Trail, which runs the length of the High Sierra, is a very crowded corridor in mid-summer, yet the climber who is willing to wander just a few miles from it will find untrammeled lake basins at the bases of peaks which see fewer than ten ascents a season.

Long ago the Spaniards saw the range and gave it its present name, which means "snowy range of mountains." In former times the 300-mile-long uplift posed a serious threat to east—west travel, and even now there are no roads across its most rugged portion for 175 miles. The crest of the range, which runs from northwest to southeast, contains scores of peaks above 13,000 feet, and eleven peaks rise above 14,000 feet. Nestled under the western side of the crest are hundreds of lakes, some set in high glacial basins and some surrounded by lush meadows.

The western side of the range slopes gently. It is nearly fifty miles from the Central Valley to the crest, and much of this distance is blanketed by heavy and varied forests. Scattered amid these forests are groves of "big trees," or sequoias. These enormous trees, endemic to the western slope of the Sierra, are one of the great tourist attractions of the West, and a national park has been named for them.

The summits themselves are often easiest from the west, and

almost every Sierra peak has at least one side which presents no problem for the climber. The north and east faces, however, tend to be steeper and have often been sculpted by glaciers.

The eastern escarpment of the High Sierra is a magnificent sight. Along its base runs U.S. Highway 395, and from it the traveler can gaze upward nearly two vertical miles to see the range's culmination, Mt. Whitney. Roads which lead into the range begin in vast fields of sagebrush, wind through the pinyon-juniper belt, and finally pass through several varieties of pine. Driving up such a road one can experience a temperature drop of twenty degrees.

Much of the rock in the Sierra is granite of excellent quality; some, in fact, is world-renowned by rockclimbers. The rock in the high country is heavily fractured, and although the rock itself may be solid, the disjointed structure makes for many loose blocks. The vast amount of rubble on ledges is proof that the mountains are continually falling to pieces. In addition to igneous rock, a few places such as the Ritter Range, Black Divide, and the Kaweahs are principally metamorphic, and some exceptionally loose rock is found in these areas. The climber must take every precaution when climbing on this type of rock.

Glaciers were active in the range for many centuries, and although only a few remnants survive, evidence of them abounds. The Kern River Valley, remarkably straight and U-shaped, is one of the finest examples of glacial action in the High Sierra, but almost every other valley shows prominent signs of the ice sheets that once scoured them.

This book covers the area from the northern border of Yosemite National Park to the southern boundary of Sequoia National Park, a distance of 135 miles. This is the rugged region generally known as the High Sierra. Included in the guide are named peaks above 10,000 feet and unnamed peaks if they are high, significant, or have interesting routes (see the following discussion on ''What is a Peak?''). Also included are a few selected rockclimbing areas on the periphery of the High Sierra. Numerous other rockclimbing areas in the low western foothills are not included. All of the region covered lies under federal jurisdiction, and permits for access and camping are required (see "Regulations").

A superb trail system is found in the High Sierra. Scores of well-marked, well-graded trails originate on both sides of the main crest and connect with the John Muir Trail, a high-level route completed in 1938.

Excellent topographical maps, published by the U.S. Geological Survey, cover the Sierra. These maps, with a scale of an inch to the mile, are indispensable for locating most of the peaks in this book since all distances and directions come from them. U.S. Forest Service maps are worthless for use in the high country but are invaluable for finding recently constructed approach roads, especially on the western slopes of the range.

Climbing History

Indians were the first climbers of the High Sierra, as has been shown by arrowhead fragments found high on many peaks, including Mt. Whitney. But the Indians left no records, and neither did the Spaniards, early military expeditions, prospectors, or sheepherders who followed. However, it is not likely that many major summits were reached during these early days, for as we all know, there are relatively few reasons to stand atop a mountain.

During the Gold Rush thousands crossed the Sierra Nevada, but they all carefully avoided the highest and most rugged part of the range. By the time of the Civil War, California had become a populated state, yet little was known about its resources or geography. It was to rectify this deplorable situation that the legislature created the California Geological Survey in 1860. For a few years the Whitney Survey, as it soon became called after its leader, Josiah Whitney, did work in other parts of the state, moving into the Sierra foothills only in the summer of 1863. After spending time in the fabulous, recently discovered Yosemite Valley, the Survey climbed up toward Tuolumne Meadows. There William Brewer, field leader

of the Survey, Charles Hoffmann, and Whitney climbed a prominent peak which they named Mt. Hoffmann. This is the first known
ascent of a major peak in the High Sierra (Mt. Tom, near Bishop,
may have been climbed in 1860). A few days later Brewer and
Hoffmann climbed a very high summit which they named Mt.
Dana, after the pre-eminent American geologist of the era. They
thought the peak was higher than Mt. Shasta, which at that time was
considered the highest point in the state. The next day Whitney
climbed the peak to see the view; it was his last important Sierra
climb, and he soon left the range to direct from afar. From then on
Brewer and his associates dominated the Survey's mountaineering.

Without question, 1864 is the key year in the history of early
Sierra climbing and exploration. That year the Survey was composed of Brewer, Hoffmann, Clarence King, James Gardiner, and
the group's packer, Richard Cotter. Leaving Oakland in late May,
they rode their mounts eastward. It was the driest summer in many
years, and the party suffered in the oppressive heat. Mummified
carcasses of cattle lay everywhere and dusty whirlwinds darted
across the grasslands. It must have been a welcome relief to reach
the mountains, which they did in early July in the vicinity of the
Kings River. Although there had been rumors of a great canyon in
the area which rivaled Yosemite, no one had yet described it to the
outside world. When Brewer's party finally came into the canyon,
they were stunned—it *was* almost as spectacular as Yosemite,
though it lacked waterfalls and monolithic cliffs. In the area of
Kings Canyon they made several climbs, and members of the
Survey immediately named one of these peaks Mt. Brewer. From its
summit they saw a very high peak to the southeast. Thinking that it
must be the highest point in the range (Mt. Dana had already been
discredited), King and Cotter longed for it, and their epic five-day
trek, described in a later chapter, was the first time in America's
history that such mountainous and inhospitable terrain had been
traversed.

A few weeks later members of the Survey crossed the range at
Kearsarge Pass and dropped down into the Owens Valley. Although

they visited a few more areas that summer, this is the last we hear of the Whitney Survey, for it soon completed its work and disbanded.

In the next few years many travelers came to the mountains to see the great canyons and big trees which had been gaining notoriety. One of these visitors was John Muir, who arrived in Yosemite Valley in 1868 for a brief stay. The following year he became a supervisor of sheepherders, a job that left him much free time to study the landscape. During the next few years Muir became a self-educated expert on the ecology of the Sierra. While in Tuolumne Meadows in 1869, he made the first ascent of the sharp and beautiful Cathedral Peak—this involved some difficult climbing of a nature not yet seen in this country. Although his mountaineering exploits are not as well known as his later geological theories, descriptive writings, and long struggles to exclude sheep and lumbermen from his beloved mountains, Muir's solo ascents of Mt. Ritter, Mt. Whitney, and many other peaks (mentioned only obliquely in his writings) place him among the first rank of early American mountaineers.

Though much country had been explored by the early 1890s, there were many blanks on the maps, and relatively few peaks had been climbed. Yet, remarkably, someone had already envisioned a trail stretching the length of the range. The idea had come to Theodore Solomons in 1884, when as a youth he had been herding cattle in the Central Valley and had been overwhelmed by a view of the Sierra on a pristine day. During the early 1890s Solomons set out summer after summer, seeking the most feasible path for his "high mountain route." Although he is best remembered for his explorations around the headwaters of the San Joaquin River and for many of the place names he bestowed in this area, the John Muir Trail, begun in 1915, is perhaps his greatest legacy to the Sierra.

Another important figure of this era was Joseph N. LeConte, the son of a famous geologist who had visited Muir in Yosemite in 1870. Barely five feet in height, "Little Joe" explored watersheds, climbed many peaks, made a splendid set of photographs, and drew the first accurate maps of much of the Sierra. Like Solomons,

LeConte was a charter member of the Sierra Club, which had been founded in 1892. His maps, distributed to club members, materially contributed to further exploration of the range. Club outings, which began in 1901 under the leadership of William Colby, brought more and more people into the mountains, in keeping with the club's by-laws "to render accessible the mountain regions. . . ."

James Hutchinson was the next prominent figure in the history of Sierra mountaineering. He was already thirty-two when, in 1899, he made his initial Sierra first ascent. During the next twenty years he compiled the most enviable first-ascent record any Sierra climber will ever have; a partial list of his peaks includes Matterhorn Peak, Mt. Mills, Mt. Abbot, Mt. Humphreys, North Palisade, and Black Kaweah.

Of all the men who have ever climbed in the Sierra, none was so legendary as Norman Clyde. A scholar of the classics, Clyde migrated west in the early part of the century, teaching at rural schools, but never staying in one place for very long. He seems to have been born with wanderlust. Clyde worked on his master's degree at Berkeley for a few years but dropped out over a dispute in curriculum. The following summer he made two first ascents in Yosemite. A curious gap of six years followed, but in 1920 he began to totally dominate the climbing history of the range. He moved to the east side of the Sierra in 1924 to become principal of the high school in Independence. He was forty years old in the summer of 1925 and later wrote, "I sometimes think I climbed enough peaks this summer to render me a candidate for a padded cell—at least some people look at the matter in that way." Clyde was involved in a Halloween scandal, in 1927, when he fired shots over the heads of pranksters who were trying to intimidate him. It was not thought proper for a high school principal to behave in such a manner, so Clyde left that job and for the next forty years worked at odd jobs in the mountains, climbing at every opportunity. It is thought that he made over a thousand ascents in the range; his first ascents and new routes number around 130. If, as someone has said, the mark of a true mountaineer is his willingness to repeat climbs, then Clyde qualifies as few others are ever likely to do. He had many favorite peaks and would climb them year after year—he apparently ascended Mt. Thompson fifty times.

Clyde was famous for his huge packs, and it was a rare day when one would weigh less than ninety pounds. Guns, axes, cast-iron pots, and books in Greek all contributed to his monstrous Trapper Nelson. Although Clyde did his last new route in 1946, he attended Sierra Club Base Camps and High Trips in the capacity of woodcutter and guide until 1970, when he retired at the age of eighty-five. Two years later he died in Big Pine.

In 1931 Robert L.M. Underhill, an East Coast mountaineer well versed in the school of European rope management, came to California at the invitation of Francis Farquhar, an early climber and later a respected Sierra historian. The two had met the previous summer in Canada, and Farquhar thought it would be a good idea if Californians learned something about proper rope techniques. The pair gathered a small group of interested and talented climbers and went on a grand tour of the Sierra. Several fine first ascents resulted and a new age of California climbing began. Rockclimber-mountaineers such as Raffi Bedayn, Dave Brower, Glen Dawson, Jules Eichorn, Richard Leonard, and Hervey Voge put up scores of difficult routes in Yosemite Valley and the High Sierra during the 1930s. These routes were of a standard little dreamed of by Muir, LeConte, or Hutchinson, involving high-angle rock and elaborate rope techniques to safeguard the participants. Few of the climbs in the High Sierra required a rope, but the confidence gained from the teachings of Underhill was invaluable. Leonard later wrote that if he were to fall, his first thought would be, "What would Underhill say of my technique?"

During the years after World War II most of the noteworthy climbing in the range was done by members of the Sierra Club outing groups. Since many of the peaks had already been ascended, the emphasis was on new routes on a multitude of virgin ridges and faces.

Rockclimbers "discovered" the big walls of the Sierra in the late

1950s. At first only the most prominent faces were climbed: Mt. Whitney's true east face in 1959, the southwest face of Mt. Conness in 1959, and the great east wall of Keeler Needle the following year. The leader of the last two climbs was Warren Harding, a legendary Yosemite rockclimber. By the late 1960s hidden walls had been ferreted out, and though these were usually not more than a thousand feet high, they were steep and difficult.

History of the Guidebook

It was during the early 1930s that the idea of collecting information on Sierra peaks was conceived. Richard Leonard wrote many years later, "I started 'Mountain Records of the Sierra Nevada' in 1932 because of a bragging, inaccurate record I found on the summit of Mt. Starr King. The fellow was claiming a second ascent about 55 years after the third ascent." Information on 890 peaks was gathered in the next few years, and in 1937 Leonard published a section on the Sawtooth Ridge in the *Sierra Club Bulletin*. Other sections appeared in subsequent issues until World War II intervened. In the early 1950s the Sierra Club gave Hervey Voge a cardboard carton full of papers and the discouraging job of collating material from what turned out to be twenty-three authors. Yet the 1954 guidebook which resulted from Voge's labors was a masterpiece of order and accuracy. A slightly revised edition was brought out in 1965. Seven years later Andrew Smatko, a veteran of 600 Sierra ascents, came out with an edition unchanged from the previous books with the exception of the addition of several hundred newly discovered peaks.

The present guidebook is totally rewritten, and it includes data on all significant Sierra summits as well as information on the hundreds of technical rock climbs which have been accomplished in the last fifteen years.

A wave of anti-guidebook feeling has surfaced in the past few years. Spearheaded by a small, elite group, the sentiment seems to be that a guidebook speeds the ruination of a climbing area. There are many differing opinions on this topic, and it is obvious that, in addition to guidebooks, added leisure time, climbing schools, mass publicity, organized outings, and the new interest in ecology have all hastened the infiltration of "our" mountains by people who "shouldn't be there." As one result of this anti-guidebook feeling, some climbers have been reluctant to part with information about new routes, thinking that this will stem the hordes, at least for a few years. In some ways I symphathize with this sentiment and have made only a half-hearted attempt to pry this information out of climbers who feel strongly about the subject. Therefore, there are a number of routes which have been done but which do not appear herein.

What is a Peak?

The 1972 guidebook to the High Sierra was somewhat controversial in that several hundred new peaks were added over the previous edition's total. These peaks didn't suddenly grow during those seven years, nor did the mapmakers go wild. Many of the new peaks were simply ends of spurs, bumps on a ridge, or sub-summits of other mountains. Most of the peaks had as their first ascenders those who in a former day would have been called explorers but now could only be thought of as peakbaggers, interested primarily in trudging endlessly over heaps of stones, building cairns, and inserting their business cards into specially designed cannisters especially carried for this purpose. But perhaps I am being too harsh. They're having their fun.

I have deleted several hundred of these peaks, partly for space considerations, but mainly because of their insignificance. The criteria used to eliminate them are as follows: north of Mono Pass, in the Mt. Abbot region, peaks under 12,000 feet which are un-named and class 1 and 2 by their existing routes have been deleted. South of Mono Pass, unnamed peaks below 12,500 feet without class 3+ existing routes have been eliminated. Therefore, if there is any question about a contour circle on the map, and it is not in this book, assume either that it has been climbed and that all routes are easy, or that it is unclimbed. The latter choice is given somewhat facetiously since by now there are probably no unclimbed peaks in the range. The lack of a cairn is not evidence of a first ascent; more likely an Indian, sheepherder, early pioneer, or perhaps Norman Clyde simply didn't think it worthwhile to risk a hernia lugging around heavy stones and arranging them into a symmetrical pile.

Many of the names in this guidebook are unofficial in that they are not on record with the U.S. Board on Geographic Names. All such unofficial names have been placed in quotation marks in their primary listing. Five different types of primary listings occur:

Mt. Whitney (14,494)—A named peak with its elevation.

Gendarme Peak (Pk. 13,241, 1 N of Mt. Aggasiz—A recent official name, not shown on the map, with its elevation and location (one mile north of Mt. Aggasiz) from a point which *is* on the map.

"Cloudripper" (Pk. 13,501, 1 ESE of Chocolate Pk.)—A local or climbers' name for a landmark, not shown on the map, plus its elevation and location.

Peak 13,356 (1.1 ENE of Chocolate Pk.)—An unnamed peak, but shown on the map as an exact elevation.

Peak 13,280+ (0.5 SE of Mt. Darwin)—An unnamed peak, represented on the map as a closed contour circle. The peak is higher than 13,280 feet but less than 13,360, since contour intervals on present Sierra maps are eighty feet.

Route Descriptions

Users of the previous High Sierra guidebooks will immediately notice a major change in the format of the route description: there is no record of the first ascent. This information, of limited interest to most climbers, has been relegated to an appendix. Scores of peaks in the previous editions have such entries as: "Class 1 from any direction. First ascent on June 28, 1914 by George Hanover III, Betty Tudor, Charlie Stuart, Mary Scott, Dick Lionheart, and seven other Sierra Club members who arrived on top ten minutes after the first group. Sierra Club Register Number 31 was placed on top. It was still there twenty-two years later when Norman Clyde led a party of eighteen Sierra Clubbers to the summit.'' This description does not seem particularly relevant to me.

Words such as chute, gully, chimney, couloir, and arete are now so much a part of the modern climber's lexicon that they will not be defined here. All geographical directions given are predicated on the vertical lines on the map (i.e., true north) rather than the needle of a compass. Directions such as right and left are given with the presumption that the climber is facing the center of the mountain.

A word should be said about variations. On most Sierra peaks there are scores of routes from which to choose. The guide often mentions that such-and-such a face has a class 2 route; in actuality, there might be ten class 2 routes within a few hundred yards. When the guide says to follow the left side of a ridge, it doesn't mean that the ridge itself or its right side won't go—it just means that someone went on the left side once and *reported* it.

Approach information has been radically shortened; the maps of the Sierra are generally very accurate and will get the climber close to his objective. Unless the information is crucial, I decline to tell prospective Sierra climbers where to cross streams, how to avoid a brushy patch, or on which side a rock band must be turned. Technical rockclimbing descriptions are often very brief also, for the same purpose: let's get some adventure back into climbing!

Rating System

Most mountaineers will be familiar with the old Sierra Club rating system, which puts all climbs into a class 1 to 5 category. Basically, class 1 is hiking. Few peaks in the Sierra are as easy as walking up a trail, so this rating rarely occurs.

Class 2 is the most common rating in this book. Most Sierra peaks are composed of talus, some of which can be unstable; therefore it's helpful to have good balance and quick reactions. The hands sometimes come into play, not so much for grabbing onto a hold as for keeping steady amid large blocks. Rubber-soled shoes are essential. Small leaps must often be made between boulders, and a spill can result in a sprained ankle or a bad scrape. When a heavy pack is carried, the balance problem can become acute, and backpackers accustomed to trail walking will find class 2 passes long and extremely fatiguing, though little potential danger is involved.

Class 3, on the other hand, begins to involve the climber in dangerous situations. Steep or large talus can be class 3; more often class 3 climbing is found among shattered blocks on a face or ridge. The exposure, or drop, is often such that a beginner feels a bit queasy about being where he or she is. Handholds and footholds are necessary; these will be quite large and easy to locate. Imagine climbing a steep, narrow staircase which has been placed on the outside of a tall building without benefit of a railing: scary but easy. A rope should be carried if there is a beginner or an unsteady person in the group.

Class 4 usually involves steep rock, much smaller holds, and great exposure. Whereas a class 3 fall might result in a broken leg, an unroped fall on class 4 could be your last. Ropes should be carried and used. Proper knowledge of knots, belay techniques, and rappelling is obligatory.

Class 5, which for the rockclimber is sub-divided into twelve categories (5.0 through 5.11), is difficult climbing requiring protection. This protection can take the form of tied-off flakes and natural projections; these are extremely common in the high country. On more monolithic rock, nuts must be used. In general, a class 5 climb is quite steep, and the available holds, often less than an inch wide, must be searched for. Techniques such as jamming and liebacking come into play. Proficient rope management is mandatory.

Aid climbing is uncommon in the high country, but most of the bigger walls have short sections of artificial work. Aid climbing is rated from A1 to A5, A1 being quite easy and A5 requiring difficult and very insecure placements.

Roman numerals from I to VI represent the Grade of the climb and are used solely with technical routes. The Grade gives an indication of the overall difficulty of a route; it includes such factors as length, commitment, strenuousness, and continuity. Grade I and II climbs are relatively easy and can be ascended in a few hours. Grades III and IV indicate a serious climb which will take most of a day. A handful of Grade V and VI climbs are found in the range— these very difficult endeavors can be compared to the big wall climbs of Yosemite Valley.

Regulations

The Sierra Nevada is a small range with many millions of people nearby, and in the past decade a remarkable population explosion has hit the back country. The John Muir Trail has begun to look like a freeway, and several hundred backpackers can sometimes be found within a mile or two of a popular spot. Campsites are becoming denuded of wood, coliform bacteria are appearing in streams, and the atmosphere of solitude, once prevalent, has vanished.

A few years ago the U.S. Forest Service and the National Park Service became aware of the overcrowding problem and came up with certain solutions, such as restricting camping at certain heavily frequented spots, banning grazing in depleted meadows, and limiting the number of visitors who could enter the back country. A reservation system was the next step. Almost every entrance point in the range now has a daily quota of permits. Reservations made months ahead of time guarantee the visitor a route of his choice on a certain day. To accommodate the traveler who wishes his trip to be a little more spontaneous, a limited number of first-come, first-served permits are reserved at selected entry points. A Wilderness Permit can be obtained by writing the headquarters of the national forest or park in which the trip will originate.

Equipment

If a person who hadn't climbed for ten years were to return to the climbing scene, the very first thing he'd notice would be the absence of pitons. Instead, his eyes would widen with amazement as he stared at odd-shaped hunks of aluminum hanging from multi-hued perlon loops. Nuts, or artificial chockstones, have taken the American climbing community by storm. Virtually every climber in the land has switched over to nuts. The phrase "clean climbing" or "doing it clean" refers to pitonless ascents.

Why the hue and cry about clean climbing? The primary reason, of course, is that pitons irrevocably scar the rock. Cracks that once took knifeblades now take two-inch angles, and old aid routes have become free because of the fist-sized excavations made by a generation of hard steel pitons. Besides saving the rock, nuts offer a fast, quiet, and challenging way to climb. They are much lighter than pitons, and the climber needn't carry a hammer.

High Sierra rock, with its multitude of fractured cracks, is such a perfect medium for nuts that the climber who carries pitons and hammers into the range must be thought of as either stubborn or ignorant. I am not speaking solely for the serious rockclimber. If a mountaineer going in to do Mt. Humphreys, for instance, carried a selection of eight nuts, six carabiners, and a 9mm rope, he would be in a position to climb with complete safety any of the standard routes on the peak.

Most routes in the High Sierra can be done clean so easily that the ego-concept of the "first clean ascent" seems ridiculous. For this reason no attempt has been made in this book to keep track of them.

Although the northern High Sierra contains many hundreds of glaciers, they can be avoided easily unless, of course, the object is to climb them. Such factors as season, time of day, elevation, and geographical setting all influence the condition of snow and ice, and the guidebook cannot tell the prospective climber when to carry or use an ice axe and crampons. However, a few general "rules" can be stated. Until about July 15 cross-country travelers who plan to go over class 3 passes will almost always need an ice axe. Later in the season, what snow remains in couloirs is icy, but can often be bypassed. Whenever the word "glacier" or "snowfield" appears in a route description, the climber would be well advised to carry an ice axe. The phrase "ice gully" or "ice couloir" can be interpreted to mean that full ice-climbing regalia is necessary.

Safety

There are several ways to die while climbing in the Sierra. Most popular seems to be what every layman suspects: the climber falls off the mountain. A handhold can break off, or a climber can stumble on a scree ledge or slip while attempting to cross an icy patch. The result, if the exposure is great enough, is death. If the fall is not far, then perhaps it will be simply a minor inconvenience. Caution and experience are important ingredients for safe climbing in any mountainous area, and the above scenarios can be avoided *if* the problem is recognized in time. Therein lies the rub, however, for an inexperienced person finds it very difficult to know when he has gotten himself into a bind. And in such a bind, common sense often disappears and the problem is compounded.

It is more than obvious that inexperienced persons should not tackle routes which are beyond their abilities. The only way to improve these abilities is to practice in a place which isn't dangerous (i.e., close to the ground) or to climb with someone who *is* experienced. Nowadays many organizations offer climbing instruction, and although a week of schooling hardly prepares one for the rigors of the mountains, the basics can be learned and the dangers can be more easily recognized.

Second only to falling, the greatest danger is being struck by a falling stone. Fortunately, natural rockfall is very rare in the Sierra, but rocks knocked down by other climbers present a distinct hazard. Gullies and couloirs, of course, are the worst places, since falling rocks ricochet erratically and have nowhere to go but down onto someone's head. For this reason, it follows that while climbing gullies suspected of containing loose rock, group members should stay close to one another. When ascending loose slopes or faces, the group should spread out horizontally. Yelling "Rock!" at the instant one is loosed and wearing a hardhat are two other methods of minimizing possible accidents.

Many accidents occur when inexperienced persons attempt to cross steep snowfields without proper equipment, or without knowing how to use their equipment. Snow is an extremely insidious danger in the mountains—although *it* can't hurt you, those rocks at the bottom certainly can. If snowslopes must be crossed, and you are under-equipped, remember that in late afternoon the snow will be softer and steps can be kicked more easily. In lieu of an ice axe, a sharp, manageable piece of stone can act as a self-arrest tool, but it is hardly an adequate substitute.

Summer storms in the high country can be uncomfortable, but they are rarely a dangerous problem for the observant mountaineer. When towering cumulus clouds are present, it is best not to be on summits or ridges. If lightning should be striking close at hand, get away from ridges and projections, squat, and either pray or scream imprecations, whichever is your style.

Solo climbing is not dangerous per se, and many of the Sierra's finest climbers did their thing alone. But it should be remembered that such incidents as a broken leg, which would be relatively minor when with someone, are uniformly fatal when you are alone and no one finds you. There are wonderful advantages to climbing solo; no one will roll rocks on you, no one will upset your pace, and the solitude is something special. If the rewards are great, so then are the hazards, and neophytes should be counseled to avoid climbing alone until they have gained more than a modicum of knowledge about their chosen environment.

Winter Climbing

Climbing during the winter months is becoming extremely popular, and a whole realm of first winter ascents await the adventurer.

Waxed skis are the preferred mode of transportation, although one will still see old-timers using skins or snowshoes. Cold-weather gear is an obvious necessity, for the Sierra is an extremely cold place in mid-winter. First winter ascents, when known, are listed in the appendix, but they do not necessarily mean much. For instance, the first winter ascent of Mt. Humphreys was made on December 28, 1956. It was a mild day in the Sierra and little snow had fallen. Skis were abandoned at 10,000 feet as a hinderance. The temperature was in the low twenties, and the wind was brisk but no problem. Was this a winter ascent? Yes, because the calendar-winter had arrived on time even if the weather-winter hadn't. And conversely, I have heard many horrendous stories of November and April ascents which were accomplished in howling blizzards. The greatest Sierra climbing tragedy occurred in late May, when a sudden blizzard of ferocious intensity trapped and killed four people on Mt. Ritter.

Fires, Horses, Ducks, and Other Small Matters

Eight years ago I ripped off the last piece of firewood from Evolution Lake, one of the most beautiful places in the Sierra. It took half an afternoon to unearth a tenacious stump, and it ruined my back for a week. In the early 1930s, Walter Starr, Jr. had warned of scant firewood at the lake, and now there is none. Or at least so little that not in the foreseeable future can anyone ever again have a roaring campfire. And what has happened at Evolution Lake is happening now at popular camping spots well below timberline. Too many people are building too many fires—it's that simple.

Two problems evolve from fire-building: First, there is a finite amount of dead wood above 10,000 feet. Second, fireplace scars are so numerous in some locales that a person can't walk a hundred feet without stumbling over blackened stones, giant boulders with two-foot-high carbon deposits, and shattered flakes, a result of premature exfoliation. These problems can be solved easily by not building fires, but this seems a bit unrealistic. Gas stoves solve the cooking problem but don't help the social scene much. What else is there to do at eight o'clock on a chilly night? If fires are to be built, they should be kept Indian-size and should not be built against mother rocks. Afterward the stones should be placed back into the holes whence they came, blackened sides down.

At the risk of offending horse-lovers who like the High Sierra as much as I do, I present these few ravings of an anti-packtrain fanatic. It must be admitted, even by horsepeople, that copious quantities of dung on the trail are offensive indeed. This might be a purely aesthetic matter except that by mid-August the beasts have torn the trail to pieces and left it deep in turd-dust. More disturbing still is that packtrains tend to ruin an area much faster than a group of backpackers. Meadows are destroyed by overgrazing and erosion sets in. Trails become roads, not paths. Packtrains bring in canned food, giant iron grills, and nails that will be pounded into trees for pot-hanging.

The Sierra is eminently suited for walking, and except in very special circumstances, it would seem indefensible to ride a horse or let a mule take one's belongings into a semi-pristine world. The Forest Service has begun to limit stock and to ban grazing in certain areas. Perhaps the day will come when a massive campaign will phase out packtrains once and for all.

Small piles of rocks—called ducks, cairns, or stonemen—have become an eyesore all over the high country. One time I was behind a pack of Boy Scouts who were ascending toward Gabbot Pass. There were about twenty of them, and as they drifted in separate packlets over high meadows and gentle talusfields they built such sturdy and so abundant a supply of ducks that it took me an extra hour and an extra mile to destroy them all. I had better things to do, and I would hate to be thought of as a duck pervert, but I genuinely shudder each time I see those little piles of stones which someone has so kindly placed to help me on my way. What arrogance the duck-builder has! Does he really believe that he has found the *only* possible route? Does he believe that he has checked out all alternate routes? Does he think we can't find our own way?

It is not only the populated areas of the Sierra which are affected, and it is not only Boy Scouts who build ducks. In the difficult-to-reach Gorge of Despair I found hundreds of ducks which must have been built by rockclimbers since few others ever see the valley. There were ducks on class 1 slabs, ducks which laboriously took me to a class 2 ledge instead of a direct class 2–3 route, and ducks which led through brushfields to a stream crossing. Hervey Voge hated ducks too, and he wrote a powerful paragraph against them in his original climber's guide. He pointed out that "it is better for a climber to judge the situation himself than to follow blindly a series of ducks." I maintain unequivocally that ducks in the High Sierra should be destroyed. They are not only unnecessary and misleading, but they ruin the sense of adventure for those who believe, however falsely, that they are explorers trodding over new ground.

Human excrement is even worse than that of equines and has become a distinct problem in popular areas. Drop your feces well away from established campsites, away from water supplies, and bury them as deeply as possible—a large, pried-up rock leaves a good sized hole that can be covered up once again.

Practices such as cutting down pine boughs for a bed and tent-ditching are fortunately almost things of the past. Both seem un-necessary in this modern age, with its floored tents and foam pads.

It goes without saying that all cans, foil, and other non-biodegradable materials should be packed out of the mountains. It is a very slovenly habit to bury them.

Wildlife

Man has destroyed, either directly or indirectly, most of the more spectacular examples of wildlife in the Sierra. The grizzly, once abundant, is now seen only on California's state flag, for the last one in the state was shot near Kings Canyon National Park in 1922. Nearly 10,000 mountain lions were killed in the first half of the century, and though they are still spotted occasionally, they are uncommon. One of the saddest stories concerns the Sierra bighorn sheep. Although these noble beasts were shot by the thousands in the early days, the biggest killer was the starvation which resulted from competition for food with domestic sheep. Hordes of the latter roamed the Sierra for sixty years before government agencies intervened (Francis Farquhar once saw 2,000 domestic sheep at Evolution Lake). By then, however, the bighorn population had been almost destroyed, and now only a few small bands exist high on mountain slopes in the southern part of the range. A belated effort to save the animals is in progress, and certain areas have restricted access.

The wolverine, whose incredible jaws can crush cow thighbones as if they were chalk, is probably extinct by now. Norman Clyde saw only one in the Sierra—this should be an indication of their rarity.

Deer and black bear are quite common in the range, though few of the latter are seen above 8,000 feet.

Of the smaller mammals, the pika, marmot, marten, ring-tailed cat, and coyote are fairly common. The fisher, arch-enemy of the porcupine, is present but rarely seen.

Relatively few species of birds are found in the high country, but several are conspicuous. The Clark's nutcracker performs comically atop pine trees as he extracts nuts from cones, and his raucous cry can be heard for half a mile. The diminutive gray-crowned rosy finch picks insects from snowfields, and flocks of these usually drab-colored birds are common at high altitudes. Those interested in *Empidonax* flycatchers can easily find the Hammond's flycatcher in the gnarled pines at timberline. Yellow-rumped warblers, dark-eyed juncos, and mountain bluebirds are extremely common.

Organization of Guide

I have divided the guide into eleven chapters, each covering a general region in the High Sierra. Eight chapters cover the crest peaks and adjoining summits, while three chapters—"Tuolumne Domes," "Kings River," and the "Great Western Divide"—treat areas west of the crest.

I have made no attempt to slavishly separate crest peaks from those mountains on either side of the divide. Previous guidebooks, for instance, listed Mt. Darwin ten pages away from its satellite, Mt. Mendel, because the latter is not a crest peak. This book treats groups of peaks and lists them roughly in north to south order. There are some problems connected with this system, of course, but only an alphabetical listing of peaks would be totally objective, and that *would* be confusing.

Each chapter has an introduction which tells something about the geography of the region, its climbing history, and its approaches. In this last category I briefly mention the trail approaches which are the best, not the only, ways into the area; the descriptions are brief because other books, most notably the Sierra Club's *Starr's Guide to the John Muir Trail and the High Sierra Region*, describe mileages, views, and campsites along these trails. And although I would not expect every climber to pack *Starr's Guide* along, I would think that everyone would have a topo map, which shows the trails in good detail.

Climbers' and knapsackers' passes are covered in more detail, but again a map is almost a necessity and a glance at it will reveal cross-country routes far easier than words could. In fact, everything but the difficulty is shown on the map. There are many passes and cross-country routes which aren't in this guide. I tended to concentrate on Sierra crest passes (since so many climbers approach from the east) and passes in the high, rugged country which should most interest mountaineers.

Each region is divided into sections and most of their names are self-explanatory. When they are not, a note is given concerning the geographical boundaries of the section.

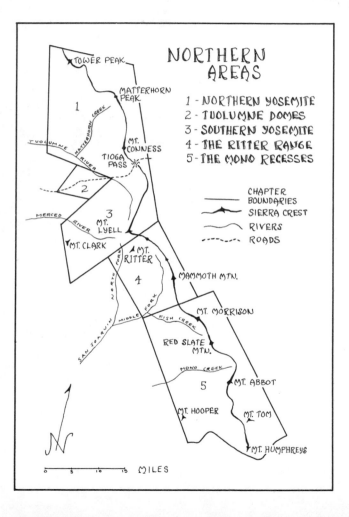

NORTHERN
AREAS

1 - NORTHERN YOSEMITE
2 - TUOLUMNE DOMES
3 - SOUTHERN YOSEMITE
4 - THE RITTER RANGE
5 - THE MONO RECESSES

CHAPTER BOUNDARIES
SIERRA CREST
RIVERS
ROADS

TOWER PEAK
MATTERHORN PEAK
1
MATTERHORN CREEK
TUOLUMNE RIVER
MT. CONNESS
TIOGA PASS
2
MERCED RIVER
3
MT. LYELL
MT. CLARK
MT. RITTER
4
NORTH FORK
SAN JOAQUIN MIDDLE FORK
MAMMOTH MTN.
MT. MORRISON
FISH CREEK
RED SLATE MTN.
MONO CREEK
5
MT. ABBOT
MT. HOOPER
MT. TOM
MT. HUMPHREYS

N

0   5   10   15   MILES

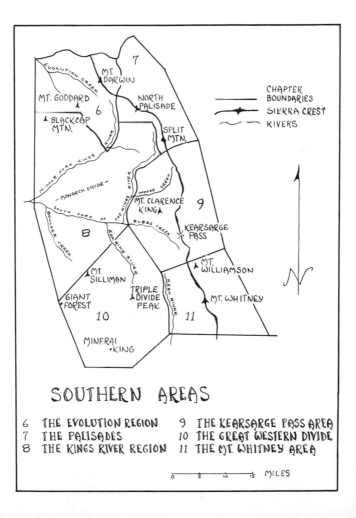

SOUTHERN AREAS

6	THE EVOLUTION REGION	9	THE KEARSARGE PASS AREA
7	THE PALISADES	10	THE GREAT WESTERN DIVIDE
8	THE KINGS RIVER REGION	11	THE MT. WHITNEY AREA

SONORA PASS	FALES HOT SPRINGS					
TOWER PEAK	MATTERHORN PEAK	BODIE				
HETCH HETCHY RES.	TUOLUMNE MEADOWS	MONO CRATERS				
	MERCED PEAK	DEVIL'S POSTPILE	MOUNT MORRISON	CASA DIABLO MTN.		
	SHUTEYE PEAK	KAISER PEAK	MOUNT ABBOT	MOUNT TOM	BISHOP	
	SHAVER LAKE	HUNTINGTON LAKE	BLACKCAP MTN.	MOUNT GODDARD	BIG PINE	
		PATTERSON MTN.	TEHIPITE DOME	MARION PEAK	MOUNT PINCHOT	
			GIANT FOREST	TRIPLE DIVIDE PEAK	MOUNT WHITNEY	LONE PINE
			KAWEAH	MINERAL KING	KERN PEAK	OLANCHA

GEOGRAPHIC ARRANGEMENT OF 15' U.S.G.S. MAPS

Maps for Major Climbing Areas

Area	Map
Sawtooth Ridge	Matterhorn Peak
Tuolumne Domes	Tuolumne Meadows
Cathedral Range	Tuolumne Meadows
Minarets	Devil's Postpile
Mt. Abbot Group	Mount Abbot
Mt. Humphreys	Mount Tom
Evolution Region	Mount Goddard
Palisades	Mount Goddard and Big Pine
Mt. Clarence King	Mount Pinchot
Kings Canyon	Marion Peak
Mt. Brewer Area	Mount Whitney
Kings-Kern Divide	Mount Whitney
Kaweahs	Triple Divide Peak and Mount Whitney
Mineral King	Mineral King
Mt. Whitney Group	Mount Whitney
The Needles	Hockett Peak

Northern Yosemite

The High Sierra begins near the northern boundary of Yosemite National Park. It is in this area that rocky summits regularly begin to poke through their cloaks of trees and take on the appearance of "Real Mountains." Pocket glaciers enliven the northern cirques, and trans-Sierra roads, with the exception of the Tioga Pass road have not been built, primarily due to the more rugged terrain.

From Dorothy Lake Pass, the point at which this guide begins to take the Sierra Nevada seriously, the crest of the range surprisingly wanders more easterly than southerly. For about fifteen miles it heads in this direction and then, at Virginia Pass, it veers and runs more or less directly south to Tioga Pass.

Many long and impressive canyons originate on the west side of the crest and fall through miles of wilderness toward the great gorge of the Tuolumne River. On the east side of the crest many small creeks drop abruptly into the watershed of the Walker River, destined for the eventual ignominy of alkaline desert evaporation.

While the Northern Yosemite region can by no means be termed the most scenic, most remote, or most *anything* of the High Sierra, it nevertheless contains much charm, and, except for the Sawtooth Ridge, has the added attraction of being less crowded than the more spectacular areas to the south.

The greatest single attraction for the mountaineer in this region is the Sawtooth Ridge, an alpine cluster of peaks known for its clean, white granite and interesting glaciers. It is a popular spot in the summer, and more and more climbers are turning to winter ascents to get away from the congestion.

The climbing history of the Northern Yosemite area is not especially fascinating. As one might predict, the highest or most prominent peaks were ascended first: Mt. Hoffmann in 1863, Mt. Conness in 1866, Tower Peak four years later, and Matterhorn Peak in 1899. During the first three decades of this century many high, easy peaks were ascended. Most of these required a sense of adventure and a degree of stamina, but none required climbing skill. Beginning in the summer of 1931, however, Sierra Club rockclimbers began technical ascents of what the old guard might have called "minor outcrops." Virtually every summit, regardless of its height, was reached by World War II. In the 1960s and 1970s, a new generation made many difficult new routes and even discovered a few "minor outcrops" of their own.

The region has a tremendous number of approaches, and perusal of the various topo maps which cover the area will show these in detail. Approaches of particular interest to the mountaineer are those into the Tower Peak, Sawtooth Ridge, and Mt. Conness regions.

Tower Peak is best approached from Twin Lakes, a resort area attainable via a short drive from the town of Bridgeport, on U.S. Highway 395. A good trail leads from the resort to Buckeye Pass. From here easy cross-country travel takes one across to the gentle pass between Wells and Ehrnbeck peaks. The head of Stubblefield Canyon, a good base camp, is just beyond. The northern section of the Tower Peak area can be reached from Leavitt Meadows, on the Sonora Pass road.

The Sawtooth Ridge is also reached from Twin Lakes: Blacksmith Creek allows straightforward access to the north group of peaks, while Horse Creek is a fast approach to the most popular cluster of climbs. A well-trodden path will be found along the latter creek.

The Mt. Conness area is very easily approached from Saddlebag Lake, just off the Tioga road.

Since much of the Northern Yosemite region is composed of relatively gentle terrain, cross-country routes abound and will not be mentioned here, with the exception of the following climbers' passes in the Sawtooth Ridge area.

Glacier Col (11,600+) lies between Cleaver and Blacksmith

peaks and is class 2 from the southwest. Moderately steep snowslopes blanket the opposite side and an ice axe should be carried.

Cleaver Notch is the obvious class 2 notch on the fin called the Cleaver; this notch is an excellent crossing point between Blacksmith and Horse creeks.

Col de Doodad (11,440+) lies on the main Sierra crest between the Three Teeth and the Doodad. There are no problems on the southwest side. Two routes exist on the glacier side. The easiest begins in a gully close against the Southeast Tooth. Once the crest is attained, move about 30 feet to the right and then drop over the edge and scramble down a class 3 chimney to the scree on the Slide Canyon side. This method is difficult to locate when approaching from Slide Canyon, so most parties head up to the main notch and rappel to the glacier. This is the more difficult way when coming from the glacier and is class 4.

Polemonium Pass (11,600+) is the obvious notch between the Dragtooth and the Doodad. From the glacier a steep snowslope, requiring an ice axe, leads to the pass. The scree slopes leading down to the upper reaches of Slide Canyon present no problem.

Horse Creek Pass (10,640+) is the low saddle between Matterhorn and Twin peaks. It offers a fast and easy cross-country route across the crest.

The following topographical maps cover the Northern Yosemite region: Bodie, Fales Hot Springs, Hetch Hetchy Reservoir, Lake Eleanor, Matterhorn Peak, Mono Craters, Tower Peak, and Tuolumne Meadows.

Tower Peak and Environs

Bigelow Peak (10,539)
    Class 1 from most sides.

Keyes Peak (10,670)
From the upper end of Tilden Lake one may proceed via numerous class 2 routes.

Forsyth Peak (11,180)
The south and west sides of the peak are quite easy. A class 3 route from Dorothy Lake has been made up the northwest ridge.

Saurian Crest (11,095)
Easy slopes lead to the class 3 summit blocks.

Tower Peak (11,755)
In 1941 fragments of arrowheads were found just below the summit—one wonders how many peaks the Indians climbed during their quest for food. A standard route climbs to the saddle one-half mile north of the peak and then ascends the ridge south to a class 3 gully which leads to the top. A more difficult route has been done on the west face, above Mary Lake. A chute on the southeast face provides yet another route.

Craig Peak (11,090)
Class 2 and 3 routes abound.

Snow Peak (10,950)
Class 2 from the Tilden Lake area.

Wells Peak (11,118)
Class 2 from the Wells-Ehrnbeck saddle.

Ehrnbeck Peak (11,240)
Class 2 from the Wells-Ehrnbeck saddle. The north ridge, approached from the West Walker River, is class 3.

Grouse Mountain (10,775)
A gully on the northwest side provides a very easy route. The east face is class 3.

Center Mountain (11,273)
   Trivial from the Thompson Canyon area.

Hunewill Peak (11,713)
   Class 2 from the trail north of Barney Lake.

Victoria Peak (11,732)
   Class 2 from anywhere.

Eagle Peak (11,845)
   This is the highest point of Buckeye Ridge. Class 2 routes may be chosen at random.

Acker Peak (11,015)
   Class 2 from Kerrick Meadow to the east.

Price Peak (10,716)
   Easy slopes lead to the summit from the environs of Thompson Canyon.

Piute Mountain (10,541)
   Class 2 from Bear Valley. The north chute has been climbed and is class 3.

Bath Mountain (10,558)
   Easy via the north-northeast ridge. A technical route has been established on the left side of the west face. Ascend a long, left-facing open book. IV, 5.10, A1.

Sawtooth Ridge and Vicinity

Cirque Mountain (10,714)
   Class 1 from Buckeye Pass.

Crown Point (11,346)

Class 2 from Peeler or Snow Lake. Rising above Peeler Lake, on the north side of Crown Mountain, is an impressive formation known as Peeler Pillar. A technical route, rated II, 5.6, has been done on this mass. Begin climbing about 100 feet right of the steep north face of the buttress. Two hundred feet of easy class 5 leads to a large ledge. Scramble upward from here to a steep, white face lined with vertical cracks. Climb this face, staying left of an open book, for four pitches of consistent, moderate climbing.

"The Juggernaut" (ca. 10,800, 0.75 SSE of Crown Pt.)

Due east of Snow Lake is a small pond. Just south of this is a very steep prow, the Juggernaut. Two routes have been done. A long, left-facing open book provides a five-pitch route, rated III, 5.10. The second route lies just to the right of the open book. Overhangs on the second and third pitches constitute the main difficulties. The fourth and last pitches ascend obvious 5.7 cracks. III, 5.9, A2.

Slide Mountain (11,040+)

Class 2 from almost any direction.

Suicide Ridge (11,089)

Class 2.

Kettle Peak (11,010)

The top can be reached via several class 2 routes. A group of four spectacular pinnacles is found on the east side of the peak. These provide excellent climbing and can easily be reached from Twin Lakes via Little Slide Canyon. From north to south these pinnacles are called Outguard Spire, the Turret, Regge Pole, and the Duck.

Outguard Spire is the lowest of the pinnacles and the easiest to approach. A short, unpleasant gully on the right side leads to the original route, rated II, 5.8. From the notch behind the pinnacle climb a rotten chimney to the crux, a narrow jamcrack. Continue up the corner via class 4 and 5 climbing to the tiny summit. A second,

Looking south into Little Slide Canyon. The Incredible Hulk is seen on the left; the pinnacle on the right is Outguard Spire.

much harder route has been established and begins on the outer, or east, face. Follow a corner on the right side of the face to a roof, and then head up and right along a ramp to a belay spot atop a shoulder on the north face. Traverse right to a terrifying chimney behind a flake; this is the crux section. From a ledge above, move to the far right and lieback to a sloping ledge on the west corner of Outguard. A bit of aid leads to a sling belay left of a prominent crack. Jam to the summit area. III, 5.10, A2.

The *Turret* can be approached by several class 3 and 4 routes. From the notch behind the formation climb to the top. This short route has one 5.8 move.

The start of the original route on *Regge Pole* can be reached by ascending the couloir on the Pole's left side. The route lies on the impressive south face. Leave the couloir and climb out on a ledge beneath a large open book. Climb this dihedral for four pitches, making excursions out to the left when necessary. Each of these pitches is 5.7; a bit of aid is also necessary. From the terrace atop the book, walk around the spire and climb to the summit via a chimney on the west face. The easiest descent is via the west chimney—two or three rappels are necessary. A second route begins from the rope-up ledge on the original route. Two bolts begin a traverse to the right; gain a crack system and climb to a small ledge. Using aid, climb over a roof and belay in slings. Move left and aid up to another hanging belay. A short pitch bypasses a giant, rotten flake on the right and ends at yet another hanging belay. More aid leads to a ledge. Next, climb up a bit; then hand-traverse left to a chimney system which leads to the summit. IV, 5.7, A3.

The last formation, the *Duck*, is quite small and can be approached with ease from Maltby Lake. Class 4.

"The Incredible Hulk" (Pk. 11,581, 1 E of Kettle Pk.)

This giant mass has no easy route to its summit and was not climbed until recently. The most feasible route begins near the headwaters of the stream one-quarter mile east of Maltby Lake. Ascend a couloir, filled with horribly loose rock, on the right side of a giant rock wall. After a while, leave the couloir and head up a steep chute. This leads to a notch high above; the summit is reached by a few class 4 and 5 pitches. In the early season this route is largely a snow climb and is consequently far easier.

A significant route has been established on the giant rock wall mentioned above. This wall is quite convoluted and routefinding is not easy. A 250-foot-high triangular section at the base marks the beginning of the route. Climb the left side of the triangle for two pitches, and then ascend to roofs and traverse to the right above them to a sling belay below a chimney. Climb this; then head up and right to terraces. From the upper right side of these climb straight up two pitches to a loose flake in an open book. Ascend this book part way; then exit right via a tension-traverse and climb to a ledge. Traverse right and climb a pillar. Next, head up and right to a notch on the skyline. Three more pitches, more or less straight up, lead to the summit ridge. The summit can be attained from here, but a preferable descent route is to rappel the route to the skyline notch and then make a series of 150-foot rappels straight to the ground. V, 5.8, A3.

A third route has been done on the Hulk; this one goes nowhere near the summit. Near the entrance to Little Slide Canyon is a conspicuous three-toothed face with an obvious gully splitting it. Climb this; then descend the back side. III, 5.7, A1.

"Eocene Peak" (Pk. 11,581, 1.3 SE of Kettle Pk.)

This peak should not be confused with the Peak 11,581 which lies a mile east of Kettle Peak. An easy ascent from the south or southwest leads to the ancient summit plateau. The summit monolith is class 3.

"Blacksmith Peak" (Pk. 11,680+, 1.3 NW of Matterhorn Pk.)

Route 1. Southwest Face. Class 3. A gully leads directly up this face to the summit pinnacles, the highest of which seems to be at the northwest end.

Route 2. Northwest Face, Right Side. II, 5.8, A2. In the center of this face one will see a very steep section with no feasible routes. To the right of this section, at a point more or less directly below the summit, is the rope-up spot for this route. Climb slabs and then steep rock to an overhang which requires aid. Above this, bear up and left to the final steep crack system, where aid is again needed. Gain the summit ridge and follow it to the top.

Route 3. Northwest Face, Left Side. II, 5.8. Start left of the central steep section described above and bear up and right over broken rock to the top.

Route 4. Northeast Gully. II, 5.5. From the base of the north arete, climb a ramp which diagonals up and left above the glacier which lies between this peak and Cleaver Peak. After 200 feet the ramp ends; traverse right and climb a short, easy class 5 wall. This brings one into the northeast gully—follow it to the top.

"Cleaver Peak" (Pk. 11,760+, 1.1 NW of Matterhorn Pk.)

Route 1. From Glacier Col. Class 3. From the col head out onto the southwest face; then traverse back left on a slanting ledge to a depression on the northwest face. Scramble up this to the summit.

Route 2. Northeast Side. Class 3. Climb steep blocks and ledges on the northeast face and meet the northeast arete (known as the Cleaver) a bit down from the summit.

Route 3. South Face. Class 5. Ascend a class 4 chute until about 150 feet below the notch which separates Cleaver Peak from the Sawblade. Turn left under a large block and climb a few class 5 pitches up the south face to the top.

The Cleaver (1.2 NNW of Matterhorn Pk.)

This is the blade-like ridge which runs down and northeast from the summit of Cleaver Peak. There are no records of a complete traverse. A 125-foot-high spire, known as *Goldfinger*, has been climbed. It lies astride the Cleaver and is climbed via aid on its west face. 5.6, A3.

"The Sawblade" (ca. 11,600, 1 NW of Matterhorn Pk.)

A class 4 or 5 traverse, involving some rappels, has been made from southeast to northwest.

"The Three Teeth" (ca. 11,600, 0.8 NW of Matterhorn Pk.)

These popular spires have many routes and even more variations. Routefinding tends to be a bit complicated because of the broken nature of the rock. The Teeth are aligned in a northwest to southeast direction. The right-hand spire, as seen from the glacier, will be called the Northwest Tooth; the Middle Tooth is next and is followed by the Southeast Tooth. The notch between the Northwest Tooth and the Middle Tooth is called the West Notch, while the notch between the Middle Tooth and the Southeast Tooth is known as the East Notch.

Route 1. Northwest to Southwest Traverse. III, 5.5. From the glacier, climb onto the face of the Northwest Tooth. Climb upward via loose rock and broken ledges, and then head up and right over to the northwest arete. From here climb up to a tunnel, or squeeze chimney, which lies beneath the imposing summit block. Pass through the tunnel to a broken area on the southeast side of the block. There are several ways to climb this final problem.

On toward the Middle Tooth. From near the broken area rappel 140 feet to the West Notch. From here climb a decomposed chimney for about 40 feet; then traverse left and ascend into another very loose chimney. Climb this to a flat ledge on the right. The summit pitch begins with a steep 5.5 lieback.

From the top of the Middle Tooth, climb down an easy-looking chimney on the east side for 75 feet; then rappel 100 feet into the gully below, and southwest of, the East Notch. Walk up the gully to the highest ledge of the imposing face of the Southeast Tooth and traverse right and proceed to a ledge. A squeeze chimney now leads to the summit area.

From near the top of the Southeast Tooth rappel 145 feet down the southeast side of the pinnacle which is located just northwest of the true summit. This takes one to the lower of two ledges; walk southeast on this for 50 feet, and then climb down to a rappel block just below a small, insecure-looking spire. Rappel 145 feet to a broken area. A short rappel leads to another broken area. Next, walk back toward the base of the Middle Tooth and rappel 80 feet into the scree couloir below the Col de Doodad.

This excellent climb is about ten pitches long. There are several moderate class 5 pitches; numerous flakes and horns provide excellent protection. It is possible to rappel using a doubled 150-foot rope, but this will involve some scary downclimbing and rather poor intermediate rappel spots.

Route 2. Southeast to Northwest Traverse. III, 5.6. From the Col de Doodad walk down the couloir toward Slide Canyon until it is possible to enter a short chimney containing a chockstone. This leads to an arete which is followed to the base of a pinnacle. Tunnel under this; then head back to the arete. Ascend the arete and chimneys to the summit of the Southeast Tooth.

Retrace Route 1 past the Middle Tooth to the West Notch. From here walk down the gully toward Slide Canyon; then climb up and right 100 feet over steeply sloping ledges and cracks. From a three-foot-wide ledge climb an exposed, 75-foot, class 5 wall. This leads to the broken area near the tunnel beneath the summit block of the Northwest Tooth. Descend via the first part of Route 1.

Route 3. Northwest Tooth, Southwest Face. Class 5. Climb a buttress just left of the couloir which leads toward the West Notch. Work diagonally toward a ledge at the top of the first (and lowest) chimney. From here make a delicate traverse across the chimney to a scree gully which lies directly above the chimney. Climb this gully until near its top; then head left on a ledge. Ascend chimneys and flakes on the southwest face and climb to the summit block.

Route 4. Northwest Tooth via the West Notch. Class 4–5. From the glacier ascend the couloir to the West Notch. Traverse right on a narrow ledge into a chimney which leads to the tunnel beneath the summit block.

Route 5. Middle Tooth, Northeast Face. Class 4–5. From the glacier, climb the couloir leading to the West Notch until about 100 feet above a chockstone. Traverse diagonally left on a ledge until well out onto the northeast face; then head into a prominent chimney. Follow this up and right to a very loose chimney. Climb this and one more pitch to the top.

Route 6. Middle Tooth, Southwest Face. III, 5.9, A1. Start climbing a bit left of the center of the face and ascend steep jamcracks for about 300 feet. Pendulum to the right across a blank section and follow a three-pitch crack system to the top.

Route 7. Southeast Tooth, Northeast Face. III, 5.7. Climb the left-leaning crack system seen in the center of the face above the glacier.

"The Doodad" (ca. 11,600, 0.5 NW of Matterhorn Pk.)

Several class 4 or 5 routes lead up the south face to the spectacular summit block. Climb this block on its southwest side. Another route has been made on the glacier face. From the lower right side of the massif, climb a long gully which slants to the left. Follow this gully, with a few deviations, until it is possible to hand-traverse left to ledges below the summit monolith. This route is class 5.

The Sawtooth Ridge from the northeast.

"The Dragtooth" (Pk. 12,160+, 0.35 NW of Matterhorn Pk.)

Route 1. South Side. Class 2.

Route 2. Northeast Buttress. Class 4. This is the long rib which divides the Matterhorn and Dragtooth glaciers. Attain the buttress from the Dragtooth Glacier and follow it to the top. On the lower section stay on the left side of the rib; higher up stay directly on it.

Route 3. North Face. Class 4. This is the wide face above the Dragtooth Glacier. Start climbing 100 feet left of the main chute which drops down the face from the summit area. Head up ledges leading left into a second chute and follow it for about 200 feet. Traverse right into the main chute and follow it until only 100 feet from the summit ridge. Climb a chimney on the left wall and hit the ridge 50 feet right of the top.

Route 4. North Buttress. III, 5.8, A2. The base of this buttress sticks farther down onto the glacier than any other part of the Dragtooth. A 200-foot triangular pedestal at the base is a diagnostic landmark. Climb chimneys and cracks on the left side of the pedestal for two pitches; then traverse left to the bottom of a very prominent dihedral. Follow this for two leads, exit up and right, and climb the easier upper ridge to the top.

Route 5. West Side. III, 5.8. From the glacier, climb up the couloir toward Polemonium Pass. When 100 feet below the pass, climb large cracks and chimneys up and then left to a large broken area. Proceed up and left and enter a large chimney. Follow this to its top; then exit up and right to the west ridge. Scramble up its right side to reach the summit.

Matterhorn Peak (12,264)

This is the peak which defeated Jack Kerouac. It is probably the most popular mountain climb in Northern Yosemite, and although badly named, it is a nice peak and commands a superb view.

Route 1. Southwest Side. Class 2. From Burro Pass contour east and climb a broad scree gully to the summit.

Route 2. Southeast Side. Class 2. An easy ascent can be made from the vicinity of Horse Creek Pass.

Route 3. East Couloir. Class 3. This is the normal route from Twin Lakes. An obvious couloir on the east side of the northeast ridge leads to the east ridge. Follow this to the top.

Route 4. North Arete. II, 5.5. Seen from the glacier below the north side of the peak, the north arete divides two nice-looking walls and is unmistakable. The lower part of the arete blends into the face. A platform several hundred feet above the glacier, and at the very base of the sharp arete, can be reached directly (5.8) or from either the right or left via class 4 pitches. From the platform, climb up broken rock on the arete for one pitch; then traverse right onto the face for about 75 feet. A beautiful, steep crack is followed for two 5.5 pitches to a large ledge a bit right of the arete. The route now traverses left past the very sharp arete to a chimney with a chockstone. Above this follow a subsidiary arete to the summit.

Several variations have been done above the large ledge. One can traverse left to the arete and follow it directly to the top (5.7). Another variation follows the arete for a pitch and then heads off right to a small notch. Shallow jamcracks above this lead to the summit ridge (5.7?). A third variation ascends a prominent dihedral above the large ledge, then moves left (5.8) to enter a thin, widening crack which leads directly to the top of the arete.

Route 5. Double Dihedral Route. II, 5.8. Two dihedrals, running up and right, will be seen on the face to the right of the obvious north arete. Ascend class 3 and 4 rock to the snow-filled bottom of the right dihedral. A steep snow pitch is followed by a 5.7 pitch in the dihedral proper. From a large flake descend 20 feet and climb a 5.7 crack which leads up 150 feet to a large ledge. The upper dihedral now rises above. One is now on a variation of Route 4. Climb the dihedral to its top; then move left (5.8) and climb a thin, widening crack to the summit ridge.

Route 6. Northwest Side. Class 3. From the notch between Matterhorn and Dragtooth climb a gully or a face to the top.

"Petite Capucin" (ca. 11,200)

When standing on the Matterhorn Glacier, facing the Matterhorn, one will see a ridge on the left containing several walls and towers. This route lies on what has been described as the "first" of these walls and towers and is supposed to resemble the fabled Grand Capucin in the Chamonix area. The four-pitch route lies on the north face of the formation and is rated III, 5.8.

"Horse Creek Tower"

As one hikes up the approach to the Dragtooth region a tower will be seen on the right. Although it is in full profile from Twin Lakes, it was not climbed until very recently. The route lies on the south face. Scramble up to a big ledge; then move up and right on bolts to a vertical aid crack. Continue up to the southeast corner of the spire; then tension-traverse into a dihedral. Mixed climbing ends on a belay ledge 60 feet above. A short bolt ladder leads to the top. II, 5.8, A3.

Finger Peaks (11,390)

Class 3 from the north. The west peak is the higher of the two "fingers."

Whorl Mountain (12,029)

The middle summit is the highest and is class 4. Both of the other summits are class 3.

"Horse Creek Peak" (Pk. 11,600, 0.95 ESE of Matterhorn Pk.)

This peak, prominent from the headwaters of Horse Creek, is the first peak east of Horse Creek Pass. The southern slopes are easy. A route has been done up the steep north buttress. Begin in a narrow snow couloir just left of the actual buttress and follow it for about 200 feet to a headwall covered with water or ice. Ascend a ramp which leads up and right onto the buttress. A class 5 pitch on the very prow leads to easier climbing. Eight hundred feet of class 4 climbing brings one onto the summit. III, 5.4

Twin Peaks (12,240+)

From the south, climb to the saddle between the two peaks. Either peak can be climbed from here; the west peak is the higher. Class 2.

Hetch Hetchy

"Wapama Rock" (Pk. 5,440+, 1.65 NE of O'Shaughnessy Dam)

On the north side of the Hetch Hetchy Reservoir, between Tueeulala and Wapama falls, is a 1,400-foot cliff. A technical route, rated V, 5.9, A3, has been done.

Hetch Hetchy Dome (6,165)

A long, hard route lies on the south face of this prominent dome. Start climbing at the base of a right-diagonaling crack system which lies a bit left of the center of the face. About 600 feet of mixed free and aid climbing leads to a very conspicuous jamcrack. This is the crux pitch. Above, an easy pitch leads to a few bolts and bat-hook holes on a slab which heads up and left. Easy class 5 rock then brings one onto a huge horizontal ledge, two-thirds of the way up the dome. A single crack system leads up above the ledge for several pitches; just before the crack ends, pendulum right to another crack system and follow it upward until a steep class 5 ramp can be followed up and right. At its end climb a hard aid pitch. The route is obvious and easier above this point. VI, 5.10, A3.

Kolana Rock (5,760+)

Across the reservoir from Hetch Hetchy Dome is a fine-looking dome with a steep face falling into the reservoir. The approach to the route on the north face must be made by circling over and around the dome to its east side. The route begins on a ledge about 200 feet above the water line. A very obvious, right-facing open book is followed for four pitches. Leave the book and climb behind a detached tower on the left. A ledge will be found a bit higher. Three pitches higher, one should traverse a full pitch to the right to avoid the summit headwall. A few more pitches of mixed free and aid climbing lead to class 4 rock and the top. V, 5.9, A3.

Virginia Canyon and Surrounding Region

West Peak (10,480+)
  Class 2 from the northeast.

Regulation Peak (10,560+)
  A popular class 2 ascent from the trail at Rodgers Lake.

Pettit Peak (10,788)
  Class 2 from either Regulation or West Peak.

Volunteer Peak (10,479)
  Class 2 from the south.

Doghead Peak (11,102)
  Class 2 from the headwaters of Wilson Creek. It is said that the summit offers a great view.

Quarry Peak (11,161)
  Class 2 from the headwaters of Wilson Creek.

Virginia Peak (12,001)
   Class 3 from the Stanton-Virginia saddle; also class 3 from the southwest or west.

Stanton Peak (11,695)
   Class 2.

Grey Butte (11,365)
   From Virginia Canyon a class 2 route can be picked out.

Camiaca Peak (11,739)
   Class 2 from the trail at Summit Lake.

Gabbro Peak (10,960+)
   Easy from either East Lake or Glines Canyon.

Page Peaks (10,880+)
   Class 2 scree slopes can be followed anywhere with impunity. The shortest route may be from Virginia Pass.

Epidote Peak (10,880+)
   Class 2 from the Hoover Lakes and probably from East Lake.

Dunderberg Peak (12,374)
   This ugly giant is a prominent sight from U.S. Highway 395 in the vicinity of Conway Summit. Class 2 from all directions.

Black Mountain (11,760+)
   Class 2 from Cooney Lake.

Peak 12,126 (0.7 NNW of Excelsior Mtn.)
   The east slopes and the south ridge are both class 2.

Excelsior Mountain (12,446)
   Class 2 from the west.

Shepherd Crest (12,015)

Class 3 via steep avalanche chutes on the south side. The northeast ridge is also class 3. At the northwest end of the peak is a rare and fascinating example of a high, unglaciated valley, the so-called Little Lost Valley of Shepherd Crest.

Sheep Peak (11,840+)

Class 2 from Roosevelt Lake.

North Peak (12,242)

Class 2 from the Conness Lakes. A 30-degree snow couloir on the northeast side of the peak has been done. Two technical routes exist, one on either side of the snow couloir. A long, deep chimney just left of the couloir provides a IV, 5.8 route—stay far back inside the chimney for the first six pitches. Another route lies quite a way to the right of the couloir, on the right side of the northeast face. Begin climbing from a small glacier and head directly toward the summit. The first three pitches are the hardest. III, 5.8.

Mt. Conness (12,590)

This peak is a prominent Sierra landmark; its sheer, white southwest face is plainly visible from the Olmsted Viewpoint on the Tioga Pass road. Many routes have been done—the mountain has something for everyone.

Route 1. From Young Lakes. Class 2. From the lakes walk up to the small lake 1.3 miles south of the top; then head due north up a gentle valley. Soon the summit plateau is reached; the route up the final monolith is obvious from here.

Route 2. From the East. From the dam at Saddlebag Lake walk to the Carnegie Institute Station one-half mile to the southwest. Head west and somewhat south from here, following a gentle valley which leads to a short headwall at the Sierra crest, some three-quarters of a mile from the top. Climb the class 2–3 headwall and follow Route 1 to the top.

As a variation, one can ascend from the Carnegie Station in a north-northwest direction, hitting the east ridge and following that to the summit plateau. This is about the same difficulty.

Route 3. Glacier Route. Class 3. From the Conness Lakes climb the glacier, and then ascend either snow tongues or rock ribs to the low point in the ridge above. This brings one to the summit plateau.

Route 4. Northeast Face. This is the steep wall rising above the right side of the glacier. Start in a gully that angles left of the prominent buttress which divides the face. At the top of the gully cross the buttress and climb several class 4 pitches to an overhang. A class 5 traverse leads to a crack—follow this to a recess. Several more pitches lead to the summit ridge, 200 feet right of the top.

Route 5. North Ridge. II, 5.6. From the saddle between Conness and North peaks climb the long ridge to the top.

Route 6. West Ridge. Class 5. This route lies on the far right side of the deeply scoured west face, and very close to the edge of the great southwest face. The ascent is very enjoyable.

Route 7. Southwest Face, Original Route. V, 5.9, A3. This ten-pitch route goes up the steep, white face somewhat left of center. An aid pitch starts things off; this is followed by an easy aid traverse up and right. The rock in this area is none too good, but it becomes excellent higher up. On the third pitch climb up and left to a ledge. Traverse left a bit and climb 250 feet (some 5.9 is found, as well as a bolt ladder) to another ledge. From its right side climb a difficult corner. Shortly after the beginning of the next pitch, head to the right above a chimney—don't follow the off-route corners straight above. A few more moderate pitches lead to a ramp; follow this up and right to the summit slabs.

Route 8. Southwest Face, 1974 Route. V, 5.9, A3. This route begins 150–200 feet right of the start of Route 7 and goes more or less straight to the top.

Route 9. Southwest Face, Right Corner. IV, rating unknown. This obscure route lies in the corner which separates the great southwest face from the less significant wall to its right. The route begins in a wide chimney. Farther up, one enters a great gully, and from this there are two exits—a hard chimney leading directly upward or an easy gully to the right. There is an inordinate amount of loose rock on this route.

White Mountain (12,000+)
Class 2 from the south.

Peak 11,255 (1.8 SW of White Mtn.)
The west slopes are easy and lead to the class 3 summit blocks.

Ragged Peak (10,912)
This peaklet is a spectacular sight from Young Lakes and has been climbed many hundreds of times. The easiest route is from the saddle east of the summit; traverse around onto the easy west or southwest slopes and climb class 2 talus to the main summit, the southernmost of three summits clustered together. Three harder routes have been established. The northwest face is class 5, the northeast face is 5.6 (start in a V-shaped trough), and the east face is class 5. The last two routes end on the lower north summit.

Peak 12,002 (1.1 SE of White Mtn.)
The slopes on the southeast side of the peak are class 2.

Gaylor Peak (11,004)
A trail from the Tioga Pass Entrance Station leads to the saddle south of the peak; a twenty-minute walk from here brings one to the top, a fine viewpoint.

Mt. Warren (12,327)
Class 2.

Tuolumne Peak (10,845)
Route 1. Northeast Side. Class 2.
Route 2. East Face, Right Side. II, 5.6. Rope up below a very prominent, left-facing open book on the right side of the face. From the top of the book traverse up and left to a tree-covered terrace.

Head for its upper left side and climb a long class 4 pitch which ends precisely on the summit.

Route 3. East Face, Left Side. II, 5.7. Start climbing about 50 feet left of the prominent chimney near the left side of the face. One easy class 5 pitch leads to the chimney, but instead of getting into it, climb the right side until it is possible to belay on chockstones back in the slot. Continue up the chimney for another long pitch; then make an improbable traverse left under a roof. Follow cracks upward 200 feet to the summit plateau.

Route 4. Southwest Face. II, 5.7. Begin climbing near the center of the face and head for a prominent, 250-foot-high chimney. From the top of this, climb up and left to the class 4 south buttress.

Mt. Hoffmann (10,850)

This peak, named for a member of the Whitney Survey, was the first summit to be reached in the Tuolumne area. It is an extremely popular ascent.

Route 1. Southeast Slopes. Class 2. From May Lake easy slopes lead to the top.

Route 2. West Slopes. Class 3. Climb to the southwest ridge from the vicinity of Wegner Lake.

Route 3. North Face. III, 5.7 or 5.8, A2. This route follows a line almost directly up to the overhanging summit blocks. Start climbing in cracks which cut through overhangs. Higher, pass through a red overhang; then traverse left to steep cracks. These lead to a belay ledge on the left. The last three pitches follow easy class 5 flakes and cracks.

Route 4. The Merle Alley Route. III, 5.7. This route, formerly known as the North Face Route, or North Chimney Route, lies about 200 feet to the right of the preceding route and follows a 600-foot crack-and-chimney system. Three overhanging areas present the main problems.

Route 5. Approach Face. II, 5.5. A climb has been made on the most obvious face to the right of the summit when viewed from the Snow Flat parking area. It is an enjoyable route and can be used as an approach to the upper slopes of Hoffmann.

Route 6. Middle Summit, East Face. II, 5.7. This is the formation which faces May Lake. Begin in cracks just right of a prominent, left-facing open book capped with roofs. Another diagnostic feature is a rib just left of the book. Climb the cracks to a recessed ramp which cuts left to the top of the formation.

Route 7. Hoffmann's Thumb. This striking spire is found part way down the southwest ridge. The upper side can be climbed by various moderate class 5 routes. A harder route has been made on the west face. The standard route lies on the side away from the summit of Hoffmann and is 5.5. All these routes are about 75 feet in length.

Route 8. Hoffmann's Turret. At the end of the northwest ridge of the peak, overlooking the lake north of the top, is a sharp pinnacle. The route lies on the northeast face. Climb the right-hand crack of two jamcracks and gain a V-shaped opening. Continue above this to the top. 5.5, A2.

Lee Vining Peak (11,691)

Easy via the southeast slopes.

Mono Dome (10,614)

Class 2 from the north.

Tioga Peak (11,513)

Easy from Gardinsky Lake. It also can be climbed without much difficulty from the Ellery Lake area.

Wildcat Point (9,455)

This peak, located a mile or two northwest of Glen Aulin, is class 2 from Mattie Lake. A route has been done on the south buttress of the peak, just above California Falls. Start just right of a prominent dihedral. Higher on the face one must zigzag to connect dihedrals. IV, 5.9 or 5.10, A4.

Cold Mountain (10,301)

This uninspiring peak is easy, as is its lower summit 1.25 miles south-southeast. On the extreme southwest flank of this lower summit is a buttress which falls away into Glen Aulin. This buttress, 0.8 mile northwest of the High Sierra Camp, has a single large dihedral, the climbing route. III, 5.8.

Tuolumne Domes

Within a six-mile radius of Tuolumne Meadows lies the most accessible, most pleasant, and most overcrowded rockclimbing area in the High Sierra. Approaches are as short as two minutes and are rarely longer than half an hour. The rock is of dreamlike quality, and "chickenheads" jut out of rough, orange granite. Most of America's top cragsmen have spent some time here, and when nearby Yosemite Valley becomes hot and crowded in June, vast numbers of hard men establish residency in the Meadows. The result, of course, is predictable. Leave the hot, crowded Valley and emigrate to the cool, crowded, and more limited area of the Meadows and what do you find? Waits in line for popular routes, glaring chalk marks which obviate routefinding skills, and cracks marred by those of us who once swung a mighty hammer.

Fortunately, piton placements have ruined only a minute number of climbs. The "high-country rock" for which Tuolumne is so renowned lends itself perfectly to the placement of nuts, and it is indefensible for climbers to carry pitons. Remember, times have greatly changed in the past decade.

An exemplary tradition has evolved in the Meadows concerning direct aid climbing. It's simple: no aid climbing. There are only a few exceptions to the "rule."

It is rather unbelievable to think that the first serious route in the now-so-popular Domes region was not accomplished until 1958, when Chuck Pratt and Wally Reed, up from the Valley for a "vacation," climbed the biggest wall in the area, the north face of Fairview Dome. When word of this ascent filtered down to the Valley, the locals thought, "Why do that when there's so much to do down here?" A fair amount of direct aid had been used, and the pair had made the first Tuolumne bivouac. These Valley practices were very soon to become anachronisms.

During the next ten years many fine first ascents were established; these generally followed obvious crack systems. Since about 1968, however, a new generation of incredibly skilled, safe, and bold climbers has pushed routes up seemingly blank, impossible faces. It is a new age of virtuosity, and names like Tom Higgins, TM Herbert, Tom Gerughty, Vern Clevenger, and Bob Kamps dominate the first-ascent list for this period. Hundreds of bolts have been placed for protection, and climbers have been known to work on routes for months, pushing their high points higher each time.

About 120 routes were done by the summer of 1975; only three-quarters of these are included in this chapter. Some routes are so short that they belong in the bouldering category, others are kept so secret that few know of their existence, and a few have been purposefully omitted. In this last category are a handful of routes which probably should fade into well-deserved oblivion. A few outcrops containing several excellent routes have been left out, so that for a while, at least, the climber may stumble onto a "new" area and recapture for a moment the feelings of the Tuolumne pioneers.

The only map necessary for this area is the Tuolumne Meadows quadrangle.

Tenaya Lake Region

"Stately Pleasure Dome"

Beginning midway along the shore of Tenaya Lake, one will notice a mile-long band of cliffs northwest of the highway. Climbers have long called the entire mass Polly Dome, but a look at the map will show that Polly Dome actually lies at the extreme end of the domed ridge. For convenience, the domed ridge can be divided into four separately named ''domes.'' Stately Pleasure Dome is the first encountered when driving east from Tenaya Lake. The dome is a clean, monolithic formation and has the obvious Great White Book as its most distinguishing feature. Most of the following routes can be easily found if the Book is located first.

A common descent is shared by all routes. When slopes of diminishing angle are reached, don't continue upward, but traverse left and descend via the giant class 3 dihedral or ramp visible from the west end of the lake. One may, of course, go all the way to the top and descend to the west, but this is much longer.

Route 1. Far West Country. 5.6. A few hundred feet up and left of the rope-up spot for the Great White Book is a large pine. Above this are several prominent straight-in cracks. A class 4 pitch leads to the pine and from here a short crack leads to friction slabs to the right of the straight-in cracks. Several moderate pitches lead to the giant dihedral or ramp used in the descent.

Route 2. West Country. 5.7. Climb the first pitch of Hermaphrodite Flake; then move left up a short 5.7 overhang. Enter an obvious, right-facing dihedral and ascend it to a belay ledge with a bolt. Next, work up and right toward twin cracks and follow these to easy friction slabs.

A major variation has been done. Climb the left edge of Hermaphrodite to its top; then move left (5.7) and rejoin the normal route. Follow this to the bolt ledge, then traverse left a bit and climb to easy slabs.

Route 3. Hermaphrodite Flake. 5.4. About 50 feet left of the Great White Book, and on a level with the one-third mark of that climb, is a detached flake. A class 4 pitch leads to a sloping ledge just beneath the gaping lower part of the flake. Moderate liebacking leads around the right edge to a bolt belay at the top. One can also tunnel behind the first half of the flake, but this is somewhat claustrophobic.

Route 4. Eunuch. 5.7. From the top of Hermaphrodite Flake, climb up and slightly right to a hard-to-see bolt 40 feet above.

Diagonal right for 80 feet (scary 5.6) to a belay bolt. Two bolts protect the next pitch, which ends at a short, prominent crack. Scrambling leads to the descent slabs.

Route 5. The Great White Book. 5.6. This unmistakable, left-facing open book is proving to be the most popular route in the Meadows. The route is quite obvious. Although the route looks intimidating from the road, the angle is embarrassingly low, and the climbing is far easier than one might imagine. There is no protection on some of the leads, however, and one must be cautious. Above the end of the book a few friction pitches lead to the unroping area.

A major variation has been done. Just above the large chockstone in the easy middle section of the book, leave the book via a 5.8 ramp which leads right. Ascend a small, left-facing dihedral; then work up and right to a belay ledge. Three more pitches lead to easy going.

Route 6. Get Slick. 5.10. Start climbing atop the pillar just right of the start of the Great White Book. Climb upward past five protection bolts to a two-bolt belay anchor. This pitch is a full 165 feet. The next pitch is easier; above is easier yet.

Route 7. Sweet Nothings. 5.10. Begin climbing on a small slab about 30 feet left of the start of South Crack. Sustained climbing leads past six bolts to a small, right-facing corner or groove. From near its top move left to the belay anchors of Route 6.

Route 8. South Crack. 5.8. About 75 feet to the right of the Great White Book is an inconspicuous, right-slanting crack. A short class 4 pitch ends at a good belay stance. Move right (5.8) into South Crack and follow it to a belay spot in the crack 20 feet below a good ledge. Easier climbing now leads along the crack until a small belay stance is reached just before the crack terminates. The fourth pitch traverses up and left at a 45-degree angle from the end of the crack, toward the left end of a roof. A bolt is seen a bit higher; the belay ledge is just to its left. Next, climb easy slabs to the unroping area. Piton scars sully this fine route, but nuts work perfectly, and it is indefensible to carry pitons.

A variation goes up and right from the end of the third pitch.

Route 9. Dixie Peach. 5.9. From the end of the class 4 first pitch of South Crack, climb straight up a left-facing flake or corner. Climb past two bolts to a two-bolt belay anchor. Continue upward to easier slabs.

Route 10. The Way We Were. 5.9. Uphill and right from South Crack is a large, left-facing arch. Start climbing atop a pillar about 150 feet downhill from the arch. Climb 20 feet (bolts will be found), traverse left 40 feet to a bolt; then climb past two more bolts to a belay spot beneath a ceiling. On the second pitch follow a black streak over a roof to a belay piton. An easier pitch leads up and right to a two-bolt anchor. Above, follow the right-hand book of two open books.

"Harlequin Dome"

Looking north from the parking area at the east end of Tenaya Lake one will see a large, rounded formation with an obvious, gull-shaped overhang near its top. This is Harlequin Dome.

Route 1. Hoodwink. 5.10. Many possible and intricate routes lead to the big ledge at the base of the right-facing corner which turns into the left "wing" of the overhang. Halfway along the arch is a 5.9 exit over it. Hard face climbing above leads to easier climbing.

Route 2. Vicious Thing. 5.10. Seen from the parking lot, this route lies in the obvious, right-curving, right-facing flake at the lower right side of the dome. A three-inch crack on the first pitch offers the stimulating possibility of a groundfall. The chimneys above are easier and safer.

"Mountaineer's Dome"

This quarter-mile-long formation can be said to begin to the right of a break in the rock band right of Harlequin Dome. This break can be seen easily from the road opposite it, some 250 yards east of the Tenaya Lake picnic area parking lot. Just right of the break, the cliffs once again assume massive proportions. The first wall encountered to the right of the break is quite monolithic; only a few wrinkles mar its golden smoothness. This wall originates from a broad ledge some 400 feet above the highway. At the right edge of the wall is its diagnostic landmark—a 200-foot-long, sinuous, left-facing dihedral.

Several routes are scattered along the remainder of Mountaineer's Dome. The dome peters out opposite the southwest end of Pywiack Dome.

Route 1. Pippin. 5.9. Well below, and somewhat left of the sinuous dihedral mentioned above, is a solitary tree some 20 feet above a ledge. A few 5.9 moves lead to the tree. From here traverse up and right along a narrow ramp to its end; then walk back left to a belay ledge. A diagonal pitch to the right leads to a large ledge near a wide dike. Climb a very difficult pitch with two protection bolts to a ledge with bushes. From the left end of this ledge climb a short crack and then a long, low-angle face to the sinuous dihedral. Several pitches (some 5.8) up this lead to the top.

Route 2. Mountaineer's Route. 5.7. About 350 yards up the road from the Tenaya Lake picnic area parking lot is a giant boulder on the southeast side of the road. This circuitous route lies on the steep wall to the north. Climb several hundred feet of diagonaling crack which leads toward the only prominent tree on the wall. When 100 feet short of the tree, cut back left and traverse for several hundred feet until it becomes obvious to drop down a ramp. From its bottom continue traversing left for about 125 feet; then turn back right and ascend ramps for many hundreds of feet to the top of the cliff. A few short 5.7 sections are encountered on this route, but most of the climbing is a lot easier.

Route 3. The American Wet Dream. 5.10. This route ascends, in a direct fashion, the wall on which the Mountaineer's Route is located. Connecting several large, right-facing corners, this route is the most obvious on the wall. Begin climbing in a shallow crack which crosses a headwall and then bears left toward a ledge at the base of the first corner. Scary 5.10 liebacks form the crux of the climb.

Route 4. Delta Squeeze. 5.8. A few hundred feet to the right of the preceding route is a very steep section of cliff marked by many shattered blocks, the most conspicuous of which has an orange base. A solitary dead tree atop the cliff is another landmark. Delta Squeeze is the narrow slot on the right side of a recess just right of the orange block. A rappel bolt has been placed above the slot to facilitate return.

Route 5. The Lieback Detector. 5.9 or 5.10. Begin climbing about 40 feet right of Delta Squeeze. A prominent, leaning, right-facing crack is liebacked for about 90 feet.

Polly Dome

This is the wall across the road from Pywiack Dome.

Route 1. The Block. 5.8. Across the road from the Tenaya Lake end of Pywiack Dome is a small bluff. A massive, 50-foot-high block, split by deep cracks on both sides, can be seen lying in a small depression. Climb the right side of the block to its top; then proceed up and left via 5.7 liebacks and face climbing to the top of the bluff. The left side of the block has also been climbed and is a bit harder. A tunnel inside the block can be ascended, but if one suffers from claustrophobia or is thicker than nine inches, forget it.

Route 2. The Cooler. 5.9. From the road opposite the main mass of Pywiack Dome one will see a very steep cliff about 500 feet above. The main landmark of this cliff cannot be discerned readily from below, but from a point several hundred yards down the road toward the lake, it will be seen as a deep slot in a large corner. Ascend a difficult lieback, then undercling around a roof. Step into an overhanging jamcrack and thrash upward to a deep, cold squeeze chimney which leads to the top.

Route 3. Deimos. 5.8. About 250 feet right of Cooler is an aesthetic crack system splitting a golden wall. A short initial pitch leads over blocks 40 feet to a belay alcove. Next, hand-jam and chimney over a difficult overhang and belay in an alcove below a bulge. Pass this; then head up and right to a fine belay ledge at the base of a large flake. The last pitch involves jamming the flake and climbing the bolt-protected face above.

Route 4. The Stairs of Cirith Ungol. 5.7. This route lies on the northwest side of the dome and is hidden from the road. Begin climbing in a chimney system just left of an enormous slot. Follow the chimney system for several pitches, occasionally wandering out on the face. On the fourth pitch turn a roof on the left and climb between large boulders to the top.

Pywiack Dome

Pywiack is the classic, free-standing dome at the northeast end of Tenaya Lake.

Route 1. The Tension Cracks. Class 4. Around the corner to the right of the slope which faces the lake is a low-angle trough sliced with many bizarre, parallel cracks. One class 4 pitch leads to easy friction and the top.

Route 2. Southwest Slope. 5.3. This low-angle slope, which faces Tenaya Lake, affords pleasant and easy climbing. Above a solitary, ancient pine there appear to be several ways to go.

Route 3. The Dike. 5.8. On the highway side of the dome, several hundred feet left of the preceding route, one will discern a sinuous dike system (often there are two dikes) leading most of the way up the face. The first pitch ends at a conspicuous, diagonal slash. The next pitch is short and follows the dike. On the next (and crux) pitch, climb to the right of the dike and wander up difficult and grossly unprotected face climbing to the summit headwall. This can be surmounted via either of two obvious cracks.

Route 4. North Face. 5.10, A1. Lying several hundred feet to the left of the Dike Route is a grass-topped flake hidden behind a grove of trees. From the flake ascend a difficult face 90 feet to a ledge on the left. Next, move up and left past bolts (5.10) to a short, left-facing flake. A belay stance lies just above. Climb up; then traverse right, using some aid, to a long jamcrack which shoots upward to the summit headwall.

"Pennyroyal Arches"

Looking south from Pywiack Dome, across the creek, one will

see a large, rounded cliff with an obvious, broken gully (the Great Fissure) splitting it. Just right of the gully, but before a large arch, are some right-facing, right-leaning dihedrals which peter out on white slabs containing a small grove of trees. Several routes ascend these dihedrals.

Most parties will probably prefer to descend via the following route: from the grove of trees (these are about two-thirds of the way up the cliff) walk down to an easy, forested ledge which begins just across the Great Fissure. As an alternative, the headwall above the trees can be climbed in several places—in general, the left side is the easiest.

Route 1. Vision. 5.9 or 5.10. Begin climbing about 40 feet right of the base of the Great Fissure. Climb easily to the top of a 60-foot slab covered with knobs; then make a few 5.8 moves up and right before working back left to a belay stance with a two-bolt anchor. Next, a long pitch protected by three bolts leads to a long, large ledge. The crux pitch follows: climb up and left past a bolt to another bolt at the base of a steep section. A third bolt lies 15 feet higher. From it work straight up; then move right to a crack system visible from the ground. A belay stance is found 15 feet up this crack. A long, sustained pitch leads to class 3 and 4 slabs.

Route 2. The Eagle Dihedral. 5.7. About 75 feet right of the start of Route 1 is an area where several dihedrals come together close to the ground. A small belay ledge 40 feet up can be reached easily. Rope up and move left into the farthest left dihedral and ascend to a tree. Continue for one pitch to a long belay ledge. Ascend a knobby face; then move left into the Eagle Dihedral, the largest open book of the area. Two pitches up this book lead to low-angle slabs.

Route 3. Euphoria. 5.7. Rope up at the same small ledge as for the preceding route and ascend the prominent open book which rises straight above. A 165-foot lieback pitch ends on a good ledge. The face above is then climbed to a long belay ledge. A very knobby lieback flake (easy class 5) is followed next and after two more easy pitches the grove of trees is reached.

Medlicott Dome Area

Medlicott Dome

This is the long formation visible east of the road a mile or so past Pywiack Dome. The northwest buttress can be said to divide the north and west faces. The north face, which lacks distinctive features, is notable for its relatively poor quality. The west face, on the

POLLY DOME CLIMBS

1 STATELY
    PLEASURE
2 HARLEQUIN
3 MOUNTAINEER'S
4 POLLY

DAFF DOME

CATHEDRAL CREEK

FAIRVIEW DOME

NORTH & SOUTH WHIZZ DOMES

THE LAMB

MARIUOLUMNE DOME

TIOGA PASS HWY

MEDLICOTT DOME

PYWIACK DOME

PENNYROYAL ARCHES

TENAYA CREEK

8800

9200

ONE MILE

N

TUOLUMNE DOMES

other hand, is much more monolithic and offers several excellent routes.

Descent from the dome can be made in two general directions. One can walk down to the notch between Medlicott and the next dome east (Mariuolumne). From this notch head down north along a stream to the road. The other route descends class 3 slabs to the south. Don't stray too far west during this descent, but rather head for a small pond nestled among the cliffs and slabs.

Route 1. North Face. 5.6. This broken, 60-degree wall can be climbed almost anywhere, but the climbing is not especially enjoyable owing to the nature of the rock.

Route 2. Another Country. 5.6. Ascend the north face just left of the obvious North Gully Route. After reaching the steep, upper headwall work up and left along the diagonal crack system easily visible from the highway.

Route 3. North Gully. 5.4. This is the low-angle gully or chimney just left of the rounded northwest buttress. The route is obvious; a four-foot-wide chimney halfway up presents a minor problem.

Route 4. Northwest Buttress. 5.7, A3. This is one of the very few aid climbs in the Tuolumne region, and for that reason is not often climbed. Climb the easy first pitch of the Yawn; then nail an obvious crack under the roof on the left. Work upward, using aid, for several hundred feet past some overhangs. The route is obvious from here.

Route 5. The Yawn. 5.9. The Yawn is the imposing, curving crack which forms the right side of the northwest buttress. An easy pitch leads to a belay alcove. Climb somewhat right of the main corner and head toward a scary-looking lieback crack. Above this is a belay spot. A short, intimidating pitch follows and ends on a chockstone. The flaring chimney above is the crux, but the difficulties ease after a short bit. Easier climbing leads to the beautiful summit dihedral. Occasional 5.7 sections are found in the remaining 180 feet. One can unrope shortly above the dihedral's top. Nut placements on this route are extraordinarily good; take big ones.

Route 6. Piss Easy. 5.7. A few hundred feet to the right of the

Yawn is a 200-foot-high pillar. Two crack pitches lead to its top, from which the summit slabs are attained by several moderate face-climbing pitches.

Route 7. Middling. 5.7. This is an obvious, dirty, straight-in crack system about 200 feet right of Piss Easy. Awkward and unsatisfying climbing leads up 125 feet to a good belay ledge. Ascend cracks on the right for about 35 feet and then move left into the main chimney. Follow this straight up to low-angle slabs and the unroping area.

Route 8. The Coming. 5.9. Begin climbing in the prominent, right-facing dihedral 150 feet right of Middling. The first belay is best placed about 120 feet out, just below a bush. The second pitch, the most difficult, begins with strenuous jamming and leads to a prominent overhang. Traverse right under this; then climb onto the face and belay. The next pitch leads straight up for 40 feet and then goes right, passing a bolt, to a belay stance beneath a roof. There appear to be several ways to go on this pitch; a few parties have been unable to find the bolt, thus committing themselves to a 140-foot, 5.6 runout. The final lead traverses around the right side of a roof to the summit slabs.

Route 9. Chartres. 5.9. Several hundred feet to the right of the preceding route is a golden wall which is so monolithic that one would immediately think "El Cap" if shown a photograph of it. Just left of this wall is a series of arches so disconnected that few climbers could have conceived a route here. A short, moderate pitch leads to a giant ramp-ledge which shoots up and left to a ledge with a large block resting on it. Work left from here; then move up into a prominent, left-facing arch. This arch is sustained 5.8, with a touch of 5.9. The next arch, which faces right, is merely sustained 5.8. An enormous, hollow roof above is passed on the left; an easy white rib then leads to the top.

Route 10. Sweet Jesus. 5.9. This excellent route goes up the right side of the golden wall mentioned in the preceding description. Begin climbing on rippled rock which rises steeply from comfortable ledges. Several bolts protect the first long lead, which ends on a small ledge with a crack. Next, climb easier rock (using a good vertical crack for protection) to a two-bolt belay. Traverse down and left about 40 feet; then climb up a bit to a belay ledge. On the next pitch climb past a bolt to a belay ledge only 50 feet above the belayer. Next, climb past two bolts and then head up and right over easier rock to the base of a long, left-leaning arch. A short traverse right allows access to the right-facing dihedral visible from the road. Follow this to the top.

"Mariuolumne Dome"

Just northeast of Medlicott Dome, and across the county line, is a dome set back a bit from the highway. Its absurd name is derived from the names of the two counties, Mariposa and Tuolumne. Two routes begin from a prominent ledge part way up the north face. Approach this ledge by circling the massive bluff below and left of the dome and then traversing out on it.

Route 1. The Hobbit Book. This pleasant route lies in the giant, left-facing open book which is so striking from the road. The 5.7 route consists of four pitches. On the upper section, don't be too dependent on the main crack; rather, wander left on the surrealistic solution pockets which abound on this route.

Route 2. Strider. This relatively ugly route begins about 150 feet left of the Hobbit Book and follows rotten, unaesthetic jamcracks and liebacks for a few pitches. A 5.8 jamcrack is found near the beginning of the second pitch.

"The Lamb"

A mile past Medlicott Dome is a pyramidal dome with prominent north and west faces. Routes 1–5 lie on the north side; the remainder of the routes are located on the west.

Route 1. North Book. At the far left side of the north face, and very prominent from the road, is a classic-looking, white dihedral, facing left. It is easier than it appears—class 4. A smaller open book to the left, similarly shaped, is apparently equally easy.

Route 2. Passover. 5.9. This nebulous route goes up the featureless wall just left of Route 3. The line is fairly direct, with minor weavings and wanderings. The last pitch traverses left on a ramp and then heads up a crack behind a light-colored flake.

Route 3. North Face, Left Side. 5.8. About 175 feet to the right of the North Book Route is the first conspicuous crack system of the cliff. A short lieback in a steep corner is the crux.

Route 4. North Face, Right Side. 5.9. About 300 feet to the right of the North Book Route is a prominent crack system. Take either of two cracks at the bottom; they converge into a left-leaning crack.

Route 5. Jog Corner. 5.7. Several hundred feet right of the distinctive north face of the Lamb is a gigantic, left-facing open book which makes a radical jog some 150 feet up. One easy pitch leads almost to the jog; the next lead passes the jog by about 20 feet and then cuts right over the corner. Two more pitches lead up easy cracks on the face above.

Route 6. Lament. 5.9 or 5.10. From the northwest base of the dome ascend a class 3–4 ramp which shoots up and right. This ramp begins just above a grove of large hemlocks. From the ramp's top climb up into a very difficult corner and proceed to a good ledge. At its left end a bolt protects a very hard move up and right. A somewhat harder variation lies up and left from the bolt. Easier climbing above leads to the top.

Route 7. Paralysis. 5.7? Ascend the ramp mentioned in the preceding description until an obvious, knobby face is seen above. On the right side of the knobby wall is a small, left-facing corner. Start here and climb upward a bit; then make an incredibly long traverse to a point where it is obvious to surmount the high-angle wall above. Small-hold climbing leads up to a belay spot. On the second pitch ascend to the only gray knob in the area; then head up and left to the top.

Route 8. Nervewrack Point. 5.8. This highly improbable route ascends the face to the right of Route 6. A solitary tree marks the rope-up spot. Climb a long pitch more or less straight up above the tree to the lower end of an indistinct fold which arches up left. On the second lead climb up a bit; then diagonal right to a belay bolt.

Next, proceed diagonally left to a ledge. Easy clambering then leads
to the right along the ledge to the unroping point.

"South Whizz Dome"

Almost totally hidden from the road, the South and North Whizz
domes are reached from the highway opposite Mariuolumne Dome
via a 30-minute walk through dense forest. South Whizz Dome is
shown on the topo map as Peak 8,924. It is not visible until most of
the approach is complete, yet most climbers seem to stumble into
the general area with little difficulty. It is best to turn the domes on
their southwest side since most of the routes lie on the west side.

Route 1. Rivendell Crack. 5.8. On the near-vertical southern
escarpment of the dome, and just right of a giant dead tree which
leans against the cliff, is a crack in a left-facing corner. Climb this to
a good ledge 60 feet above the ground; then move right around the
corner and zigzag to the summit.

Route 2. The Prow. 5.7. Begin climbing in a thin, right-slanting
crack which lies just left of the rounded corner which separates the
south and west faces. Wander up a pitch toward the obvious prow on
the right and follow it to the top.

"North Whizz Dome"

Route 1. Deception. 5.10. Rope up immediately left of the corner
which separates the south and west faces and climb a thin crack
which, after 30 feet (some 5.9), eases back a bit. A roof is found 40
feet higher — traverse left under it to a belay ledge. Climb a small,
right-slanting corner on the left (5.10) to easier rock.

Route 2. Thy Will Be Done. 5.10. Midway along the overhanging lower west face, a steep, left-facing open book rises to a
horrendous roof split by a thin crack. Begin this intimidating route
by climbing a tree to pass the initial overhang. Next, traverse right
to the book and follow it (5.8) to the roof. This is the crux and is
surmounted by a strenuous, jam-undercling technique.

Route 3. West Side. 5.6. Near the left side of the west face is a
very obvious chimney leading to a low spot on the summit ridge of

the dome. From the base of this chimney diagonal up and right onto a broad, sloping ledge. Traverse right for about 100 feet and then ascend a short chimney to the summit slopes.

Route 4. North Face. 5.7. About 50 feet left of the corner which cleanly divides the north and west faces of the dome is a bulky flake detached from the main face. Climb above this for three pitches.

Route 5. Cuckoo's Nest. 5.9. Standing at the base of the north face, some 200 feet left of the preceding route, one will see a large ceiling above. Start here and climb an easy ramp to an arching, right-facing open book. Climb up this, passing a ceiling on its right side, to a grassy belay ledge. Next, climb cracks on the left to a small, sloping ledge which lies beneath the large ceiling. Traverse right 20 feet to a bolt; then ascend to the ceiling and traverse under it to the right. A short section then leads to the top.

Fairview Dome and Vicinity

Fairview Dome

This is the largest and most spectacular of the Tuolumne domes and offers long and serious routes. Many of the routes lie on the 800-foot-high north face; the west face, to the right, is much more monolithic.

Descent from the summit is most easily accomplished by walking southeast off the back side via steep friction slopes.

Route 1. Northeast Margin. 5.7. This route ascends the short face just right of the large gully at the extreme left side of the north face. Moderate climbing leads up past blocks, cracks, and tree-covered ledges. A short 5.7 section is the only difficulty of the route.

Route 2. Always Arches. 5.10. A prominent feature of the left side of the north face is a series of thick, stacked arches some 250 feet above the ground. Class 3 slabs are ascended to a point just beneath these arches. A break appears about one-third of the way from the left; pass through this (5.10) and continue under a second arch until it rises vertically and becomes thinner. Step left over the arch to a good belay ledge. The next pitch diagonals up and right below a thick, indistinct arch to a belay spot. Climb a headwall above a bolt, move down and left for a bit, and then climb to a bushy ledge. Next, traverse straight left around still another arch (the

The north face of Fairview Dome. Route 2 (Always Arches) ascends the prominent arches at the lower left side of the wall. To their right are the two parallel cracks which form the starts of Routes 4 and 5, respectively. Routes 6-9 lie on the smooth wall to the right.

climber becomes aware of the significance of the route's name at this point!) onto a fine, steep face with a belay bolt. The enormous arch above is crossed at a difficult spot directly above the belayer. The fifth and final lead ascends a face to a long, flat ledge prominent from the road. From its left end easy climbing leads to the summit slabs.

Route 3. The Inverted Staircase. 5.10. This intimidating route ascends the steep but broken rock just right of the major arch of the lower north face. Five hundred feet of climbing takes one to an obvious, wide ledge. Traverse right off this ledge; then climb up and somewhat right past three bolts to the Inverted Staircase, three step-like ceilings visible from the road. This section is desperately hard. Easier climbing above the Staircase leads to the summit slabs.

Route 4. Powell's Route. 5.9. The most striking features of the lower north face are two very similar, white, parallel cracks, some 300 feet in length. This route begins in the left-hand crack and follows it to a distinct ledge 250 feet above the ground. From the right side of this ledge the route proceeds more or less straight up, passing over the right edge of some ceilings. At the 600-foot level the route joins Route 5 and follows it to the top.

Many parties join Route 5 at the 250-foot level—a friction face leading to the right is the crux of this variation.

Route 5. North Face. 5.9. This very popular route was the first major climb to be established in the Tuolumne Meadows area. The route begins in the right-hand crack mentioned in Route 4. The crux of the route lies on the third pitch, where face climbing bypasses overhangs in the main crack. At the 500-foot level one reaches Crescent Ledge. Follow steep books and cracks on the left side of this ledge until nearly level with the enormous roof on the right. Pass through small ceilings at a knobby area. Easier climbing leads to the summit slabs. Nuts protect this climb perfectly.

Route 6. Fairest of All. 5.10. Two hundred feet to the right of the preceding route is a small, left-facing dihedral. Climb this; then traverse right to a bolt. Climb to a ledge and ascend a crack; then

make an improbable traverse left to a bolt. From here climb up past a
ledge to a small belay stance. Now head up and left past a bolt to
another small belay stance. Climb upward, belay below a large
dike, and then head up and right, past bolts, to a good ledge. From
this point proceed up a right-curving arch to ledges. Higher, make a
long traverse right to a right-facing corner. Climb this and then head
up past a bolt to easy slabs and the top.

Route 7. Pièce de Résistance. 5.10 or 5.11. Start climbing at the
lowest-angle section of cliff several hundred feet up and right from
the start of Route 6. A few tiny ledges, some containing grass, will
be seen just above the ground. Climb past these to a bolt about 75
feet up. Make a difficult traverse right; then head up to a belay
ledge. A pitch leading more or less straight up takes one to a belay at
a bolt. Pitch 3: climb up to a bolt, traverse right to a little arch, and
climb up past another arch to a giant belay ledge. A short class 4
pitch up a trough leads to a belay spot. A very difficult pitch next
leads to a nice belay dike. Pitch 6 is the crux and is protected by
seven bolts. This pitch ends on a ledge with an unsteady block. The
next three pitches lead up to, then follow, an enormous right-facing
arch. Belay near the end of the arch, where it thins. Pitch 10: make a
few hard moves over the arch; then traverse far left from a bolt to a
rounded ledge. Belay here. Next, climb a pitch to a long, flat ledge.
Start the final section in a short lieback crack. The summit is 200
feet above.

Route 8. Lucky Streaks. 5.10. This excellent route lies near the
right-hand margin of the west face. A continuous crack system,
with one jog to the left, can be picked out easily from the highway.
Although the route is obvious for the most part, one must take care
to avoid horrendous sections of the main crack by making use of the
knobby areas to the side. The first 20 feet of the third pitch is
especially crucial in this way: step right below a thin crack, climb 15
or 20 feet, and then work back left into the crack. The belay
positions on the upper section of the route are minuscule.

Route 9. Pumpkin Eater. 5.9. This short route lies to the right of

Lucky Streaks, and just before the southern slabs begin. Class 3 scrambling leads to the base of a small crack. Climb the crack, past three bolts, to a belay ledge. Wander up and right to easy slabs.

"Daff Dome"

The name comes from the initial letters of the succinct statement: Dome Across From Fairview. This aesthetic formation is shown on the map as Peak 9,153. Unlike the other Tuolumne domes, Daff has no walk-up route. The easiest route lies on the east side and involves 100 feet of class 3–4 scrambling. This is also the normal descent route.

Route 1. West Crack. 5.8. On the west face one will immediately see the prominent Crescent Arch. About 100 feet left of the arch is a remarkable crack which extends almost unbroken for 400 feet. The single most difficult move is about 20 feet off the ground and is protected by a bolt. The remainder of the first pitch involves continuous 5.6 and 5.7 on beautiful knobs. A wild but relatively easy overhang must be passed on the second pitch. The last lead entails jamming a thin crack.

Route 2. Crescent Arch. 5.9. This striking feature is easily seen from the highway. Rather than stay in the main arch all the time, make use of the edging possibilities on the right.

Route 3. El Condor. 5.8. Rope up about 100 feet right of a group of three trees at the base of the smooth face right of Crescent Arch. Climb a tiny, right-facing corner for 75 feet to a belay ledge. An unprotected but fairly easy face is climbed up and left toward an obvious flake. Just above this is the "Condor," a remarkable knob. It can be tied off and used to protect the remaining 25 feet to a belay stance with a bolt. Next, climb up to a horizontal crack-ledge and follow it left for about 40 feet. Make a few difficult moves up and right to a belay ledge. One easy pitch follows.

A variation has been done: from the belay stance with the bolt, climb directly up knobs to easy friction slopes. This variation is 5.7.

Route 4. The Cooke Book. 5.10. Hidden from the road, this obvious route follows a huge, left-facing open book around to the left of Route 1. Begin climbing at a group of trees below an angular, 100-foot-high dihedral. Climb this and then drop down to the left a bit and follow the main book for two pitches to the crux. This consists of a difficult, flared section followed by an awkward lieback.

Route 5. Beverly's Route. 5.7. Several hundred feet left of the Cooke Book is a rounded buttress which leads toward the very top section of the book. Begin climbing below a solitary tree with a white snag. Pass over a headwall and belay at the tree. Traverse left and climb a crack to a sloping belay ledge. One more pitch leads to the crux lead—a bolt will be found for protection.

Lembert Dome Area

Lembert Dome

For many travelers this dome is the principal landmark of Tuolumne Meadows. In August one can find numerous parties climbing the varied routes. The summit is popular with hikers—there is a class 1 route on the eastern slopes. Low-angle slabs at the eastern side of the south face provide an enjoyable class 3 route; this is the usual descent route also.

Routes 1–6 lie on the broad northwest face, much of which is hidden from the commercial zone on the highway. From the main highway bridge one gets a good view of the southwest face and its dominant feature, the Water Cracks. Routes 7–11 are found in this area. Five more routes lie far to the east.

Route 1. Beginner's Route. 5.4. Around the corner to the left of the Water Cracks is the start of the long northwest face. Route 1 lies near the far right side of the face and just left of the rounded corner. Ascend an obvious class 3 ramp which leads up and right to ledges about 250 feet off the ground. These ledges are about 150 feet below and left of a gigantic pine. A foot-wide cleft can be climbed from the ledges; an alternate is a less strenuous face 40 feet to the right—a bolt protects the only hard move. Both routes lead to the huge ledge with the pine. Walk right to the rounded corner and ascend class 3 friction slabs to the top.

Route 2. Northwest Books. 5.5. Follow the class 3 ramp mentioned in Route 1 until just below a huge ceiling. Rope up and climb a low-angle slab at the left edge of this ceiling. Lieback the ceiling, which turns into a left-facing book. A big ledge is soon reached. From here climb the right-hand wall of a steep open book toward easier climbing and the top.

Route 3. Interrogation. 5.9. About 100 feet left of Route 2, and 40 feet left of some trees which grow out of a steep wall, is a short, left-facing corner. One pitch leads to the base of this corner. Climb it halfway; then move right to a short crack. Proceed straight up past a bolt to a belay ledge. Next, traverse far to the right. Reach a corner and climb it to a terrace. Move back left across the face and climb to the top.

Route 4. Direct Northwest Face. 5.9. This classic route follows the only continuous crack system on the broad northwest face; it lies about 500 feet left of the Beginner's Route. Scramble up slabs to the obvious rope-up spot. Climb up and right for 30 feet; then head straight up to a huge ledge with bushes. The wall above steepens radically and is climbed using a slender, right-facing dihedral.

Route 5. Northwest Buttress. 5.8. About 50 feet left of the start of the very obvious Route 4 is a giant fir growing close to the base of the cliff. Ascend a 200-foot, class 4 ramp which shoots up and left to sloping ledges. The steep wall above is festooned with old pitons and bolts. Several variations exist: the easiest seems to be on the left, beginning in a right-diagonaling crack. This crack, split into two sections, leads to easy ledges which blend left into a moderate open book.

Route 6. North Slabs. 5.6. All of the routes thus far described do not lead to the true summit of Lembert, but rather to the southwest summit. A broad gully on the northwest side of the dome separates the two summits. Various routes may be found on the low-angle face left of this gully.

Route 7. The Water Cracks. 5.7. Seen from the highway bridge below the southwest face of Lembert, these cracks stand out quite well. Although the angle is only 55 or 60 degrees, the rock is so polished as to make this route very deceptive. Climb increasingly difficult slabs toward the cracks and belay near the base of the right-hand crack. From a bolt a few feet higher move into the left hand crack and follow it to easy slabs 110 feet higher. Several bizarre techniques must be used to overcome the giant solution pockets on the upper part of this popular route. Bolts protect the pitch.

The left crack can be ascended directly from its base, and the right crack can be followed for its entirety, although this is more difficult.

Route 8. Truckin' Drive. 5.8 or 5.9. Just left of the Water Cracks is a small arch. Climb up to the lower right side of the arch and belay. Climb over the arch; then work left along an easy crack to a bolt. Ascend the face above, passing several more bolts, to the end of the roped climbing. A belay can be set up from two bolts midway up this last section.

Route 9. Rawl Drive. 5.9. Not far left of the point where the Truckin' Drive Route crosses the arch is a tongue of rock which is conspicuous from afar. This scary and hard route ascends to, crosses, and climbs above this formation. The golden wall above the tongue is the crux: sustained and not well-protected 5.9 face climbing. From a ledge 60 feet above the tongue climb up and left to a thin water crack. Follow this to the easy slabs.

Route 10. The Lunar Leap. 5.9. This fine route lies about 100 feet left of Rawl Drive and passes through the main headwall or arch at an obvious, lower-angle section. A fantastic ledge at the base of the headwall can be attained by following the main arch for two pitches from the base of the Water Cracks. A nicer and more direct route ascends the face, past four bolts, to the fantastic ledge. From here either climb or make a wild leap to reach an obvious handhold. Above, ascend a ramp up and left to a bolt which protects the crux—20 feet of sustained, small-hold climbing.

Route 11. Werner's Wiggle. 5.8. Just right of the Water Cracks are several much less distinct water cracks. This route ascends the left-hand crack. Bolts protect the main difficulties.

Route 12. Alive at Leads. 5.7. Many hundreds of yards to the right of the Water Cracks area is a 175-foot-high section of cliff capped with roofs. A 10-minute walk from the Tioga Pass road leads to the cliff. A large, dying lodgepole pine which splits into two trunks high up is an essential landmark for finding the five routes which have been done in the area. All five routes lie left, or downhill, from the pine.

Just left of the pine, and 20 feet above the ground, is a flake with a hole through it. Climb to here; then work up and right over a series of small ledges for about 100 feet to the last ledge which has adequate anchors. Move right 30 or 40 feet and climb an unprotected section to the giant roof which lies above. Surmount this at the only possible break and wander up easy slabs to the top.

Route 13. Patsy's Safari. 5.8. This route lies immediately left of the preceding route. Climb to a belay ledge 60 feet up and then go straight to the summit.

Route 14. Elephant Massacre. 5.8. This improbable route begins about 20 feet left of the dying lodgepole described in Route 12 and proceeds up and left 30 feet to a bolt. From here climb to a flake on the left; then move up to another flake on the right. A bolt is found 25 feet higher. Wander upward to another bolt, head right, and climb to the top.

Route 15. Second Choice. 5.7. Begin climbing in a short, right-facing open book some 200 feet downhill from the dying lodgepole (see Route 12). Ascend a jamcrack in the book to its top and belay. Move up and right toward the only obvious protection point; then proceed straight up to a roof. This can be surmounted at two places—the right one is easier and more conspicuous.

Route 16. Names in the Guidebook. Rope up about 40 feet left of the preceding route and ascend a difficult face which is protected with two glaringly obvious bolts. From the belay ledge 30 feet above the ground follow a dike to the overhang above. The overhang is 5.9; the face with the obvious bolts is 5.10.

"Dog Dome"

This tiny dome lies at the extreme northeast end of the Lembert Dome massif but is separated enough from it to warrant its own name. The trail to Dog Lake passes close by the formation.

Route 1. North Face. 5.7. This short route follows the prominent crack system near the center of the face.

Route 2. Mongrel. 5.9. Begin climbing about 50 feet right of the preceding route and ascend a delicate 5.9 lieback to sloping ledges. After surmounting overhanging blocks on the right, proceed over a 5.8 step. Climb upward left of a prominent open book to slabs which lead back toward the book. From a platform atop the book follow a diagonal ledge system to the top.

Route 3. Dirty Dog. 5.7. This route lies on the west side of the dome. Walk down and left from the high point of talus under the face. Begin climbing up and right from several large, loose blocks. Ascend past a loose-appearing block on the left; then head up a small corner. Belay at a tree on slabs 150 feet above the ground. Class 4 scrambling leads to the top.

Southern Yosemite

Three splendid sub-ranges comprise the southern section of Yosemite National Park. On the east is the Sierra crest, reaching 13,000 feet for the first time at Mt. Dana and culminating with Mt Lyell, the highest and most alpine peak in the park. West of the crest is the Cathedral Range, which begins as a striking array of sharp summits, and then gently curves eastward, joining the main crest at Mt. Lyell. It is between the Cathedral Range and the main crest that the Tuolumne River, one of the mightiest of the Sierra, begins its journey to the reservoirs below. Ten miles to the southwest of the Cathedral Range lies the isolated Clark Range, whose northern peaks overlook Yosemite Valley.

The peaks of the main crest are largely enormous mounds of talus and have little to offer the serious mountaineer. The few exceptions occur in the Lyell group. The Cathedral Range, however, is noted for its cockscomb formations, and these spectacular peaklets not only offer fine climbing, but are apparently curious geological phenomena. A half-century ago the noted geologist François Matthes wrote an article describing the formations and proposing for them the name "cockscomb." He apologized for the name: "The writer does not claim to be a connoisseur in poultry, nevertheless, he believes that the likeness to a lobate cockscomb is fairly close—as close as one might expect to find in a piece of mountain sculpture." The third sub-range, the Clark Range, is noted more for its varied colorings than for any significant climbing. Mt. Clark itself is an exception and offers a few fine routes.

The Southern Yosemite area was the locale of the first real mountaineering accomplished by white men in the High Sierra. During the summer of 1863 members of the Whitney Survey camped in Yosemite Valley, Tuolumne Meadows, and points

87

south. Mt. Dana was climbed and Mt. Lyell attempted. Peaks were surveyed and named, and the age of mountaineering began. John Muir's solo ascent of the class 4 Cathedral Peak in 1869 marks the first instance of difficult climbing in the Sierra. Lyell was climbed a few years later, and slowly the peaks began to succumb to prospectors looking for riches, packers looking for lost stock, and soldiers looking for an escape from boredom.

Clarence King and James Gardiner climbed the Obelisk (now Mt. Clark) in 1866, and the story which King later wrote is a superb example of the type of adventure writing which was so popular in those days. The account bears little resemblance to reality, but it is certainly guaranteed to make the palms sweat. A gap in the summit ridge gave the climbers second thoughts about continuing, and King imagined that he was "sure to fall and be dashed to atoms." He made a wild leap, however, and turned to watch Gardiner: "I shall never forget the look in his eye as he caught a glimpse of the abyss in his leap. It gave me such a chill as no amount of danger or even death coming to myself could ever give." Back safely in camp, they were "well pleased that the Obelisk had not vanquished us."

In 1931 a few members of a Sierra Club outing group began to "practice climbing with ropes" in the Cathedral Range. On July 12 Francis Farquhar and five others did a roped climb on the northeast side of Unicorn Peak. This incident later became a Sierra legend— the first use of ropes in the range. Moreover, the legend stated that Robert Underhill, of the Appalachian Mountain Club, had come west to show the neophytes how to climb and had taken them up Unicorn. Unfortunately, a glance at the old *Sierra Club Bulletins* of the era shows a few flaws in the legend. Underhill, for instance, wasn't even in the Sierra on July 12. And, more important, the year before had seen a class 4 climb on Laurel Mountain, south of Mammoth Lakes. John Mendenhall, a member of the team, had written: "My companion and I were roped, moved one at a time and employed the belays." This account sounds suspiciously like it might be "the first roped climb in the Sierra." And yet it must be remembered that Clarence King and Richard Cotter used a rope in 1864. The Underhill-Unicorn myth does contain an element of truth, for later that summer Underhill taught a new generation of California cragsmen *proper*, textbook-style rope techniques, and, by doing so, ushered in a radical change in the climbing history of the range.

During July 1931 first ascents were made of two outstanding crags, Eichorn Pinnacle and Matthes Crest. Both these climbs, the first continuous technical routes in the area, were done by Jules Eichorn and Glen Dawson, two of the leading lights of a generation which was to establish hundreds of rock climbs in Yosemite Valley and the High Sierra.

There are many approaches into the Southern Yosemite region. Peaks on the main crest are very easily reached from the Tioga Pass road or from the John Muir Trail. The crest peaks can also be reached from spur roads off U.S. Highway 395 on the east. The Cathedral Range is accessible from Tuolumne Meadows in a matter of hours. The Clark Range, not nearly so accessible as the other two sub-ranges, can most easily be reached from the Yosemite Valley area. The last few peaks of the chapter, those south of Triple Divide Peak, are best approached from the south via good dirt roads which originate near Bass Lake, in the western foothills.

Cross-country travel is relatively easy in the region; a look at the map will reveal many non-technical routes and passes. A climbers' trail which deserves mention is the Budd Lake trail. This well-trodden path leaves the John Muir Trail about one-quarter of a mile from the highway. The path follows the west bank of Budd Creek for several miles to the lake and offers a short, pretty, and not overcrowded route to climbs in the Cathedral-Echo group.

The following topographical maps are needed to cover the region: Devil's Postpile, Merced Peak, Mono Craters, Tuolumne Meadows, and Yosemite.

The Crest and Environs

Mt. Dana (13,053)

This giant peak, once thought to be the highest in the Sierra, is without a doubt the most often climbed in the northern part of the range. It is a walk-up from Tioga Pass—stay to the right of the buttes part way up. A hidden glacier on the northeast side of the mountain offers an enjoyable, 40-degree ice climb late in the year. The wall to the right of the glacier has been climbed and is loose class 3.

At least two technical routes have been established on the northeast side of the Dana Plateau, some two miles north of Dana's summit. The routes can be seen easily from portions of the Tioga Pass road as it winds down Lee Vining Canyon. A prominent pillar provides a good seven-pitch route—III, 5.9. A buttress to the right of the pillar is smaller but offers a 5.7 route.

Peak 12,568 (1.55 SE of Mt. Dana)

Class 1 from the Dana Fork of the Tuolumne River.

Mt. Gibbs (12,764)

The first ascent was made by a horse—this should give an indication of the difficulty of most sides of the peak. The ridge from the Dana-Gibbs saddle is easy class 3.

Mt. Lewis (12,296)

Class 1 or 2 from either Mono or Parker Pass. On the northeast slope of the peak, approximately a mile and a half from the top, is a series of spectacular crags. One route has been reported: from the Bloody Canyon trail, about one-half mile above Walker Lake, one will see a black open book on the easternmost pinnacle. Climb the face to the right of the book as well as the book itself—eight pitches of climbing lead to the top of the route. II, 5.6.

The Dana Glacier as seen from Dana Lake.

Mammoth Peak (12,117)

Class 2 and 3 routes will be found up the open slabs of the north face; easier routes can probably be found on the west side.

Kuna Crest (12,207)

Class 2 or 3.

Kuna Peak (12,960+)

Class 3 from Helen Lake.

Koip Peak (12,979)

Class 2 from the pass between Koip and Parker peaks. The glacier on the northwest side of the mountain can also be climbed. This glacier, by the way, is noted for its near-perfect multiple moraine structure.

Parker Peak (12,861)

Trivial from the Parker-Koip saddle.

Mt. Wood (12,637)

This peak is easily climbed from nearby Parker Peak. It is an easy but quite long climb from the east.

Blacktop Peak (12,710)

Class 1 via the enormous Eocene plateau on the west side. Class 2 from Crest Creek.

Koip Crest (12,668)

The two-mile-long jagged crest contains about sixteen pinnacles. The nine pinnacles to the north of Point 12,668 have been traversed in a day and are class 4. Point 12,668, the high point of the crest, is class 2 from the east and class 3 via the southeast arete. A prominent chimney on the southwest face is class 5. Little is known about the pinnacles to the southeast except for the following route: from the northern Lost Lake climb a buttress on the third-from-left pinnacle. Six pitches; II, 5.6.

Peak 12,223 (0.6 NE of Donohue Pk.)

From the stream which drains the largest Lost Lake climb the class 2 southeast ridge.

Donohue Peak (12,023)

A horse made the first ascent from the northwest. Class 2–3 from Donohue Pass.

Mt. Lyell (13,914)

This much-desired peak is the high point of Yosemite National Park. In 1863, the first climbers to attempt the climb had this to say: "We toil on for hours; it seems at times as if our breath refuses to strengthen us, we puff and blow so in the thin air. After seven hours of hard climbing we struck the last pinnacle of rock that rises through the snow and forms the summit—only to find it inaccessible." Thousands have proven otherwise.

Route 1. Regular Route. Class 2–3. In the high summer one can find five parties a day slogging up the glacier. From the headwaters of the Lyell Fork of the Tuolumne River, climb onto the glacier and proceed to the saddle between Lyell and Maclure. From here climb onto the ridge and scramble to the top. There are several possible variations, since the exact point where one leaves the glacier varies from year to year.

Route 2. East Arete. Class 3. From the vicinity of Upper Marie Lake climb onto the east ridge and follow it to the top. This is a fine and seldom-done route. The final part of the east arete can also be reached from the glacier of Route 1.

Route 3. South Face. Class 4. From the lake basin south of the peak, climb a steep talus chute to the summit area.

Route 4. Southwest Ridge. From the head of Hutching Creek

climb to a col on the ridge. Follow this ridge until it merges with the upper south face. A bit of class 4 leads to the summit ridge about 100 feet west of the top.

Route 5. West Face. Class 5. Seen from the head of Hutching Creek, the west face is a steep, wide wall which ends in a vertical prow. Begin climbing directly beneath this prow. Climb a rotten chimney; then ascend several class 4 pitches to the steep upper section. Work up and left until almost at a "diving board" prominent from the base. A couple of class 5 pitches lead to the fractured summit blocks. A short class 4 pitch up and right brings one to the summit ridge just left of the prow.

Route 6. From the West. Class 3. From the head of Hutching Creek climb an obvious, class 3 gully which leads to the Lyell-Maclure saddle. Follow Route 1 to the top.

Mt. Maclure (12,960+)
Class 3 from the Lyell-Maclure saddle. This is the normal route. The class 4 ridge from the Simmons-Maclure pass has been done. Another route has been established on the southwest face: climb a conspicuous gully for several hundred feet; then traverse right to the east ridge. Follow this to the summit. Class 3.

Peak 12,358 (0.75 WSW of Mt. Maclure)
Class 2 from the saddle to the northeast.

Peak 12,720+ (0.8 SW of Mt. Lyell)
Class 2 from the pass to the southwest.

Peak 12,132 (1.8 SW of Mt. Lyell)
Class 2 from the pass to the northeast.

Rodgers Peak (12,978)
This peak is misspelled on some current editions of the Merced Peak quadrangle. Class 3 from the Marie Lakes, class 3 from the basin to the west, and class 2–3 from the headwaters of the North

Fork of the San Joaquin. The easiest and most accessible route is as follows: from the Davis Lakes to the east cross the easy pass northwest of Peaklet 11,627 and proceed into the cirque west of the tiny lake 0.8 mile due east of the summit. Head south onto the east-southeast ridge and climb to the top. Class 2 with a few spots of class 3.

Peak 12,560+ (0.75 S of Rodgers Pk.)
Class 2 from the southeast.

Electra Peak (12,442)
Class 2 via the west side and north ridge; also class 2 from the southeast.

"Mt. Ansel Adams" (Pk. 12,760+, 1.25 WSW of Electra Pk.)
This peak, named for a prominent Sierra Club outing leader and explorer of this region, is a spectacular sight from the Lyell Fork of the Merced. From the creek ascend slopes to the west of the mountain; then climb a gully south of the top. The south face is followed for the last bit. Class 3.

Foerster Peak (12,058)
The south slopes are quite easy. The west side of the north ridge is class 2 or 3.

Long Mountain (11,502)
Class 2 from the south.

The Cathedral Range

Tenaya Peak (10,301)
This slabby peak is prominent from Tenaya Lake. The "back

side" is class 2. At least two routes have been done on the broad
northwest face. A 5.6 route is as follows: ascend near the left corner
of the face, passing two snowfields that linge until late season.
Higher, follow friction ramps to the right of a cirque. Another route
begins about 300 feet right of the preceding route. Scramble up to a
prominent ledge system one-third of the way up the face; then climb
a steep, triangular face. Pass overhangs on the third pitch and
ascend a rib right of an easy gully. Exfoliation roofs and friction
slabs are encountered in the next section, which leads to small trees.
Traverse right from here and climb a few pitches to the top. III, 5.7.

Columbia Finger (10,320+)

Class 3 from the west. Another route has been established: from
the base of the south buttress walk 150 feet right to an open book.
Climb this for two pitches, turn an overhang, and reach small
ledges. From the right end of the highest ledge climb up cracks to
the ridge. II, 5.4, A1.

Tresidder Peak (10,560+)

From the south a class 4 arete leads to the south summit, the
higher of twin summits. The north arete is also class 4.

Cathedral Peak (10,940)

As John Muir camped below this magnificent peak just after
having made the first ascent, he wrote, "This I may say is the first
time I have been at church in California. . . ." Many have felt that
way since.

Route 1. Regular Route. Class 4. From the Budd Lake area ascend brushy scree slopes to the right of the summit towers. Once the
ridge is attained head over toward the notch between the main summit spires and the prominent west summit, called Eichorn Pinnacle.
From near the notch work up and left along ramps to the final
summit block, which is on the far left. The climbing is class 3 to this
point. From a small notch just below, and west of, the summit,
traverse around the corner onto the south side of the tower and climb

a short, class 4 crack to the top.

There are many variations. The notch between the main tower and Eichorn can be reached via class 2 slabs from the Muir Trail to the west. And, if arriving from Budd Lake, one doesn't have to go all the way over to the notch—it's possible to climb easy class 4 slabs directly to the summit tower.

Route 2. North Face. 5.5. Follow Route 1 from Budd Lake until only about 100 feet below the ridgecrest. Begin climbing in a chimney-like depression and ascend two pitches to the summit tower. A 5.8 variation lies just left of the depression.

Route 3. Northeast Face. Class 5. This route lies somewhere on the face to the left (downhill) of the preceding route. In fact, the route may be only a variation of the Southeast Buttress Route, described next.

Route 4. Southeast Buttress. II, 5.4. This extremely popular route ascends the wide, indistinct southeast buttress. There are numerous ways to begin; the easiest lies about 175 feet uphill from the base of the buttress and ascends myriad right-leaning flakes and books. Midway up the route one can escape left via easy, broken gullies. This is a distinct mistake, for the climbing on the upper part of the route is very stimulating and not too hard.

Route 5. South Face. Several short routes, some class 4 and some medium class 5, can be found on the 300-foot face which leads toward the saddle between the main summit towers and the western satellite, Eichorn Pinnacle.

Route 6. Eichorn Pinnacle, Regular Route. 5.3. From the notch between the main summit towers and Eichorn Pinnacle (Cathedral's spectacular west summit), traverse around the right side of the spire and ascend steep cracks and ledges to the top.

Route 7. Eichorn Pinnacle, Southwest Buttress. II, 5.8. Rope up above sandy ledges and slabs on the south side of the buttress and head upward until it is possible to traverse into a prominent crack. Climb this for three pitches; then scramble over to the left side of the buttress and climb a wide chimney. Move left to a sloping ledge and finish with steep jamcracks.

Route 8. Eichorn Pinnacle, West Pillar. III, 5.9. A four-inch-wide jamcrack will be seen as the obvious first pitch of this route. Climb the crack for one pitch and then ascend a rib. After a while, traverse down and right to another crack. Ascend this until easier climbing is reached.

Route 9. Eichorn Pinnacle, Direct South Face. III, 5.7, A2. This route begins in a moderate chimney near the southwest base of the pinnacle. Climb the chimney and then a prominent 5.7 crack. Higher, a bit of aid leads to a ledge. Next, traverse left to the shoulder west of the summit. Climb a short chimney to the top.

Echo Peaks (ca. 11,000)

The accompanying map shows the numeration of the nine Echo Peaks, located a mile south of Cathedral Peak.

Peak 1 is class 3 via the combination of east face and south ridge. The west face can also be climbed: head up to the 1–2 notch and then proceed to the top. The direct west face is 5.8; the north arete is easy class 5.

Peak 2 is climbed via its class 3 east face and north ridge.

Peak 3 is the highest point of the nine Echo Peaks. Attain the 2–3 notch from either the west (class 3) or the east (class 4); then climb the north ridge to the top.

Peak 4 can be reached via a class 4 traverse from Peak 3. The summit can also be reached from a prominent row of shrubs under the northeast face.

Peaks 5 through 8 are all class 3 via their northern sides.

Peak 9 is the most massive, prettiest, and most difficult of the lot. A 5.5 route lies on the southwest side and is fairly obvious.

Echo Ridge (11,120+)

The slabby northern escarpment is prominent from Budd Lake. The peak is easy via the west, south, and east sides. A route has been done on the north face: start in the left-hand chimney of the lower cliff and climb to the ridge left of the summit. Follow the ridge to the top. Class 4.

Cockscomb (11,040+)

This small, spectacular peaklet has several routes. The standard route lies on the west side and is class 4.

Matthes Crest (10,880+)

This superb example of a knife-edge fin was named for Francois Matthes, the pre-eminent Sierra geologist. There are scores of possible routes on the sides of the fin; many short routes have been done, but they will not be recorded here. The usual routes attain the summit ridge from the east or the west, and then traverse the knife edge to the top. The most pleasant route is a complete traverse of the ridge from south to north; this is 5.3 and a true classic.

The southern segment of the fin is actually quite separated from the main massif. A striking tooth on this segment (east of Echo Lake) has a 5.9 route on its west face. The opposite side of the tooth has a route rated III, 5.8.

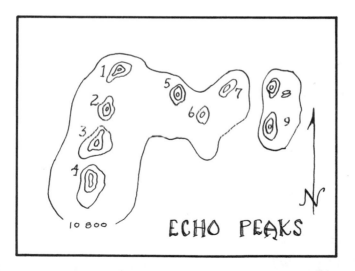

10 800

ECHO PEAKS

Unicorn Peak (10,880+)

Although the peak has only one summit tower when viewed from the north, there are actually three nearly equally high summits, the northern one being the highest. The regular route ascends from Elizabeth Lake to the notch between the middle and north summits. A class 3 scramble leads to the top. The northeast face, the original route, is class 3 or 4. Various short and unaesthetic routes have been done on the north and northwest faces. A three-pitch route, 5.8, A3, has been done on the direct north face.

Johnson Peak (11,070)

Class 1 or 2 from any direction.

Rafferty Peak (11,120+)

Class 2 from Tuolumne Pass.

Peak 11,282 (1 SW of Rafferty Pk.)

Class 2 from the east. The northwest side of the peak has a surprising array of ribs and buttresses. A route has been done on the northernmost and cleanest-looking of these buttresses. A single crack system drops down from a point just right of the western summit of Peak 11,282. Climb into a very deep chimney and follow it for a few pitches. When the chimney ends, follow the dihedral above. The crux is a bulge on the final pitch. II, 5.8. Another route, a three-pitch 5.9, lies near the northwest corner.

Fletcher Peak (11,408)

From Vogelsang Lake a class 2 ascent may be made. A couloir on the northwest face has been done and is class 4.

Vogelsang Peak (11,516)

Class 2 from Vogelsang Lake.

Potter Point (10,278)

Class 2 from the Lyell Fork of the Tuolumne. Easier from the west and south.

Amelia Earhart Peak (11,982)

The north-northeast ridge is class 2. A class 4 couloir on the west face has been climbed; when the couloir abuts a steep wall, traverse left to the north-northeast ridge.

Parsons Peak (12,080+)

Class 2 from Ireland Lake. Also class 2 from the lakes above Bernice Lake.

Simmons Peak (12,053)

Class 2 from the west.

Mt. Florence (12,561)

From the trail to the west, climb shale-covered slopes to the summit. Class 2.

The Clark Range

Mt. Clark (11,522)

Formerly known as the Obelisk, this fine peak dominates the northern Clark Range.

Route 1. Southeast Arete. Class 3. Approach the arete either from the Illilouette Creek area or from Obelisk Lake. The arete is a bit exposed in places—a rope might be carried for the unsteady.

Route 2. Southwest Face. IV, 5.8, A2. A single crack-chimney system will be seen leading up the southwest face to a ridgecrest. Rope up just left of the chimney and climb two pitches to loose blocks. Move right into the chimney and go up it to an alcove. Leave the chimney temporarily; then climb it to a ledge 200 feet above the alcove. Pendulum left into a small dihedral and follow it to a ledge. Climb a ramp up and right, cross the chimney, and gain the south ridge. Keep on the right side of this ridge and climb a mixed free and aid pitch to the ridgetop. Follow this several hundred feet to the summit.

Route 3. Northwest Arete. Class 4. This route is a classic, long ridge—mostly class 3.

Route 4. North Face. III, 5.7. This route goes up the wall at the head of the striking cirque north of the peak. An icefield is usually found at the base of the face. Gain the ledge system which runs across the lower section of the cliff. Several routes have been done on the face above: "vertical chimneys" have been climbed and a "steep open book" has been done. Difficulties have been reported as low as 5.6 and as high as 5.8.

Route 5. Northeast Face. Class 3. This is probably the easiest route on Clark. The route is seen easily from the lakes above Obelisk Lake. Stay on the right side of the face and follow broad, easy ledges to the top.

Gray Peak (11,574)
The southwest slopes of the peak are quite easy.

Red Peak (11,699)
Class 2 or 3 from the Ottoway Lakes.

Ottoway Peak (11,440+)
Easy from the trail pass to the northwest.

Merced Peak (11,726)
This is the highest peak of the Clark Range. One day in the autumn of 1871, John Muir was "following the footprints of the ancient glaciers that once flowed grandly from their ample fountains, reading what I could of their history." He approached the cirque under the north face of Merced Peak and, to his delight, found a living glacier, the first ever discovered in the Sierra Nevada. By 1949 this glacier was deemed a "fossil glacier."

Three routes have been done on this peak. The west arete is class 3; the northeast arete is class 2. The north face has a route rated III, 5.7. Climb loose rock to a ramp which diagonals up and right. A short class 5 section at the top of the ramp leads to easier climbing and the summit.

Triple Divide Peak (11,607)
   Class 2 from the northeast.

Post Peak (11,009)
   Class 1 from the nearby trail.

Isberg Peak (10,996)
   The name of this peak is misspelled on present editions of the Merced Peak quadrangle map. Class 1 or 2 from all directions.

Gale Peak (10,693)
   The northwest ridge is easy.

Madera Peak (10,509)
   Class 2 from the southwest.

The Ritter Range

South of Yosemite the Sierra crest lies low for about twenty-five miles and offers little of interest to the climber. As if to make up for this "Low Sierra," the dark and massive Ritter Range rises precipitously to the west. In spite of its loose, mottled rock, the range invites the climber toward its two great sentinels, Ritter and Banner, and its cluster of needles, the Minarets.

Although one could hardly refer to the Minarets as a climber's paradise, it is a very popular area, and the scenery is equal to the best in the High Sierra. Most of the routes are class 3 and 4, and they tend to assail high-angle gullies and troughs as well as airy ridges. The rock is extremely shattered, and there is an outrageous amount of debris on ledges. The Minarets are not known for being a safe place in which to practice the sport. A few glaciers adhere to the east faces, adding an alpine touch to the region and making ice-climbing equipment mandatory for some routes.

The great hulk of Mt. Ritter attracted Clarence King as early as 1866. Bad weather defeated him about 500 feet below the top; he regarded this last section as inaccessible. In 1872 John Muir guided a group of artists into the Yosemite back country, got them settled in a "sublime" setting, and told them that he was off for an "excursion to the untouched summit of Ritter." And so, alone, with his blanket and bread, he set off through the wild country west of the peak. Although he had warned his comrades not to expect him for a week or ten days, he was back in three, successful.

Banner Peak was the next to be climbed, and Mt. Davis was soon to follow. By 1891 the major peaks had been climbed, but the many spires of the Minarets lay absolutely untouched. It was not until 1923 that the first person ventured onto the pinnacles. Charles Michael was probably the foremost California rockclimber of the early 1920s; he often climbed alone and did so on his very bold climb of what he thought was the highest Minaret. It was not until six years had passed that Michael Minaret was shown to be a few feet lower than the highest point, Clyde Minaret. Michael, however, was not disappointed by this fact: "Whether my peak was the highest or not does not matter to me so much, for I can at least recommend it as a grand and thrilling climb."

Norman Clyde visited the Minarets in 1928 and characteristically managed to solo climb to the high point which now bears his name. Most of the other summits of the group succumbed in the early 1930s to the onslaught of Sierra Club rockclimbers, and most of the pinnacles bear the names of their first ascenders. Six first ascents were made during a brief period in mid-August 1933, when many of California's leading climbers gathered to search for the missing Walter Starr, Jr., another famous solo climber. Teams went out to search for four straight days, climbing standard routes to check summit registers, making first ascents, and scanning the range with binoculars. Unsuccessful, they left the Minarets. Clyde stayed on, however, and after a week, using patience and classic detective skills, found Starr's remains high on Michael Minaret. The body was later interred on the ledge where it lay, and Walter Starr, Sr. is said to have rewarded Clyde with a stipend for the rest of his life.

Few first ascents were done in the next twenty-five years, but in the early 1960s Allen Steck was the leader of various groups which put up technical routes on three major Ritter Range faces, the finest of which is the popular south face of Clyde Minaret.

Approaches to the Ritter Range are invariably done from the east and are extremely short and simple. Leave U.S. Highway 395 at the Mammoth Lakes turnoff and drive west over Minaret Summit to either Agnew Meadows or Red's Meadow. From the former roadhead good trails lead in six or eight miles to fine campsites near Ritter and Banner. The southern Minarets are best approached from Red's Meadow via the easy seven-mile trail to Minaret Lake.

There are many climbers' passes across the Ritter Range; they are listed here from north to south.

Glacier Lake Pass (11,158) lies three-quarters of a mile northwest of Banner Peak and separates that peak from Mt. Davis. It provides access to Route 1 on Davis, Routes 6 and 7 on Banner, and the "back side" route on Ritter. The pass, which contains the desolate Lake Catherine, is class 2 from both directions.

The *Ritter-Banner Saddle* (12,000+) is reached via an easy glacier on its northwest side. The more common approach, from Ediza Lake, is harder and involves cliff bands and steep snowslopes. On the main cliff band, pass to the right of the watercourse via class 3 ledges. Carry an ice axe.

Ritter Pass (11,200+) lies between Waller Minaret and Mt. Ritter and is 1.2 miles south-southeast of the latter. The pass provides a class 2 route between Ediza Lake and the North Fork of the San Joaquin River.

The Gap (11,200+) is the wide, deep low point just southeast of Waller Minaret (Peak 11,711). Steep talus is found on the western side; slabs, cliff bands, and snowslopes are found on the Ediza side. Class 2; an ice axe is often needed.

North Notch (11,600+) is the most prominent break in the main Minaret chain and provides access to several routes on Michael Minaret as well as other routes on the spires which adjoin the notch. From Ediza Lake climb onto the ridge which leads toward the notch until it is possible to traverse into the chute which heads up to the notch. One chockstone in this chute offers momentary difficulty. The west side of the notch is composed of steep talus. Class 3; carry an ice axe in early and mid-season.

South Notch (11,360+) is a deep col 0.4 mile southeast of Clyde Minaret (Peak 12,281). The col lies at the junction of the main Minaret chain with the picturesque spur which shoots out toward Minaret Creek. The col is used mainly as the southerly approach to Michael Minaret. From the south end of Cecile Lake climb talus and/or snowslopes to the obvious saddle left of the impressive east face of Ken Minaret. An ice axe is generally taken on this class 2 pass. From South Notch easy talus slopes lead down and south into the Iron Creek drainage. To reach the base of Michael Minaret, traverse north from the notch to Amphitheater Lake, a small ice pond in the bowl between Ken and Adams minarets. See Michael Minaret for routes from this point.

Beck Lakes Pass (10,800+) is located one-half mile northwest of Upper Beck Lake and offers a convenient class 2 method of crossing the Ritter Range.

In addition to these climbers' passes, there are many easy cross-country routes suitable for backpackers. Most significant of these is the well-traveled route from Ediza Lake to Minaret Lake. The class 2 route is quite obvious; both of the lakes passed en route are turned on their east sides. Another easy route between Ediza and Minaret lakes can be made across the pass in Volcanic Ridge just north of the Minaret Mine.

The Devil's Postpile quadrangle is the only map one needs for this region.

Ritter–Banner Region

Mt. Davis (12,311)
Route 1. Southeast Side. Class 2. From Glacier Lake Pass follow the stream which flows into Lake Catherine. This leads north to the gentle summit slopes.

Route 2. North Buttress. Class 4. This buttress is located immediately east of the north glacier. Climb the right side of the rib at first; later follow it directly to the top.

Route 3. Northeast Buttress. Class 4. This buttress is bisected by the Mono-Madera county line. Climb the left side of the buttress; then climb a chute up onto it. Follow the rib to the gentle summit talus field.

Route 4. Annie's Spire. This small formation lies 0.85 mile southeast of the top, on the eastern flank of Davis's southeast ridge.

It is visible from the west end of Thousand Island Lake as a curving fin in a broad couloir near the top of the ridge. The 5.4 route lies on the sloping west face.

Banner Peak (12,945)

From many vantage points Banner is a more beautiful mountain than its companion peak, Mt. Ritter, although the latter is higher, more popular, and more revered.

Route 1. East Cliff. Class 3. From the east climb to the Banner-Ritter saddle—this section requires an ice axe. From the saddle steep but easy talus is followed to the summit.

Route 2. Southeast Face. Class 5. From Ediza Lake one gets a good view of this route, which lies near the center of the face. Start in the first couloir right of a deep chimney and ascend easy rock. It soon becomes advisable to traverse left into the couloir above the chimney. Continue up and right over steep rock to a big ledge with a snowfield. Traverse right about 300 feet; then climb straight up to

Mt. Ritter and Banner Peak from the east. Route 3 for Banner begins at the saddle right of the minor peak at the lower left. Routes 4 and 5 lie on the face above the obvious glacier.

the summit ridge, meeting it a few hundred feet left of the top. Much of this fine route is class 4.

Route 3. East Corner. Class 4. This route lies on the vague corner which separates the southeast face from the east face. Begin climbing near the saddle which lies between Banner and a peaklet due east. Ascend a chimney or chute on the left side of the buttress which rises above the saddle until it is possible to attain the ridge above the buttress. Climb this until stopped by a very steep section; then make a diagonal traverse across a steep, smooth, 80-foot wall. After this is climbed proceed up steep chutes to the summit area.

Route 4. East Face. III, 5.6. From the top of the glacier (not shown on the map) nestled under the east face, climb onto the wall about 40 feet right of a snow tongue which extends upward into a prominent couloir. One is more or less directly under the summit at this point. Steep class 5 climbing leads up for two pitches. Now work up and right for three easier pitches until an obvious, fairly easy route can be seen above. Hit the summit ridge about 200 feet right of the top.

A variation has been made. After the "three easier pitches" have been passed, move to the right around a prominent arete. Climb this and the wall above to the summit area. 5.7.

Another variation, or perhaps an entirely separate route, lies a short distance left of this route. A headwall halfway up is the main obstacle.

Route 5. East Face, Right Side. III, 5.8. Start climbing about 200 feet to the right of the preceding route. Ascend the left side of a prominent rib for two pitches; then climb the rib upward for many class 4 and 5 pitches until a few hundred feet below the summit ridge. Work up and left for two easy pitches and climb a short, difficult pitch to the ridge.

Route 6. Northeast Buttress. III, 5.6. This route begins atop the shoulder which lies just right of the pocket glacier under the east face. Attain the shoulder from the north (class 3–4) or from the south (class 5). From the top of the shoulder climb up and left into an obvious gully. Two moderate class 5 pitches in this bring one to several hundred feet of scrambling. Above this is a talus-filled notch overlooking a steep drop on the north. Three pitches above here take one to the summit ridge.

Route 7. Northwest Shoulder. Class 4. Follow the ridge from Glacier Lake Pass.

Route 8. From Lake Catherine. Class 2. This is the easiest route on the peak. From the lake ascend the easy glacier to the Ritter-Banner saddle and follow Route 1 to the top.

Mt. Ritter (13,157)

The highest peak of the Ritter Range is a striking Sierra landmark and can be seen from peaks 80 miles down range. John Muir made the first ascent more than a hundred years ago. Part way up he found himself "with arms outspread, clinging close to the face of the rock, unable to move hand or foot either up or down. My doom appeared fixed. I *must* fall." Fortunately, "life burst forth again with preternatural clearness," and his limbs once more "moved with. . .positiveness and precision. . . ."

Route 1. From the Ritter-Banner Saddle. Class 3. Attain the saddle as in Routes 1 or 7 for Banner Peak. From the saddle climb steep snow to the right-hand chute of two chutes on the north side of Ritter. From the top of the chute cross to the top of the left chute and follow a wide, diagonaling ledge which leads over to an arete. Follow this to the top. This is a hazardous route and has claimed many lives.

Route 2. Northeast Buttress. Class 4. Climb the lower band of cliffs leading toward the Ritter-Banner saddle. Just after passing the cliff move left to the buttress. Two thousand feet of class 3 and 4 climbing brings one to the top.

Route 3. East Face. Class 4 or 5. This route lies on the left side of Ritter's biggest face. From the lower left side of the wall, traverse up and right on a ledge which shoots toward a prominent scar. Wander upward above here; there are many possible routes.

Route 4. Southwest Glacier. Class 2–3. Ascend slabs and talus until just below the snout of the glacier. Work around to the right and skirt the glacier until an easy chute leads up and right to talus slopes and the top. An ice axe should be carried during times of high snow.

A slightly harder route has been done. Climb the cliffs left of the glacier's snout and pass around pinnacles; then drop onto the glacier. Walk up this for a while, wander back onto the rock at the left, and finally reach the northwest end of the snow. Easy talus slopes lead to the top from here. Class 3.

Route 5. West Slopes. Class 2. This is the easiest route, although it is infrequently climbed because of its relative inaccessibility. Ascend talus slopes from the lakes under the base of the peak.

Peak 12,344 (0.9 SSW of Mt. Ritter)

This jagged, good-looking mountain is class 4 or 5 from the south. It is entirely possible that it was the last major Sierra summit to be reached.

The Minarets

Volcanic Ridge (11,501)

The easiest route is probably from Minaret Lake: ascend talus-and-willow-covered slopes to the prominent saddle due north of the lake. Scramble up loose talus to the top, which lies near the far right side of the ridge. An easy route, also class 2, can be made from the canyon above Minaret Mine (wrongly placed on the map—it should be one-half mile downstream). Also class 2 from Ediza Lake. A class 4–5 route has been done somewhere on the northwest face. The view of the Minarets from the summit can only be called fantastic.

"Starr Minaret" (Pk. 11,319, 0.6 SW of Deadhorse Lake)

Class 2 from South Notch. A route has been made on the east face; much of the climbing is class 3 and 4, although the summit pitch is a mite harder. An incredible 700-foot chimney called the Sleeping Beauty Chimney, located on the south face, has also been climbed and is rated III, 5.9.

"Watchtower" (Pk. 11,200+, 0.5 SSE of Starr Minaret)

This pinnacle lies on the ridge which divides Beck and Deadhorse lakes. The east face has been climbed—II, 5.5.

"Riegelhuth Minaret" (Pk. 10,560+, 0.25 S of Minaret Lake)

This pinnacle is a striking sight from the west side of Minaret Lake. From the lake climb to the Riegelhuth-Pridham col; then ascend class 4 rock up a broad trough to the top. The north face has also been climbed: follow a prominent, left-diagonaling chimney or chute to the top of the east ridge. Class 4. As a variation, one can leave the chute about 200 feet below the ridge and climb a 5.5 wall on the right. This leads directly to the summit. A third route has been established on the east face and is 5.6.

"Pridham Minaret" (Pk. 10,960+, 0.2 W of Riegelhuth Minaret)

Easy from the Pridham-Riegelhuth saddle.

"Kehrlein Minaret" (Pk. 11,440+, 0.65 W of Riegelhuth Minaret)

Class 4 from South Notch. The north face is also class 4. The east ridge has a class 5 route: reach the base of the ridge via Pridham Minaret and the Pridham-Kehrlein notch. The west summit is the highest.

"Ken Minaret" (Pk. 11,760+, 0.2 S of Pk. 12,281)

The northeast face is the popular route and is class 4–5. Climb the couloir between Ken and Clyde until it splits. Take the left branch for a few hundred feet; then climb the face on the left, keeping to the right of the large rib which descends from the right-hand (true) summit. The actual summit rocks are best approached from the north, where a short class 4–5 crack must be climbed. Another route lies on the southeast ridge: from the South Notch traverse in the direction of Michael Minaret and head for the notch just left of a conspicuous tower. Keep on the left side while climbing the wall above the notch; then follow the ridge to a tower below the big, obvious step in the ridge. A short rappel leads to the base of the step. Next, work out onto the east face and climb to the top. Class 5. A third route lies on the west face and is class 3 until the summit rocks are reached.

"Clyde Minaret" (Pk. 12,281, 0.5 SW of Cecile Lake)

By a matter of a few feet, this is the high point of the Minaret group. It is by far the most popular of the major summits.

Route 1. Starr's Route. Class 4. From the south side of Cecile Lake climb talus toward a prominent area of red rock. Ascend a class 3 slope just to the right of the red rock; then traverse around to the right, above a permanent snowpatch. Keep traversing upward past two wide gullies or chutes to the third one. Ascend this gully

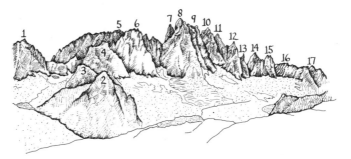

The Minarets from the southeast. 1. Starr 2. Riegelhuth 3. Pridham 4. Kehrlein 5. Adams 6. Ken 7. Michael 8. Clyde 9. Eichorn 10. Rice 11. Bedayan 12. Dawson 13. Dyer 14. Jensen 15. Turner 16. Leonard 17. Waller.

about 1,000 feet to the summit ridge; then proceed left some 200 feet to the top.

Route 2. Rock Route. Class 4. From the northwest end of Cecile Lake climb upward to a deep chute which lies immediately left of the left edge of the glacier. Enter the chute via one of several ways; then climb it nearly to its top. At this point leave the chute and work diagonally up and left to the summit area.

Route 3. Glacier Route. Class 4. Ascend to the top of the glacier north of the peak; then cross onto the rocks. Climb class 4 chutes and ribs to the summit ridge. Routes 1, 2, and 3 all work up the same general area for their upper 500 feet.

Route 4. Traverse from Eichorn Minaret. Class 3.

Route 5. Southwest Face. Class 3–4. From Amphitheater Lake climb steep blocks to the low point between Clyde and Eichorn—the summit lies a few hundred yards to the right. One can also reach the upper part of this route via the class 3–4 gully which leads to the Clyde-Ken col from the east.

Route 6. South Face. IV, 5.8. From the southern end of Cecile Lake climb talus toward the Ken-Clyde notch. The south face, the most impressive wall in the Minarets, looms above during this approach. Start climbing a bit uphill from the actual base of the wall. The first pitch is not too obvious: traverse almost straight right onto the face (5.6) until a gully-depression 125 feet out is reached. Climb up and right; then head straight up for four pitches (moderate class 5) to a large ledge left of the base of a hidden chimney. Move right and climb a pitch up this chimney (5.7). Next, a long pitch (some 5.8) takes one to the base of the prominent upper dihedral. A 90-foot pitch up this leads to a small belay ledge. Now, instead of continuing up the dihedral (although this has been done), traverse left about 55 feet over improbable rock; then climb upward about 110 feet to a small ledge. Another small ledge lies 60 feet higher. From here make an improbable traverse right to a broken, overhanging corner. Climb this and reach the class 3 summit ridge just left of the top of the prominent dihedral.

"Eichorn Minaret" (Pk. 12,255, 0.25 WNW of Pk. 12,281)

This unspectacular formation lies at the junction of the main Minaret ridge with the spur which shoots across to Michael Minaret. Class 3 to 4 from either Michael or Clyde Minaret. Also class 3–4 from Amphitheater Lake. Class 3 from the Rice-Eichorn notch (see Rice Minaret). A class 5 route has been done on the northeast face.

"Michael Minaret" (Pk. 12,240+, 0.1 SW of Pk. 12,255)

Hidden from the usual vantage points, this spire is one of the more spectacular sights in the Ritter Range. From U.S. Highway 395 near the Mammoth Airport, Michael is seen as the thin needle just left of the slightly higher and much more massive Clyde Minaret.

The eastern escarpment of the central Minarets. 1. South Notch 2. Ken 3. Clyde (the wide chutes of Route 1 are conspicuous) 4. Eichorn 5. Rice 6. Bedayan 7. Dawson 8. Dyer 9. North Notch.

Route 1. Michael's Chute. Class 4. This route and the two which follow it lie on the northwest side of the spire. This relatively inaccessible side can be reached from either North Notch (obvious) or South Notch (not so obvious). From the latter notch work into the Amphitheater, the bowl which contains a small lake. Climb to the Adams-Michael notch. Drop down the back side (class 3) to talus; then circle around the west face to reach the northwest base.

Two chutes lead up to the twin spires in the notch between Eichorn and Michael minarets. The right-hand one is Michael's Chute: follow it past chockstones to the very top chockstone in the notch. This is known as the Portal, and six of the seven routes use this point for beginning the final summit tower. There are at least three ways to go, but the easiest seems to be to follow a ledge heading out left. After a short bit, work up and right via exposed class 3 and 4 rock to the summit area.

Route 2. Eichorn's Chute. Class 4. Take the left-hand chute mentioned in Route 1. Near its top work around right, under the twin spires, to the Portal. Continue as in Route 1.

Route 3. Starr's Chute. Class 4. This was the last climb of Walter Starr, Jr. He fell to his death a few hours after this first ascent. Climb the second chute left of Eichorn's Chute until it branches; then take the right branch until near its head. Traverse right across the wide face to the Portal and follow Route 1.

Route 4. From Eichorn Minaret. Class 4. The traverse takes about an hour.

Route 5. Amphitheater Chute. Class 4. From Amphitheater Lake climb the conspicuous chute which leads to the Michael-Eichorn notch. Drop down the other side of the notch and circle around to the Portal. Follow Route 1 to the summit.

Route 6. South Face. III, 5.7, A1. From the Adams-Michael notch climb an obvious chimney system for three pitches; then head up and right toward a small notch. Two easy pitches lead to the top.

Route 7. Clyde's Ledge. Class 4. From the Adams-Michael notch drop down the west side to the southwest base of the spire. Ascend the west face for a while; then follow a slanting ledge which leads left around the corner to the central section of Michael's Chute. Continue as in Route 1.

"Adams Minaret" (Pk. 12,000+, 0.1 S of Pk. 12,255)
Class 3 from the Adams-Michael notch.

"Rice Minaret" (Pk. 12,160+, 0.05 NW of Pk. 12,255)
Two routes have been put up on the west side of the pinnacle. One ascends Starr's Chute (see Michael Minaret, Route 3) to the branching and then heads up and left to the top. The other route lies in the next chute to the left. The hardest route yet done, and the only one from the east, is as follows: climb the glacier to the snow chute leading up to the Eichorn-Rice notch. Class 5 climbing is found in the upper portions of this chute. From the notch climb the first chute on the left to a short, vertical wall which can be climbed on the right. Next, follow an open book to the summit ridge.

"Bedayan Minaret" (Pk. 12,080+, 0.1 NW of Pk. 12,255)
Route 1. Traverse from Rice Minaret. Class 3-4.

Route 2. West Face. Class 4. Climb a chute which heads toward a notch northwest of the pinnacle. When 300 feet from the notch, cross over into the next chute to the right and climb the south face to the top.

Route 3. East Couloir. Class 4. From the glacier, climb the very loose and dangerous chute which leads to the Bedayan-Dawson notch. From the notch climb the ridge to the top.

Route 4. Northeast Face. Class 5. Start at the high point of the glacier, between a watercourse in the middle of the northeast face and the chute which leads to the Bedayan-Dawson notch. Climb up and somewhat left to a sloping ledge which can be followed to the watercourse. Climb the right side of this to a seasonal snowfield. Easier climbing above here leads to the summit ridge.

"Dawson Minaret" (Pk. 11,920+, 0.2 NW of Pk. 12,255)
Class 4 from the Bedayan-Dawson notch. The standard route,

also class 4, is from North Notch. Bypass Dyer Minaret on its right side and enter the next chute. Head up this a while; then go up and right to the south side of the spire. The final portion of the climb is done on the south face.

"Dyer Minaret" (Pk. 11,680+, 0.25 NW of Pk. 12,255)

This is the very sharp spire best seen from Cecile Lake. Approach from North Notch; turn North Notch Minaret and climb one 5.6 pitch up the exposed northwest face. Another route has been done: from North Notch traverse around onto the east side of the spire. From a large, sloping platform climb two pitches to the top. 5.7.

"North Notch Minaret" (just NW of Dyer Minaret)

This is the tiny pinnacle in North Notch. It is easy class 5 from the notch between this spire and Dyer.

"Jensen Minaret" (Pk. 11,760+, 0.35 SE of Pk. 11,711)

A loose, unattractive class 4 route can be done from North Notch. A better route seems to be the following: from Iceberg Lake one can see a 300-foot chimney which leads directly toward two small spires in the notch between Jensen and Turner. Climb this chimney; then follow the arete to the top. 5.4.

"Turner Minaret" (Pk. 11,600+, 0.25 SE of Pk. 11,711)

The climb is class 3 from Jensen Minaret. Another route can be followed: ascend the crack system of Route 1 on Leonard Minaret; then continue up and left to a large, curving open book which runs up all the way to the notch right of Turner. Climb this class 4 book for several pitches; then turn a huge block on the right to gain the notch. Traverse out on the west face and climb a 5.4 pitch up to the broken summit ridge.

"Leonard Minaret" (Pk. 11,600+, 0.3 ESE of Pk. 11,711)

Route 1. East Side. II, 5.3. From Iceberg Lake, Leonard Minaret is seen as the pretty pinnacle with a deep, conspicuous chimney or slot on its lower east face. Ascend a less prominent crack system just left of this slot. When an obvious, wide ramp shoots up and right, head left onto the crest of an arete. Follow this to the top.

Route 2. West Ridge. Class 4. From the Gap climb onto the ridge and follow it left to the summit.

Route 3. South Face. A class 4 route lies somewhere on this face.

"Waller Minaret" (Pk. 11,711, 0.9 W of Iceberg Lake)

This is the most isolated of the Minarets, contains the best rock, and is an excellent vantage point.

Route 1. Regular Route. II, 5.4. Begin climbing down and east from the Gap where a ledge runs out to the right. Follow the ledge; then start wandering up steep faces, aretes, and chutes to the summit ridge. This is an enjoyable and airy route.

Route 2. East Face. Several routes have been done on this face. By choosing the easiest-appearing way, a 5.5 route can be found. A direct route has been done and is 5.8.

Iron Mountain (11,149)

Class 1 from the south. Another route has been done: from Ashley Lake ascend a snow tongue which rises above the southwest end of the lake to the summit ridge. Class 3; carry an ice axe.

The Crest and Environs

Carson Peak (10,909)

Class 1 from Agnew Pass. The north face, as viewed from the June Lake loop road, has three major ribs. A route has been done on the left rib and is rated III, 5.9, A1. Start on the left side of the rib and work up toward the center. Loose rock is a problem. The central rib has also been climbed and is rated IV, 5.8.

San Joaquin Mountain (11,600)

Class 1 from any direction. A good view is had from the top.

Two Teats (11,387)

This appropriately named peak is an easy stroll to the summit nipple. This sensuous formation is class 2–3.

Mammoth Mountain (11,053)

Best known as a ski area, this rounded mass is a pumice walk from all directions.

The Mono Recesses

Two of the principal mountaineering attractions of the High Sierra, the Mt. Abbot group and Mt. Humphreys, are found in the Mono Recesses region. In addition to offering fine climbing, the area encompasses some of the most elegant scenery in the range. The cross-country traveler will discover remote lake basins and high mountain meadows. The Mono Recesses themselves, while terribly overcrowded, are a geological masterpiece and should not be missed. Four classic glacial valleys fall in quick succession into the giant U-shaped trench of Mono Creek. To travel up the Second Recess toward Gabbot Pass is to take a fascinating journey through many of the life zones of the Sierra landscape. Leaving the main trail and its aspen groves at Mono Creek, one meanders uphill alongside the stream, past cascades and pools, and into meadows traversed by silent threads of water. Midway up the recess a faint path ascends the canyon wall into a hanging valley containing timberline lakes. Farther up, and not so pleasant as the terrain below, lie the talus slopes so common at this altitude. Higher still, one reaches the alpine zone; glaciers and steep granite prevail, and the climber is home at last.

East of the Ritter Range, the Sierra crest, which has been lying low for many miles, begins a gradual rise back to High Sierra standards, and soon peaks such as Mt. Morrison and Red Slate Mountain dominate the skyline. In fact, the latter peak is the first one higher than 13,000 feet in over thirty miles.

A few miles to the south of Red Slate Mountain a long spur known as the Silver Divide shoots off westward. This ridge, which contains several nice peaks, separates Fish and Mono creeks, two major west-side streams.

Mono Creek is the major watershed of the region, and it runs a dozen miles in a near-perfect straight line from the crest to a premature death in Lake Edison. Paralleling the creek on the south is the Mono Divide. The junction of the divide and the main crest results in a fine cluster of peaks known as the Abbot group.

South of the Mono Divide, where Bear Creek has its headwaters, the elevation of the peaks diminishes once again, but the region is one of the more rugged and charming places in the Sierra. Mt. Hooper, Seven Gables, and Royce Peak are the major landmarks of this area.

Ten miles southeast of Mt. Abbot lies Mt. Humphreys, one of the highest and most striking Sierra peaks. Not only is the peak isolated, but it is difficult by any route, and thus has earned the respect of many a Sierra climber.

The first recorded climbing in the region was in 1860, when Tom Clark probably reached the summit of Mt. Tom, the enormous mass which so dominates the head of the Owens Valley. This was unquestionably the first ascent of a major Sierra peak by a white man. A few years afterward, the Whitney Survey visited the area briefly and climbed, or almost climbed, a few peaks. During the remainder of the nineteenth century, relatively little climbing was done in the area, but the first decade of this century saw several major peaks climbed in swift succession—Humphreys in 1904, and Mills and Abbot in 1908. James Hutchinson added these three peaks to his impressive list of Sierra first ascents. He climbed Humphreys with his brother; two other members of the party stopped 300 feet below the top. Not willing to take the risk of the final steep wall, they instead built a large cairn on a nearby point and christened it "Married Men's Peak."

In the mid-1920s Norman Clyde began a run of first ascents which in eleven years was to net him nearly twenty peaks, including Mt. Morrison, Bloody Mountain, Four Gables, and Mt. Emerson. In 1927 he ascended a lesser-known peak, Piute Crag 5, the highest of a group of rotten, unaesthetic crags near Mt. Emerson. Twenty-two years passed before modern rockclimbers decided the crags were worth climbing.

Sierra Club outing groups cleaned up what Clyde and his compatriots had left, and by 1955 there were no unclimbed peaks worthy of mention. Surprisingly few technical routes have been made on the high peaks. True, there are no great walls, but there is a wealth of class 4 and 5 routes awaiting the future climber.

Off to the west of the Recesses area, near where the three forks of the San Joaquin River merge, are several spectacular domes which offer fine rockclimbing. Climbers "discovered" Balloon Dome and Fuller Buttes in the early 1970s, and have established some very difficult routes.

Approaches to this region of the Sierra are most easily made from the east, where spur roads off U.S. Highway 395 lead to good trails. For the northern part of the area, take the Mammoth Lakes road, the short Convict Lake road, or the dirt road up McGee Creek. The north and west sides of the Abbot group, and also the cluster of peaks surrounding Pioneer Basin, are easily reached from the high roadhead above Rock Creek Lake. The Mono Pass trail is one of the easiest crossings of the Sierra crest and leaves from this roadhead; it quickly takes one into the heart of the high country. The east side of the Abbot group is reached in a few hours from the same roadhead via the scenic Little Lakes Valley. The country south of the Abbot group contains peaks such as Seven Gables and Royce and can be reached most easily via either Italy Pass or Pine Creek Pass. Good but arduous trails over these passes begin above the modern mining village of Scheelite, west of Round Valley on U.S. Highway 395. Pine Creek Pass also gives access to the Mt. Humphreys area, though most climbers will prefer the far easier route over Piute Pass. To reach this trail, take the main road west out of Bishop and follow signs to North Lake, the 9,200-foot-high roadhead.

The region is also accessible from the west side of the Sierra. The western peaks of the Silver Divide can easily be approached from Lake Edison, and the Mt. Hooper area can be reached from Florence Lake via the trail up the South Fork of the San Joaquin River.

Climbers' and knapsackers' passes abound; the more significant include the following, listed in approximate north to south order.

Pretty Pass (11,840+) offers a convenient main crest crossing in the Convict Lake area. The class 2 pass lies just north of Peak 12,277, southwest of Dorothy Lake.

Gemini Pass (12,080+) is the broad saddle just west of Red Slate Mountain. This is the best cross-country route between upper Convict Creek and Fish Creek and is class 2 from the south; the north side contains permanent snowfields and an ice axe can prove useful.

Corridor Pass, at an elevation of 11,760+, lies 0.9 mile east of Red Slate Mountain and provides a class 2 route between Convict and McGee creeks.

Grinnell Pass, which crosses the Silver Divide just west of Red and White Mountain, allows one to travel easily between the headwaters of Fish Creek and the Mono Recesses. The 11,600-foot-high pass is class 2.

Hopkins Pass (11,360+) lies on the main Sierra crest between Red and White Mountain and Mt. Crocker. The very easy pass separates the Hopkins and McGee creek drainages.

Stanford Col (11,600+) lies three-quarters of a mile west of Mt. Stanford and connects Pioneer Basin with upper McGee Creek. Class 3.

Huntington Col (11,760+) is located 0.4 mile northwest of Mt. Huntington and provides an excellent class 2–3 route between Pioneer Basin and Hilton Creek.

Half-Moon Pass, immediately east of Golden Lake, is an excellent short route across the main crest. It is lower, less tedious, and much less traveled than the nearby Mono Pass trail. From the east, start near the pack station at Rock Creek Lake and head west up a small canyon. The 11,440-foot-high pass is class 2, with one very short class 3 section.

The Mono Divide may be crossed in at least three ways. *Recess Pass* (11,840+) lies between Recess Peak and Peak 12,205 and is class 2. *Hilgard Pass* (12,400+), 0.6 mile north-northeast of Mt. Hilgard, provides a class 2 route between the Second Recess and Lake Italy. *Gabbot Pass* (12,240+) crosses the divide between

Mts. Abbot and Gabb and is much easier than Hilgard Pass. The route from the Second Recess goes past the Mills Creek Lakes. Easy slopes are found on the Lake Italy side. Class 2.

Peppermint Pass (12,320+) is located about one-half mile east of Bear Creek Spire. This class 2–3 col offers a good route from the Rock Creek watershed to Morgan and Pine creeks.

Many class 2 and 3 passes will be found in the lake basins to the south of Lake Italy, and these offer scenic and convenient north-to-south "high routes" near the main crest. Especially popular is the class 2 *Feather Pass* (12,320+), located 0.65 mile west-northwest of Royce Peak.

Several very easy passes lead from Granite Park, east of Italy Pass, to the upper Royce Lakes. These routes give quick access to Royce and Merriam peaks.

Farther south, it is possible to travel cross-country from the tundra near Pine Creek Pass to Humphreys Basin. A 12,080-foot-high saddle south of Steelhead Lake is probably the easiest way to cross the ridge.

Nine topo maps cover the region: Blackcap Mountain, Devil's Postpile, Kaiser Peak, Merced Peak, Mt. Abbot, Mt. Goddard, Mt. Morrison, Mt. Tom, and Shuteye Peak. Three of these maps— Abbot, Morrison, and Tom—show the main areas of interest to the climber.

North of Mono Creek

Crystal Crag (10,364)

This small but nice-looking formation lies to the south of the Mammoth Lakes. The south arete is class 2. Class 3 routes may be picked out from Crystal Lake. Both the north buttress and the northeast face are class 4. On the left side of the east face is a 5.9 route.

Peak 12,052 (1.9 W of Bloody Mtn.)

Class 2 from the west. A steep chute near the left side of the east face is class 3.

Peak 11,760+ (1.6 WSW of Bloody Mtn.)

The east face is class 3 or 4.

Peak 11,894 (2.1 WSW of Bloody Mtn.)

Class 3 via the northeast ridge. A chute on the southwest side of the peak is also class 3.

Bloody Mountain (12,544)

Class 2 from the south. Also class 2 via the north-northeast ridge. A 1,500-foot, 45-degree couloir on the north-northwest side of the peak offers good introductory snow and ice climbing.

Laurel Mountain (11,812)

Class 1 from the north; class 2 from Convict Lake via the "northeast trough." A class 4 route has been done on the northeast side of the peak: a steep gully will be seen midway between the northeast trough and the arete which splits the east cliffs. Climb the class 4 gully to an arete, turn right, and head for the top.

Mt. Morrison (12,268)

The striking north and northeast faces of this peak are very obvious to travelers on U.S. Highway 395. The rock on this peak is mostly of volcanic origin and can be exceptionally loose. Bad limestone is also found. The summit one-half mile south of the one indicated on the map is probably the highest point.

Route 1. East Side. Class 2. From Convict Lake climb an arduous slope which leads into the classic hanging valley east of Morrison. From the head of this valley ascend to a saddle; then work up easy talus to the top.

Route 2. Northeast Face. Class 4–5. Several routes have been done on this large wall. In general, the farther left one goes, the easier.

Route 3. North Buttress. IV, 5.7, A3. Ascend a 200-foot, right-diagonaling traverse to the base of a crack system on the prow of the buttress. Several pitches directly up the buttress bring one to a headwall; this is overcome with a bit of aid. Continue up the ridge for a few hundred feet; then traverse left on a wide ledge to a reddish chimney. Couloirs above this lead to the summit.

Route 4. North Face. IV, 5.8. Several hundred feet up and right from the prow of the north buttress is a squat, black rock. Begin climbing near the middle of this rock and climb more or less straight up, tending to the right wherever the black rock blends to gray. Traverse down and left (5.8) to avoid a clean, sharp dihedral; then ascend broken rock to the base of a white section shaped like the state of California. Next, move left on friction to an exposed corner. Another pitch takes one almost to the prow of the north buttress. Easier climbing leads to a gold-colored chute. This brings one to a headwall and a thin arete. The summit is just above. After the first four pitches, this route fails to attain 5.6.

Route 5. Northwest Chute. Class 3. To the right of the north buttress and face is a steep snow chute. Climb this to the ridgecrest; then head left to the top.

Route 6. Northwest Ridge. Class 2. This is a long, uninteresting route. From Convict Lake climb talus to the ridge and follow it forever.

Mt. Aggie (11,561)
     Class 2 from McGee Creek.

Peak 12,240+ (0.6 SW of Mt. Aggie)
     This peak is briefly prominent from U.S. Highway 395 as a spectacular, flat-faced formation. A gully to the right (north) of the flat face provides a class 3 route.

Mt. Baldwin (12,614)
     From the vicinity of Mildred Lake climb the class 2 northwest side of the peak. The north ridge is a bit harder.

Peak 12,227 (1.4 SW of Dorothy Lake)
Class 2 or 3 from the north.

Peak 12,354 (0.8 W of Pk. 12,227)
A class 2 route can be made up the south slopes and then the east ridge.

Peak 11,915 (0.9 E of Lake Virginia)
Large granite blocks on the north ridge form a class 2 route. The south side is class 3.

Peak 12,160+ (1.35 NW of Red Slate Mtn.)
Class 2 or 3 from the main Sierra crest via giant blocks. The north-northwest ridge is of the same difficulty.

Red Slate Mountain (13,163)
This massive, rounded peak totally dominates the region. To the north all peaks are lower; to the south eight miles go by before a peak rises above Red Slate's height.

Class 1 and 2 routes can be found almost anywhere. A snow couloir on the north side provides enjoyable 40-degree snow and ice climbing.

Peak 12,400+ (0.85 ESE of Red Slate Mtn.)
Class 3 from the saddle between this peak and Red Slate Mountain. The arete is composed of very loose shale.

Peak 12,320+ (1.05 E of Red Slate Mtn.)
Class 2 from the saddle between this peak and Peak 12,400+ to the west.

Sharktooth Peak (11,639)
Class 2 from the south.

Silver Peak (11,878)
From Margaret Lake one may pick out several class 2 routes.

Graveyard Peak (11,520+)

Class 2 or 3 from Graveyard Lakes. The benchmark (11,494) indicated on the map is not on the true summit.

Peak 12,21 (0.8 ESE of Silver Pass)

A scree slope on the south side of the peak is the normal route.

Peak 11,840+ (0.9 NE of Silver Pass)

The summit blocks on the peak are class 4. Reach them via the class 3 northwest ridge or the class 2 south slopes.

Mt. Izaak Walton (12,099)

This peak, named for the author of *The Compleat Angler*, is class 3 via either the southwest slopes or the northeast ridge.

Peak 12,238 (0.7 SW of Red and White Mtn.)

Class 2 from the saddle between this peak and Red and White Mountain. Also class 2 from the north. A route has been done on the southwest face. Follow a shallow chute which ends on the northwest ridge some 50 feet from the top. Class 5.

Red and White Mountain (12,850)

Class 2 from Little Grinnell Lake. The ridge which leads up from the saddle between Peak 12,238 and this peak is class 3. The northeast and southeast sides of the peak are class 2 or 3.

Peak 12,426 (1 N of Red and White Mtn.)

Class 2 via the north ridge.

Mt. Crocker (12,457)

Easy slopes are found on the southwest and south sides of the peak.

Peak 12,408 (0.7 SE of Mt. Crocker)

Class 2 from Hopkins Creek; the northeast chute is a bit harder.

Mt. Hopkins (12,302)
   Sand slopes are found on the Pioneer Basin side. The peak is also trivial from the south and from the west.

Peak 12,178 (1.95 SW of Mt. Hopkins)
   Class 2 from the north.

Mt. Morgan (13,005)
   This is the northern, and lower, of two Mt. Morgans in this region. The traverse from Mt. Stanford is class 2; an easier route can be made from Davis Lake.

Peak 12,894 (0.65 WSW of Mt. Morgan)
   Class 1 from Mt. Morgan. Class 2 from Mt. Stanford.

Mt. Stanford (12,851)
   Class 2 from all directions except the northwest.

Peak 12,522 (0.95 E of Mt. Stanford)
   The southwest ridge is class 2 or 3.

Peak 12,318 (0.9 SE of Mt. Stanford)
   Class 2 from almost anywhere.

Mt. Huntington (12,405)
   The southwest ridge is class 2. Class 3 routes have been made on the south and northwest ridges.

Peak 12,240+ (0.9 SSE of Mt. Huntington)
   Probably class 2 from most directions.

Peak 12,252 (1.4 SE of Mt. Huntington)
   The summit mesa can be reached easily from Rock Creek or from Golden Trout Lake.

Mono Divide and Environs

Round Valley Peak (11,943)
   An easy peak from any direction.

Mt. Morgan (13,748)
   This giant mass is the southern of the two Mt. Morgans in the area. It is an easy but arduous climb from many directions. The view is supposedly rather nice.

Peak 13,265 (1 NE of Mt. Morgan)
   Class 1 or 2 from Tamarack Lakes.

Broken Finger Peak (Pk. 13,120, 0.85 E of Mt. Morgan)
   From Tamarack Lakes climb a couloir to the col northwest of the peak. From here traverse the ridge to the top. Class 3. The name was made official in 1968.

Mono Rock (11,555)
   From Fourth Recess Lake climb class 2 slopes to the low point south of the rock; then head right to the top. Another route begins from the same lake and ascends the class 4 east face. The north face has a class 5 route.

Mt. Starr (12,870)
   An uninspiring peak bears the name of the great Sierra figure, Walter Starr, Jr. Class 2 from Mono Pass via unstable talus slopes. Another easy route can be made from the roadhead at Rock Creek.

Peak 13,198 (1.05 SSW of Mono Pass)
   Two routes lie on the west side of the peak. One of them ascends a couloir which drops down from the highest point. Class 3. The other can be seen from a point between the two Snow Lakes as a

chockstone-filled chimney which leads to a col north of the peak. Climb the chimney to the col; then follow the right side of the ridge south to the top. Class 4–5. A third route has been done on the east buttress.

A series of class 5 gendarmes south of the peak, on the main crest, has been traversed.

Mt. Mills (13,468)

Route 1. North Glacier. Class 3. From the head of the Fourth Recess climb onto the glacier. Ascend the couloir between the central and western of three rock ribs. Cross into the central rib for a while; then, near the top, cross right again and climb the western rib to the summit plateau.

Route 2. East Couloir. Class 3. Three couloirs cut the east side of Mills. Take the third couloir (counting from the Abbot-Mills col) to the summit ridge. Cross over this and then turn left toward the summit plateau.

Route 3. South-Southeast Ridge. Climb from the Abbot-Mills col. A short bit of aid is necessary on the otherwise class 4 arete.

Route 4. Southwest Face. Ascend chutes near the right side of the face. The last section is class 4.

Mt. Abbot (13,715)

This is the highest point of the Sierra crest in this region. Several fine routes have been done.

Route 1. West Ridge. Class 4. Follow the ridge from Gabbot Pass. A few deviations from the ridgecrest make things class 4 instead of 5.

Route 2. West Chimney. Class 4. From Gabbot Pass ascend easy slopes toward the main peak. Climb a left-slanting chimney or chute which ends at a notch between Abbot and an obvious, over-hanging spire to the northwest. From the notch climb up and left to the plateau.

Route 3. Southwest Chute. Class 3. This is the most popular route on the peak. From Gabbot Pass scramble up to a talus fan to the right of the steep summit mass. From the top of the fan climb the broad central chute of three chutes. The headwall at the top of the chute is exposed class 3.

Route 4. Southeast Buttress. Class 3. From the glacier which lies between Abbot and Dade climb the left side of the buttress or spur which is seen at the left edge of the east face. At times one must wander onto the right side of the buttress.

Route 5. East Side. Class 3. Climb an ill-defined ridge just left of a prominent snow couloir on the east face.

Route 6. East Couloir. Class 3. This appears to be the easiest route from the east. Climb the prominent snow gully on the east face until it is possible to exit right on easy class 3 rock. Angle up and right, gain the north ridge, and follow it to the top.

Mt. Dade (13,600+)

Route 1. South Slopes. Class 2.

Route 2. Southwest Chute. Class 2 or 3. This chute leads almost directly to the summit. The rib immediately to the right of the chute can also be climbed.

Route 3. West Chute. Class 3. A chute left of the preceding route can be followed to the northwest ridge.

Route 4. North Couloir. Class 4. From the glacier between Abbot and Dade climb steep snow to a rock rib which forks at the top of a broad couloir. Improbable class 4 climbing leads up the left side of the rib. The summit lies just above.

Route 5. Northeast Face. Class 4. Climb a large gully which lies just left of a steep face. Ascend steep snow until it is possible to exit right on a ledge. This leads to easier climbing and the top.

Route 6. East Face. Class 4. Climb the face via the second chute from the right. Two-thirds of the way up, the chute ends; head left a short bit; then climb to a depression on the summit ridge. Lots of bad rock will be found on the climb.

Peak 12,975 (0.55 NE of Mt. Abbot)

From the saddle southwest of the peak, climb the class 4 ridge to the top. The west face is class 3.

Mt. Gabb (13,711)

This giant, isolated peak is visible from many spots in the Sierra.

Route 1. South Side. Class 2 from Lake Italy. A rock band at about 12,000 feet is overcome by means of broad chutes.

Route 2. Northeast Ridge. Class 3 or 4 from Gabbot Pass.

Route 3. North Face. Climb the north glacier until just right of an obvious, diagonal split in the center of the face. Ascend slabs to the split; then climb its right side to a large chockstone. Passing this is class 4. Continue upward to the northwest ridge and follow it to the summit.

Route 4. Glacier Route. Class 2–3. Climb the north glacier and its scree headwall to the northwest ridge and follow it upward.

Route 5. Northwest Ridge, East Spur. Class 3. From Upper Mills Creek Lake ascend steep, unstable talus to the notch right of a conspicuous gendarme on the east spur of the northwest ridge. From the notch follow the ridge to the top.

Mt. Hilgard (13,361)

Class 2 from the south; class 3 from the southeast. From Second Recess a route has been made on the class 3–4 northeast ridge.

Peak 12,720+ (0.7 NNW of Mt. Hilgard)

The northeast arete is class 4. Class 2 from Hilgard Lake.

Recess Peak (12,836)

This peak has been climbed via aretes on its northeast, southeast, and southwest sides. All routes are class 3.

Peak 12,145 (2.8 NE of Recess Pk.)

Class 3 or 4 from the Second Recess.

Volcanic Knob (11,168)

Class 1 from the west.

Bear Creek Spire (13,713)

Route 1. Northwest Side. Class 3–4. This is by far the most

popular way up the peak; only the last 100 feet or so are at all difficult. From Lake Italy head northeast until past a subsidiary peaklet; then walk up sandy slopes to the summit area.

Route 2. North Arete. III, 5.8. From the vicinity of Dade Lake (the usual approach) this fine prow will be seen leading directly toward the top of the peak. Climb straight up the center of the prow on excellent rock.

Route 3. Northeast Ridge. Just left of the north arete is a ridge with a tower at its base. The ridge is class 3 or 4.

Route 4. Northeast Face. Class 3–4 via the wide face between the northeast and east ridges.

Route 5. East Ridge. Moderate class 5. This is the spectacular step-like ridge which rises from the col between Bear Creek Spire and the peaklet southwest of Spire Lake. It is an enjoyable and lengthy climb.

Route 6. South Face. IV, 5.9, A1. This steep, 1,000-foot-high wall is hidden from most vantage points. The wall to the right of the summit is split by two major cracks— a serrated fin separates these. This route ascends the wall just right of the right-hand crack. Climb steep, rough rock; finish the hard climbing at a notch on the east ridge. This notch is at the top of the right-hand crack.

Route 7. South Side. Class 3–4. A relatively low-angle wall abuts the south face on the left side. Climb this wall to the broken southwest ridge and follow it to the top.

Peak 13,120+ (0.55 S of Bear Creek Spire)

From the small lake northwest of the summit, diagonal across the face of the north ridge. When below the lowest point of the ridge, make a sharp left and climb to the summit plateau. Class 4. The west-southwest ridge is class 3. The southern slopes are easy.

Peak 12,866 (0.7 NE of Bear Creek Spire)

Class 2 from the saddle between Bear Creek Spire and this peak.

Peak 12,744 (1.5 NE of Bear Creek Spire)

Class 2 from the saddle to the southwest.

Mt. Julius Caesar (13,196)

The south and west sides of this peak are easy. The southwest ridge is a classic class 3 climb. Another route has been done from the small lake to the northeast: climb the face to the east arete and follow it to the top. Class 3.

Peak 12,756 (1.3 SW of Mt. Julius Caesar)

The northwest ridge is class 3. The southeast slope has been described as "one of the better sand-climbs in the Sierra."

Peak 12,400+ (2 SSE of Mt. Julius Caesar)

This peak, lying due north of the largest Royce Lake, has a class 4 summit block. The southwest ridge up to this block is class 2 or 3.

Peak 12,563 (2.3 SE of Mt. Julius Caesar)

The west, south, and east slopes are quite easy, but the summit block is class 3. Two technical routes have been established on the steep northwest face of the mountain. A 5.7 route begins in a steep corner which ends in a bowl. A more difficult route lies a bit farther to the left and ends at a pinnacle high on the face. Climb a steep aid crack past an overhang; then free climb to the top of the pinnacle. 5.7, A2.

"Feather Peak" (Pk. 13,242, 0.7 NW of Royce Pk.)

This spectacular peak well deserves a name; Feather Peak has been the climbers' name for over 40 years. The southwest ridge is class 3–4; careful routefinding is necessary to avoid harder climbing. An easier route has been done up the southeast side. A direct route has been done on the east-northeast face: scramble up to a large, sloping ledge beneath a conspicuous cleft; then rope up and climb up and right until easy clambering brings one to the final, steep 300-foot section. Climb a corner to a belay stance below a ceiling. A difficult pitch goes left into a jamcrack which leads to the summit area. 5.8.

Royce Peak (13,253)
Class 2 or 3 from most directions.

Merriam Peak (13,077)
Class 2 from the Royce-Merriam saddle. Class 3 routes can be worked out on the east, south, and southwest sides of the mountain.

Seven Gables (13,075)
This fine, isolated peak dominates its surroundings. Class 2 talus slopes are found on the west side, but the eastern escarpment is a striking sight. Two routes have been established on this side of the peak. From the first lake north of Stub Lake climb slabs to a chute which ends at the saddle 0.3 mile north of the summit. From here follow the ridge to the top. Although the true east face is unclimbed, a route has been done just to its right. Ascend the steep, broken wall which leads to a point just right of the north summit. The lower section of this route is class 4; the middle 700 feet is stimulating class 3; the upper headwall is again class 4. The summit ridge is attained about 200 feet north of the top.

Peak 12,287 (1.8 N of Seven Gables)
A class 2 or 3 route has been done on the west side.

Gemini (12,866)
Easy from the broad saddle between Seven Gables and this peak. Another route has been done from Aweetsal Lake: climb class 2 slopes to the south ridge and follow it to the top.

The Pinnacles (12,240+)
This mile-long ridge south of Gemini contains many pinnacles, some of which probably remain unclimbed. Two formations at the southern end of the ridge have been done; so has another, unidentified one. The best routes appear to be on the east side, not the west.

Mt. Hooper (12,349)

Easy slopes lead to the summit monolith from nearby Selden Pass. The top block is usually done by spurious methods—a ladder has been placed for the climber's convenience. A jamcrack to the left of the ladder is probably climbable for those desiring a pure ascent.

Peak 12,014 (0.9 SE of Mt. Hooper)

Easy from Sally Keyes Lakes. Class 2 or 3 from Selden Pass— swing to the southwest of the east shoulder of the peak. The traverse from Mt. Hooper is class 3.

Mt. Senger (12,271)

This peak was named for Joachim Henry Senger, the driving force behind the formation of the Sierra Club. An easy slope leads to the summit from the John Muir Trail in the vicinity of Sally Keyes Lakes. Class 2 from the east.

Turret Peak (12,000+)

This is a relatively easy ascent from all directions.

Mt. Humphreys Area

Pilot Knob (12,245)

Class 2 from Humphreys Basin.

Four Gables (12,720+)

From the lakes southwest of the top, climb onto the east ridge and follow it toward the summit. From the same lakes an approach can be made to a technical route. A long wall, which might as well be called the east face, lies due west of the upper lake. Near the right edge of the wall is a prominent buttress; cracks and chimneys lead up about 800 feet to the summit. III, 5.8. Another buttress, to the right of this route, has been climbed. II, 5.6.

Mt. Tom (13,652)

This enormous, dry hulk of a mountain is perhaps the most prominent sight to travelers of U.S. Highway 395. The easiest way to the top is from Horton Lake, where a jeep road can be taken to the Tungstar Mine at 12,000 feet. Class 2 slopes lead to the top from here. A much more strenuous route is found on the northwest side. Follow the trail up Gable Creek; then follow a tramway. Cross the creek and ascend an old, scree ridden "trail" which works its way upward for thousands of feet to the Tungstar Mine. This route requires an elevation gain of 6,200 feet.

Basin Mountain (13,240)

Class 2 from Horton Lake. Another route begins from the basin northeast of the peak: climb a snow-filled couloir to the east ridge and follow it to the top. Class 4 or 5.

Peak 13,224 (0.9 WSW of Basin Mtn.)

Class 2 or 3 from the plateau to the southwest.

Peak 12,160+ (1.2 NE of Mt. Humphreys)

When viewed from the east, this peak is a miniature replica of nearby Mt. Humphreys. The summit rocks, from any direction, are class 4. These rocks can be reached via the class 2 south slope or the class 3 terrain above McGee Lake. A technical route, rated III, 5.7, has been done on the 1,800-foot-high northeast face. Half the route is class 4; the crux is a 200-foot dihedral midway up the face.

Mt. Humphreys (13,986)

Dominating the Piute Pass area of the High Sierra is Mt. Humphreys, a spectacular and massive peak which even by the easiest route is class 4. Part of its appeal to the mountaineer lies in the very fact of its relative inaccessibility—no organized youth groups writing inane comments in *this* register, that's for sure.

Most people climb the mountain from the Humphreys Basin side, and from here one can see several routes. From the first notch left of the summit a 45-degree ledge and talus system will be seen diagonaling down to the right. At the exact point where this system intersects the talus fans, another gully slices upward diagonally to the right, ending at a very deep notch to the right of the summit mass. These landmarks should help to locate Routes 1 through 4.

Route 1. Regular Route. Class 4. Walk up to the base of the endless southwest face and ascend the left-diagonaling ledge system mentioned above. Loose class 2 climbing eventually brings one to the notch just left of the summit mass. Variations exist everywhere on this lower section—the face to the left can be climbed by numerous class 2–4 routes. From the notch climb the shallow gully to the right of the main summit ridge. After about 250 feet a steep section is reached. Traverse right onto a ridgecrest and climb a 100-foot section of class 4. The summit is a just above.

Route 2. Southwest Face. Class 5. This 800-foot face rises above the approach ledges of Route 1. Not much is known about this seldom-done route, but it looks like there are several moderate routes available.

Route 3. South Couloir. Class 4. Climb the aforementioned right-diagonaling gully until about 400 vertical feet have been gained. Leave the main gully and enter a well-defined subsidiary gully which cuts up and left between two large black formations. This gully leads to the south couloir, a gash which eventually ends at a notch immediately right of the summit cone. From this notch move left a few feet and climb a short class 4 pitch. There are several ways to go in this area, but after about 50 feet the difficulties ease and the summit is but a 10-minute scramble.

Route 4. South Ridge. Class 4. Follow the right-diagonaling gully mentioned above to the deep notch southeast of the summit. Three hundred feet of obvious, specimen class 4 climbing leads to easier ground. Scramble along the ridge to the notch just beneath the summit cone and follow the last part of Route 3 to the top.

A major variation has been done. The deep notch can be reached from the headwaters of the south branch of the south fork of McGee Creek by means of a steep, loose class 3–4 chute.

Route 5. East Arete. Class 4. From the headwaters of the south branch of the south fork of McGee Creek climb to the right of a permanent snowfield and head for the obvious notch in the east arete of the mountain. Follow the arete upward to a steep step which can be turned on the left. Higher, the northeast arete joins the east arete and the combined ridge leads to the plateau just south of the summit.

A major variation exists. From the left side of the glacier under the northeast face, climb up just left of a couloir which shoots toward the skyline ridge. After a short bit cross the couloir and follow a ledge which diagonals up and right. Leave this after a few hundred yards and climb the face above to the east arete. Class 4.

Route 6. Northeast Face. At the base of this wall is a large glacier with a prominent snow tongue extending upward. Start at the base of this right-trending couloir, but instead of following it, head up and left on broken rock and snow. After about 500 feet begin traversing up and right on a snow-covered ledge. Shortly after turning a rib, head upward and eventually up and right to hit the summit area very close to the top. III, 5.7. Crampons and auxiliary gear should be taken.

Route 7. Northeast Couloir. Class 4. Ascend the couloir mentioned in Route 6. After a few hundred feet take the right branch and follow it to the main summit ridge. Pass over a minor peaklet and follow Route 1 to the top.

The main couloir apparently can be followed all the way.

Route 8. From McGee Lake. Class 4. From the lake ascend to the tarn to the west; then continue west to the plateau. Follow the long north-northwest ridge until Route 1 is joined just below the summit.

Peak 13,112 (1.1 SE of Mt. Humphreys)

Class 2 or 3 from Humphreys Basin. On the northern flank of this peak are two snow couloirs. The right-hand one has been climbed and involves about 800 feet of 50-degree snow or ice climbing.

Mt. Emerson (13,225)

This high, isolated peak rises north of Piute Pass and offers a great view.

Route 1. North Face. This rarely done climb was the route of the first ascent and is probably class 3.

Route 2. West Ridge. Class 3. From Piute Pass head toward the small lakes to the northeast; then scramble up the ridge to the top.

Route 3. South Face, Left Side. Class 3. Leave the Piute Pass trail about one-quarter of a mile west of Loch Leven and ascend a rib toward the top. Reach the summit ridge just left of a prominent overhang. There are many possible variations on this route.

Route 4. South Face, Right Side. Class 4. Just left of the couloir which separates Emerson from the Piute Crags one will see two cracks which shoot up the face. Take the left crack or chimney and follow it to the summit ridge.

Piute Crags (ca. 12,300)

A series of large but basically uninteresting pinnacles lies on the east ridge of Mt. Emerson. The accompanying sketch shows the numeration system used. All approaches are from the trail.

Crag 1. From the south ascend the 1–2 couloir to the 1–2 notch. Head up and left across the steep northeast and north faces to the summit ridge. Class 5.

Crag 2. Three routes have been done. From the 2–3 notch climb up very loose class 4 rock to the top. From the 1–2 notch the original route ascends the west face toward the west arete. After a class 4

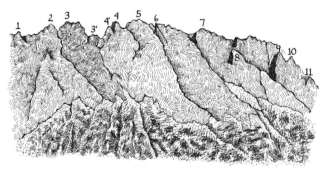

The Piute Crags from the south.

pitch, climb a huge slab on the right. Gain the arete and scramble to the top. The third route begins just below the 1–2 notch. Traverse up and right onto the south face and climb a few easy class 5 pitches to the top.

Crag 3. From the 3–3' notch scramble to the base of the east face. Traverse around the corner to the right; then climb up and right onto the north face. Climb to the ridge and the top. Class 4. Another class 4 route has been done—climb the arete from the 2–3 notch.

Crag 4. From the 4–4' notch traverse across the north face to a platform; then ascend straight up to the east ridge. Easy climbing then leads to the top. Class 5.

Crag 5. This was the first crag to be climbed and it predated the next climbing in the area by 22 years. From the 5–6 notch traverse onto the class 3 south ridge and follow it to the top.

A minor but very sharp spire between Crags 5 and 6 is class 4.

Crag 6. Class 4 from the 5–6 notch; easy from the 6–7 notch.

Crag 7. Nothing is known about this crag.

Crag 8. This is the red pinnacle seen on the south face of Crag 7. Climb the gully to the right of Crag 7; then head over left to the notch behind 8. Class 3 climbing leads to the summit.

Crag 9. East of the red Crag 8 are two pinnacles on approximately the same level. Crag 9 is the western and higher of the two. The easiest route is from the notch behind the crag–class 3. A class 5 route has been done: from the notch between 10 and 11 the south ridge is followed.

Crag 10. Class 3. Climb to the notch between 9 and 10; then head up the easy north face. Another route is as follows: from the 10–11 notch descend a few feet to the obvious route on the south face. 5.4.

Crag 11. Class 4–5. From the couloir east of the crag one will see a broken buttress facing southeast. Climb this to a chute which diagonals up and left behind a small crag. From a notch an easy pitch is climbed to the top.

The White Tower, a prominent formation on the south side of Crags 1 and 2, is a trivial ascent from the west.

The Western Domes

Balloon Dome (6,881)

In 1864, William Brewer, of the California Geological Survey, was in the region south of Yosemite and spied a dome which to him looked like "the top of a gigantic balloon struggling to get up through the rock." The dome is one of the most conspicuous in the Sierra and is located just above the confluence of the San Joaquin River with its south fork. There are two approaches to the dome. The first starts from near the Clover Meadow Ranger Station, located on the Mammoth Pool road, which starts near the town of North Fork and parallels the river for many miles. From the ranger station follow an old dirt road south to a trailhead (this trailhead can also be reached by a walking route from McCreary Meadow on the Mammoth Pool road). The trail drops 2,200 feet to the river, crosses it on a bridge, and then winds up the opposite side. From Cassidy Meadows the route over to the dome is clear.

The other approach begins from Lake Edison, at the end of the highway which starts in Fresno. Dirt roads lead northwest from the reservoir toward the Hertz Meadow Ranger Station. Logging roads, sometimes impassable, lead over toward Cassidy Meadows. This is by far the best route *if* the correct roads can be found and *if* they are not washed out.

Route 1. Southeast Side. Class 2–3. From the left side of the east face ascend friction slabs up onto the gentle south ridge of the formation.

Route 2. West Face. IV, 5.9, A3. In the center of this face, above a big ledge, one will see a very prominent, left-facing open book. This somewhat dirty route is seven pitches in length; half of the climb involves aid.

Route 3. Northeast Pillar. IV, 5.8, A3. A classic pillar leans against the northeast face of Balloon. Five pitches up the left side of this pillar lead to its top. Hard slab climbing and jamming are encountered in this section. From the pillar's top, rappel 50 feet to the notch behind it; then pendulum to the right into a long crack (mostly aid) which leads to easier climbing and the top.

Route 4. Northeast Face. III, 5.9. Immediately to the left of the pillar of the preceding route is a smooth face marred only by a sinuous dike which curves up and left. Follow this dike for nine excellent free pitches. Nine bolts will be found.

Route 5. East Face. III, 5.9. Farther to the left of the dike mentioned above is a chimney system. Climb this for three pitches; then traverse to the right across a steep section to a crack. Follow this to the upper two pitches of Route 4.

East Fuller Butte

The Fuller Buttes are a major landmark on the north side of the San Joaquin River and are located just north of the upper segment of the Mammoth Pool Reservoir. Of the two buttes, the eastern one is the principal attraction. The approach to the dome is quite straightforward: from the town of North Fork take the road toward Mammoth Pool. After many miles Jackass Creek will be crossed. Just beyond this, turn right on a logging track which, after a mile or two, leads to a point very close to the top of the buttes. Hike down the east slopes to reach the following routes.

Route 1. Southeast Face. IV, 5.8, A2. High on the face one will see a huge, right-facing arch or open book. The route begins below this feature. Start climbing on the right side of a large flake and proceed up awkward free and aid climbing to a bushy ramp. Follow this up and left. A bolt ladder (carry 3/16" hardwoods) leads up a blank wall to a sling belay. Next, climb a flake to a ramp and belay below a long chimney. This chimney is strenuous but not particularly difficult. From chockstones atop the chimney use aid up a wide crack; this narrows after 50 feet and a hanging belay can be established higher at a bolt. Forty feet above this, exit left at a horn which is lassoed. Free climb up a groove to the easy upper pitches.

Route 2. Southwest Dihedral. IV, 5.9, A3. A crack system which leads to a prominent open book on the upper face is the most obvious climbing route on East Fuller Butte. Walk out right on a bush-covered ramp to this crack system and climb it. A wide, flared crack on the third pitch calls for a strange aid technique. Above, the route in the book is obvious and involves chimneys and overhangs. The summit mass is turned on the right via a long, horizontal ledge and then a chimney.

The Balls

A few miles below the southern border of Yosemite National Park, and just west of Jackass Meadow, is a group of six or eight small domes called the Balls. Some of these rocks have steep south faces which provide fun climbing on superb rock. Over a dozen routes have been established; most involve three or four pitches of 5.6 to 5.10 climbing. To reach the Balls, leave Bass Lake and follow dirt roads northeast through Beasore Meadows to Jackass Meadow. The rocks are quite obvious from the road and are only a very short distance away.

The south side of Fresno Dome. The satellite dome is on the left.

Fresno Dome

Six miles east of Fish Camp, on the Fresno-Yosemite highway, is a large dome with an expansive southern escarpment. Good roads lead from Fish Camp toward the dome; from a campground below the rock a dirt road can be followed up to a saddle behind the dome. When seen from the south, the dome has a massive satellite dome attached to its western flank. Several moderate to difficult routes have been made on the south face of this satellite. Farther east, on the south face of the main dome, at least three routes have been established. A sheer, left-facing open book is 5.10. To the right of this obvious route is a steep, 40-foot-wide alcove with cracks up either side. Both the cracks have been done; both are 5.7. The right-hand crack leads to a prominent pillar 300 feet above the ground.

The Evolution Region

Although not particularly distinguished when viewed from afar, the Evolution group is one of the most famous and popular areas in the Sierra Nevada. The lakes and meadows along Evolution Creek, just west of the crest, have long been acclaimed as gems of the range. Walter Starr, Jr. wrote that the Evolution country was "the region where the grand crescendo of the Sierra touches at once the heart of the mountaineer and the artist."

The peaks which rise so elegantly above Evolution Creek have attracted the mountaineer for over a century. Many of these peaks have no walk-up route, and this fact undoubtedly adds to their appeal. While the west side of the group used to be described as one of the most remote spots in California, the freeway-like John Muir Trail and easier access from the west have combined to make the region a heavily overused one. The area has lost some of its original charm, but the climber who is here for the peaks will soon leave behind the four-foot-wide trails and old campfire scars. There are, as yet, few technical routes in the Evolution country, but the climber interested in class 3 and 4 ridges and faces can hardly find a more concentrated region in which to practice his dangerous and rewarding sport.

From Piute Pass, the northern limit of the Evolution area, the Sierra crest rises almost immediately to 13,000 feet, and it continues at or above this level throughout the region, which can be said to end at Bishop Pass, twelve miles southeast of Piute Pass.

Two gigantic spurs shoot west from the crest in the Evolution country. Glacier Divide, named for the many permanent snowfields under its north side, joins the main crest just a few miles south of Piute Pass and forms such an effective east-west barrier that the John Muir Trail is forced into the "lowlands" to circumvent the

151

obstacle. Glacier Divide, incidentally, forms the northern boundary of Kings Canyon National Park. The other spur is the Goddard Divide, named for the black mass at its west end. This divide leaves the Sierra crest near Mt. Wallace and separates two great Sierra watersheds, the San Joaquin and Kings rivers. The divide also presents a barrier to north-south travel, and it was not until 1917 that a trail was constructed over Muir Pass.

Another significant sub-range in the Evolution region is the well-named Black Divide, an eight-mile-long metamorphic ridge which extends from near Muir Pass southward to the junction of Cartridge Creek with the Middle Fork of the Kings River. The divide contains some interesting and remote peaks, and the rockclimber will appreciate the Devil's Crags, near the south end.

The eastern side of the Sierra crest in the Evolution region falls sharply away into the various forks of Bishop Creek. Two large artificial lakes, Lake Sabrina and South Lake, dominate the area and offer untold pleasures to boaters and fishermen, as well as to climbers who like high roadheads with nearly year-round accessibility. Above these dammed lakes lie scores of beautiful lakes and tarns. Whoever named some of these lakes certainly had a creative streak: Hungry Packer, Baboon, Topsy Turvy, and Dingleberry are just a few of the more original. Because of the rugged character of the main crest in this area, there are no trail passes over it between Piute and Bishop passes.

Owing to its great height and isolation, Mt. Goddard was the first peak in the Evolution region to be coveted. Richard Cotter, of the Whitney Survey, and a soldier named Spratt attempted the peak in 1864 but were stopped 300 feet below the top. It is certain that difficulty did not stop them, for the summit cone of Goddard is a talus slope on most sides. The two explorers had approached their peak from a base camp some twenty miles distant and had set out with great determination but little food. It is quite probable that they simply ran out of time and energy. Goddard was finally climbed in

1879 by Lilbourne Winchell, a member of a family that made extensive explorations of the Kings River country in the 1870s.

Certainly the most prominent historical figure of the region was Theodore Solomons, who first explored the headwaters of the South Fork of the San Joaquin River and gave the peaks their distinctive names. Solomons had conceived of a pack trail the length of the Sierra, a trail which would stay as close to the crest as possible. During the 1890s he and various partners spent several summers in the range, working out a high-level route. In 1895 he and Ernest Bonner decided to explore the rugged terrain which lay between the San Joaquin and Kings rivers. Solomons was fascinated with recent theories of evolution, and he soon began naming major peaks for those philosophers, scientists, and historians prominent in the field.

On July 16 the pair climbed Mt. Wallace and, back in camp by noon, decided to ascend Mt. Darwin, the highest peak of the Evolution group. They were only two or three hundred feet below the top when they "finally came upon a little platform of rock from which farther ascent is barred to all human beings." Interestingly enough, John Muir had been in the area in 1873 and had "climbed the highest peak at the head of the San Joaquin." Presumably this was Darwin; Muir didn't deign to mention the difficulty, or location, just the view!

After exploring and mapping the Evolution Creek area, Solomons and Bonner made the third ascent of Mt. Goddard and then dropped down into a place still regarded as the most remote in the Sierra—the Enchanted Gorge. Most of the place names in this region are also Solomons'. The team had succeeded in finding a route across the Goddard Divide, but it was obviously too rough for stock, and it is still a route chosen by very few.

Although such noted mountaineers as James Hutchinson, Walter Starr, Sr., and Joseph N. LeConte had visited the region around the turn of the century, they did no significant climbing. Members of a survey party made the first recorded ascent of Darwin in 1908, overcoming the final summit monolith by means of a "monstrous icicle.'' The two nicest-looking peaks in the area, Mt. Haeckel and Mt. Huxley, were climbed in July 1920; the latter peak was done by none other than Norman Clyde.

During the next twenty years all the main peaks were ascended, and subsequent first ascenders learned to be content with small, unnamed peaks and new routes on the steep north and east faces of the group. The great ice couloirs on the north face of Mt. Mendel offered challenging ice climbing and were ascended in 1958 and 1967, respectively. Less spectacular ice gullies are presently falling to a new generation.

From the western foothills of the Sierra there is only one really feasible approach to the Evolution group—the 25-mile-long trail which leaves Florence Lake and travels first up the South Fork of the San Joaquin and then follows Evolution Creek.

The east side of the group is very easily approached from North Lake, Lake Sabrina, or South Lake, all of which are quickly accessible from Bishop via good roads. Trails lead from each of these lakes into scenic basins below the crest. The best base camp for climbs on the east side of the Darwin-Haeckel group is either at Hungry Packer Lake or Midnight Lake. Both have trails leading to them from Lake Sabrina.

To reach the western side of the region from the east, one has a choice of at least four passes which cross the Sierra crest. From north to south, these are as follows.

Piute Pass (11,423) is regarded as one of the easier east-side passes in the range and quickly places the climber in the back country. North Lake is the roadhead. The pass is located at the far north edge of the Evolution group and is therefore used primarily for peaks of the Glacier Divide. To reach the Darwin group from Piute, one must cross the divide at either of two passes which will be described later.

Lamarck Col (12,880+) is a regularly used backpackers' pass which allows one-day access into the heart of the Evolution region.

The route was misdrawn on the maps in both the 1965 and 1972 guidebooks (but curiously not on the map in the 1954 edition), and some confusion has resulted. The popular route involves a rise of 3,700 feet and is mainly off-trail walking. Thus, even though it is only class 2 in difficulty, the trip should not be taken lightly. From North Lake take the trail (not shown on the map) toward Upper Lamarck Lake. From a point just below its outlet, leave the trail near a stream crossing and pick up a fairly well-worn path which heads south. Traverse toward the headwaters of the small creek which drains into Grass Lake. After a while one must ascend a short, steep slope containing sparse brush. This leads to a gentle, sandy, mile-long valley which rises to the southwest. A butte with a curious obelisk is passed; soon the final sandy basin beneath the crest is reached. A small tarn here provides water until mid-August. At the head of the basin is a peaklet with a steep left side. To its right is a series of small notches; Lamarck Col is the first one to the right of the peaklet, though any of the other notches will do. From the col a descent of 1,300 feet brings one to lakes in upper Darwin Canyon. Evolution Lake and the John Muir Trail can be reached from here in about two hours.

When climbing to Lamarck Col from Darwin Canyon, make sure that the subtle notches close to Mt. Lamarck are chosen, not the more gentle saddle to the right. This saddle will deposit the traveler in the Lake Sabrina watershed. This route is class 2–3 and takes an hour or two longer than Lamarck Col.

Another mistake made by some is to continue down the sandy, mile-long valley too far, where a loose and very steep slope drops to the southwest end of Upper Lamarck Lake. This slope lies just east of Peak 12,396 and is not recommended.

Echo Pass (12,400+) provides a long one-day route to the Muir Pass region. From Lake Sabrina follow the middle fork of Bishop Creek to its headwaters at Echo Lake. The class 2 pass lies one-half mile to the south, between Peak 13,267 (Clyde Spires) and the Mt. Powell massif.

Bishop Pass (11,920+) separates the Evolution and Palisade groups and is a very popular crest crossing. From the roadhead at South Lake it is just over seven miles to the pass. The trail offers excellent access to the southern peaks of the Evolution chain.

Several crest passes in the vicinity of Mt. Haeckel and Mt. Wallace have been used by climbers, but they are extremely loose and time-consuming and are not recommended.

The Glacier Divide, as mentioned earlier, is crossed by two passes. Both are class 2 and contain inordinate amounts of talus. *Alpine Col* (12,400+) lies just southwest of Muriel Peak and offers a route between Goethe Lake and lower Darwin Canyon. The *Keyhole* (12,560+) is located just southeast of Muriel Peak and is higher and more arduous than Alpine Col.

The Goddard Divide can be crossed at several places. *Muir Pass* (11,955), of course, is the route of the John Muir Trail. At the pass is the Schwarz Hut, built by the Sierra Club in the summer of 1930. The total cost was $5810, of which over half was for the rental of the pack animals. The hut offers succor in emergencies, but it should not be used for routine overnight stays because of the sewage problem. *Wanda Pass* (12,400+) lies 1.2 miles west-southwest of Muir Pass and offers a convenient class 2 route between Wanda Lake and the Ionian Basin. The steep section just south of the lake should be turned on the west. This pass is often used by would-be Goddard climbers.

The Black Divide can be crossed in two ways. *Black Giant Pass* (12,160+) lies 1.05 miles southeast of Muir Pass and allows the traveler speedy access into the Ionian Basin and to peaks such as Scylla and Charybdis. Class 1–2. *Rambaud Pass* (11,553) is located 0.65 mile southeast of Wheel Mountain. A trail once led up Rambaud Creek to the pass, but the traces are hard to find. The Devil's Crags are readily accessible from the pass, as is Wheel Mountain. Class 2.

The Mt. Goddard quadrangle covers the Evolution region; the Blackcap Mountain topo is necessary for the western approaches.

North of the Goddard Divide

Pavilion Dome (11,846)
   Class 2 from the south.

Peak 12,873 (1 S of Packsaddle Lake)
   A class 4 route can be found on the north arete.

Peak 12,498 (0.4 SE of Paine Lake)
   A class 2–3 route has been done on the northwest ridge.

Peak 12,971 (1 SW of Goethe Lake)
   The north ridge is class 2, as is the ridge leading up from the saddle between this peak and the next peak to the southeast. The east couloir and northeast ridge have also been climbed and are class 3.

Mt. Goethe (13,200+)
   This, the high point of the Glacier Divide, is an easy ascent from the south and east. The ridge from Alpine Col is class 3. A class 5 route has been made on the north face, above the central lobe of the glacier.

Muriel Peak (12,942)
   From Goethe Lake class 2 and 3 routes may be picked out. The ridge from the Keyhole has been followed and is class 2 or 3.

Peak 13,120+ (0.8 E of Muriel Pk.)
   Class 3 from Piute Pass—simply follow the gentle main crest south to the summit crags.

Peak 13,360+ (0.8 NW of Mt. Lamarck)
   This mountain lies at the extreme south end of the immense plateau southeast of the Keyhole. The ascent is trivial from the plateau.

Mt. Lamarck (13,417)

Class 2 from Lamarck Col. The highest point is on the northwest side of the summit plateau. Another route has been done on the north side of the peak. On the right side of the north face are several gullies. The left-hand gully leads to a notch just left of a serrated ridge. This gully provides 1,000 feet of snow or ice climbing at a moderate angle.

Peak 13,198 (0.7 ESE of Mt. Lamarck)

The north and northwest slopes are class 2.

Peak 13,248 (0.9 NE of Mt. Darwin)

The north ridge provides an interesting class 3 route.

Peak 13,385 (0.5 NW of Mt. Mendel)

This rugged peak, an outrider of Mt. Mendel, has several routes. A chute on the southwest side is class 3. A few class 3 and 4 routes lie on the north and northeast sides of the peak.

Mt. Mendel (13,691)

Route 1. Southwest Face. Class 3. This is the route most favored by mountaineers and is often climbed by those seeking the summit of nearby Mt. Darwin. Leave the John Muir Trail about one-quarter of a mile south of the peninsula which juts into the north end of Evolution Lake. Ascend a massive buttress which rises from near the lakeshore (in contrast to the large talus fields which border most of the shoreline). After about 1,500 feet, during which the buttress angles up and to the right, the glaciated rock gives way to the broken upper part of the peak. Cross right into the first talus fan and ascend it to the chute from which the fan emanates. Keep in the left branch higher up. A notch is soon reached; turn left here and traverse the serrated ridge to the top.

Route 2. Central Chute. Class 4. From the lower end of Evolution Lake this route lies in what could be termed the central chute of the southwest face. The chute leads directly up to the highest visible point.

Route 3. Right Mendel Couloir. Class 5. On the north face of Mendel lie the two most spectacular snow couloirs in California. In the late season they present formidable ice-climbing problems. Little need be said about the route in the right-hand couloir: belays can be established on the sides of the gully, and ice pitons and more sophisticated ice-climbing gear are necessary. The angle in this gully approaches 60 degrees.

Route 4. Left Mendel Couloir. Class 5. A short section of ice reputed to be angled at 80 degrees is found low in this couloir. Generally, the route is between 40 and 60 degrees.

Route 5. Northeast Ridge. Class 3. At the base of the ridge, start up a sloping slab which leads into a shallow chute on the nose of the ridge. Ascend this until about 50 feet below the crest of the ridge. At this point traverse left to the ridgetop and follow it to the summit.

Route 6. East Side. Class 3. Traverse the lower part of the Darwin Glacier to the east face. Obvious ledges and chutes lead to the summit plateau. There is an abundance of loose rock on this route.

Mt. Darwin (13,830)

Darwin, the giant of the Evolution country, has no walk-up route and has thus attracted the attention of many Sierra mountaineers. John Muir probably climbed the peak in 1873, but the first ascent is credited to others in 1908. The large summit plateau is a classic reminder of what the Sierra was like before the great uplifts and extensive glaciation. Curiously, a small pinnacle detached from the southeast side of the plateau is the highest point, though many who have come this far do not attempt it because of its considerable exposure. A short chimney on the northern side of the pinnacle provides a class 3 route.

Route 1. West Side. Class 3. Leave the John Muir Trail near the south end of Evolution Lake and ascend broad avalanche chutes or gullies to a ridge just northwest of the summit plateau. There are many variations possible on this route, especially on the lower section, where chutes may be followed, crossed, alternated, or climbed directly. Higher, the route angles generally to the right. All in all, the climb is a classic exercise in routefinding.

Route 2. Northwest Ridge. Class 3. On the Darwin-Mendel ridge is a large notch with a smaller notch about 300 feet to the southeast. Cross the Darwin Glacier and climb to either notch. Follow the northwest ridge to the summit. If one wishes to avoid the glacier, it is possible to skirt it on the right and then traverse over to the notches.

Route 3. North Face. Class 4. Two giant ribs run down the face, partly dividing the glacier. Climb the left side of the left rib until it merges with the face above; then work up and left to the summit plateau. The steep snowslopes on either side of the left rib offer enjoyable snow or ice climbing to those who are equipped.

Route 4. Northeast Ridge. Class 4–5. The base of this fine ridge can be reached either from the Darwin Glacier or from Blue Heaven Lake. From the latter, climb either to the flat saddle just right of Darwin (class 4) or to the next notch to the right, which is easily reached via a wide scree gully. Walk over to the ridge and follow it closely to the top. It is possible to escape onto the easier east face at many points.

Route 5. East Face, Right Side. Class 4. Attain the northeast ridge as in the preceding route. After a few hundred feet of easy slabs and blocks, one will reach a definite class 4 pitch in a shallow gully. Above this, exit left onto the face and traverse gently upward for many hundreds of feet on ledges to the second major wide chute. Climb this to the summit plateau. Most of the climbing on this popular route is class 3.

Route 6. Direct East Face. Moderate class 5. Begin a few feet to the right of a prominent, dark watercourse which descends from the broad, central avalanche chute on the east face and climb up and left to a large ledge 90 feet above the ground. Traverse left on rounded holds and then climb upward to class 5 cracks. Move right after 100 feet; then wander up into the central avalanche chute. This leads to the summit area.

Route 7. East Face, Left Side. Class 4. From Midnight Lake, in the afternoon light, one will see a wide band of dark rock crossing the east face from its lower left side to the summit plateau. Follow this band for about 500 feet; then cross right into the central avalanche chute. A steep, broken, 200-foot class 4 section at the beginning of the dark band presents the major difficulty.

Route 8. Southeast Ridge. Moderate class 5. Attain this ridge from either Lake 11,592 to the southwest or Blue Heaven Lake. A gendarme very high on the ridge is the main obstacle; otherwise the ridge is class 3 and 4.

Peak 13,280+ (0.5 SE of Mt. Darwin)

The southeast face has a class 2 route.

Mt. Spencer (12,400+)

Class 2 from the saddle east of the peak.

Mt. Haeckel (13,435)

Route 1. West Shoulder. Class 3. From the basin west of the peak ascend a chute to the ridge which joins the crest south of the summit. A short but steep face is the only obstacle between here and the top.

Route 2. Northwest Arete. Class 4. From the col northwest of the peak ascend either the arete directly or the chute to its left. This is a thrilling and enjoyable route.

Route 3. North Face. Class 4. From the small lake north of the peak ascend snow and slabs; then traverse to the right through a notch in a sharp rib. Finish via Route 2.

Route 4. East Ridge. Class 3. From the saddle east of the peak traverse under the ridge along the southeast slopes to the summit.

Route 5. South Ridge. Class 3. From the saddle between Haeckel and Wallace climb the serrated ridge to the top.

"Picture Peak" (Pk. 13,120+, 0.7 E of Mt. Haeckel)

Seen from Hungry Packer Lake, this is one of the most beautiful Sierra peaks.

Route 1. Southwest Side. From the cirque above Echo Lake several class 3 chutes provide routes.

Route 2. North Face. Class 4. From the cirque north of the

mountain ascend scree slopes about two-thirds of the way to the deep notch between the main peak and the northeast buttress. From this point proceed diagonally toward the top and ascend a chute to the summit.

Route 3. Northeast Face. IV, 5.9 This route begins with class 3 and 4 chimneys on the lower part of the face. Eventually a smooth wall is reached, above which are two large flakes split by a squeeze chimney. Difficult climbing leads to a point about 75 feet below the flakes. From this belay spot climb between the flakes (5.7); then head up a face with a steep corner (5.9). Now climb up and right to a 5.9 move which takes one to the corner of a buttress. Next, climb left along a steep ramp. The last pitch goes up a series of ramps and open books; the rest of the route is easier (class 4).

Route 4. East Side. The notch between the main peak and the northeast buttress can be reached from the stream below Echo Lake. A few hundred feet of class 5 climbing has been reported.

Mt. Wallace (13,377)

The west slopes of this peak are class 2. The ridge leading up from the Haeckel-Wallace saddle is class 3. The south ridge is easy.

"Clyde Spires" (Pk. 13,267, 0.6 SE of Mt. Wallace)

Two small spires stand atop Peak 13,267. Both have been climbed, but the rating is unknown—probably class 4 or easy 5. A tiny granite sliver about 100 yards west of the spires is apparently the actual high point of the peak and is class 4.

Mt. Fiske (13,524)

From Helen Lake the peak is a walk-up. Class 2 from the Warlow-Fiske saddle. Also class 2 from the lakes immediately to the west. Another route has been done from the lake west of Mt. Wallace: climb the class 2–3 northeast ridge to the east summit; the west summit is a short walk.

Mt. Warlow (13,231)

This recently named mountain is quite impressive from some

directions. Class 1 and 2 routes will be discovered on the south and west slopes. The ridge from Huxley is class 2–3, and the jagged, exposed ridge coming up from the Warlow-Fiske saddle is class 4.

Mt. Huxley (13,117)

Route 1. West Shoulder. Class 3. From the Muir Trail on the bench above Sapphire Lake climb the south side of the west shoulder until the angle steepens appreciably. Continue up a shallow chute which ends almost on the shoulder; gain this and scramble up the sharp summit arete.

Route 2. North-Northwest Buttress. Class 3. A prominent feature of the north side of Huxley is a wide, indented talus slope which contains snow until late in the season. This talus slope merges into the upper north face. On either side of this slope are buttresses or ridges. The route lies on the right buttress. Begin by climbing the talus slope; then exit right onto the buttress and follow it to the top.

Route 3. North-Northeast Buttress. Attain the left buttress (see preceding route) from the east and climb to the top. Class 3.

Route 4. South Ridge. Class 3 from the Huxley-Warlow saddle. To reach the saddle from the east, however, is class 4.

Emerald Peak (12,543)

This peak, and the three which follow, are located several miles west of the Darwin group, across Evolution Creek. The upper west slope of this peak is class 2 and is best reached by heading due south from Evolution Meadow and then contouring on the west side of the massif until the west slope or the northwest ridge is attained.

Peter Peak (12,543)

The east side offers several class 2 routes. The peak is composed of dark, metamorphic rock which is quite unsound.

Mt. McGee (12,969)

Route 1. North Chute. From upper McGee Canyon head toward the north face. At the right side of this face, and to the right of a small glacier, is a steep cleft which contains snow. Climb this cleft (the upper part is class 4) to the notch at its top; then head left along the jagged summit ridge to the top.

Route 2. West Side. The west face of the western summit is easy, but a class 4 traverse is necessary to reach the true summit.

Route 3. South Chute. Climb to the notch between the two summits from the south and scramble east to the top. This class 2 route contains much nasty scree and is a fine descent route.

The Hermit (12,360)

Seen from the north, the Hermit is one of the noblest of Sierra peaks; its symmetry and monolithic nature have attracted generations of climbers. Not everyone gets to the top, for the summit boulder is a difficult problem; a rope should be taken and will be used by most. The south side of the boulder is a friction problem; a 5.6 jamcrack on the east face is more secure but is a bit strenuous. The ratings given below will not take the final problem into consideration.

Route 1. From Evolution Lake. Class 2–3. From the lake head southwest toward the base of the east face. Either climb this face or, easier, head for the notch in the south ridge, which is then followed to the top.

Route 2. West Side. Class 2. From Lake 11,065, southwest of the peak, climb to the notch south of the summit and follow Route 1.

Route 3. North Ridge. Class 3. From Colby Meadow ascend to a shelf on the north shoulder; this shelf usually shelters a prominent snowbank. From here traverse left under steep cliffs; then diagonal right to easier rock and the top.

Route 4. Northwest Face. Class 3. From the shelf of the preceding route follow a broad ledge which leads up and around the west face. A chute is soon reached which leads up and left to a point overlooking the shelf. Continue up the broken ridge to the top.

Mt. Powell (13,360+)

The actual high point of this mountain has been the subject of some controversy, and during the past 40-odd years the register has been transported back and forth between several summits, all of which are within a few feet of the same height. Recently, the use of an Abney level has solved the problem; the high point is at the northeast side of the summit plateau, 1.8 miles east-southeast of Mt. Wallace. The other main summit in contention is located just left of the printed name on the map and will be referred to here as the southwest summit.

Route 1. South Side. Class 2. From Lake 11,710, at the southern base of the peak, climb talus to the summit plateau. The southwest summit will be on the left; the main summit is straight ahead.

Route 2. Northwest Chute. Class 3. Climb the chute on the wall just left of the glacier which lies under the northwest face.

Route 3. East Face. III or IV, 5.8, A2. This route ascends the 1,000-foot face which lies above the glacier under the northeast side of the peak. The first pitch involves 5.8 climbing in a dihedral, and much of the remainder of the route lies in similar, but easier, dihedrals and cracks.

Route 4. Northeast Side. Class 2–3. Ascend the rock rib which forms the western border of the northeast glacier. From the glacier ascend a steep, prominent, scree-filled chute on the left side of the face. Above, an easy slope leads to the main summit.

Route 5. East Ridge. The ridge from the Powell-Thompson saddle is class 3.

Peak 12,960+ (0.5 ESE of Echo Lake)

Follow the ridge from Echo Lake. Class 3 if the route is carefully chosen, class 4 otherwise. The east face is class 4.

Mt. Thompson (13,440+)

From the cirque above Lake 12,132 (south of the peak) ascend the southwest face. Class 2. A second route is as follows: from Sunset Lake ascend the glacier which lies under the northwest face. Leave the glacier and climb a chute to a notch between Thompson Ridge and Thompson. From the notch ascend just left of the ridge to the summit. Class 3. Another class 3 route has been done: from the basin northeast of the peak, head up scree slopes to the Thompson Ridge and follow it to the top.

Peak 13,323 (0.4 NNE of Mt. Thompson)

This is the high point of Thompson Ridge, a prominent three-mile-long spur which divides the middle and south forks of Bishop Creek. The peak is class 2 from the east.

Peak 12,993 (1.6 NNE of Mt. Thompson)

The east ridge and southeast face are easy, but the twin summit rocks are exposed class 3.

Mt. Gilbert (13,103)

Class 1 via the southeast slopes. Class 2 via the east ridge, which may be reached from the basin above the largest Treasure Lake by means of a prominent and loose chute. The northeast couloir route ascends the left side of the north glacier and enters an obvious, 900-foot-long ice gully. The angle of the ice varies from 50 to 60 degrees. III, 5.6

Mt. Johnson (12,868)

The northwest ridge is class 3. An easier route can be made by following the southeast slopes from the basin above Lake 11,586. The west ridge is class 2.

Peak 12,960+ (0.4 W of Mt. Goode)

Route 1. West Ridge. Class 3 from the saddle between Johnson and this good-looking peak.

Route 2. Northwest Face. Also class 3.

Route 3. North Ridge. From the tiny lake just above the first "d" in the word "Saddlerock" (on the Mt. Goddard topo), climb onto a buttress which heads southwest. When the main ridge is gained, turn south toward Peak 12,960+ and climb to the top. This excellent and airy route is class 4 in spots.

Mt. Goode (13,092)

Class 2 from the east or south. A route has been done on the north buttress and is rated III, 5.8. Start in an open book on the right side of the buttress. Two traverses to the left are found in the first few hundred feet. The final four pitches are class 4 and ascend a beautiful, blocky ridge to the summit. Another route is found on the buttress, but little is known about it.

Hurd Peak (12,219)

From Treasure Lakes climb the class 3 west face. A somewhat harder route has been done on the south ridge.

The Goddard Divide
and the Black Divide

Peak 12,913 (0.9 NNW of Mt. Goddard)

From the basin above and southeast of Davis Lake ascend a steep, blunt buttress which leads to the ridge between this peak and the Goddard Divide. When the ridge is gained, turn right and wander and weave to the top. Class 3–4.

Mt. Goddard (13,568)

This dark, brooding giant is visible from many Sierra points and was one of the first peaks climbed in the central part of the range.

Route 1. East Slope. Class 2. From Wanda Lake cross the saddle 1.2 miles west of Muir Pass; then traverse for a long distance along the south side of the Goddard Divide to the enormous talus slope which leads to the summit. There are many variations on this route. From anywhere in the Ionian Basin one can find a feasible route.

Route 2. Northeast Side. Class 2–3. From the basin southeast of Davis Lake climb onto the ridge between Peak 12,913 and the Goddard Divide. Climb this ridge or buttress until it becomes very steep and then head left on a ledge above a long, permanent snowfield. From the divide proceed west over talus to the top.

Route 3. South Side. Class 2. From the lake just southeast of the peak, climb to the southwest ridge and follow it to the top.

Peak 13,081 (1.1 E of Mt. Goddard)

Class 1 from anywhere except the north.

Mt. Solomons (13,016)

Class 2 from Muir Pass. The south-southeast ridge is easy also.

Scylla (12,939)

From the lake 0.3 mile northwest of the summit, climb the class 2 northwest slope.

The Three Sirens (ca. 11,800)

About one-half mile east of Scylla are three semi-isolated pinnacles. All can be climbed via class 3 and 4 routes.

Charybdis (13,091)

The northeast side of this rugged, remote peak provides a class 3 route.

Black Giant (13,330)

Class 1–2 from the west. Another, more interesting, route has been made: under the eastern escarpment lie four pocket glaciers. Climb the north one to its top and follow a loose chute for 100 feet. This brings one to a diagonal ledge which leads to the summit ridge. Class 4.

Peak 13,046 (1.2 SSE of Black Giant)

The northwest slopes are class 2. A steep class 2 and 3 chute on the southwest side of the mountain has also been done. From the lake southeast of the peak a third route is as follows: ascend north for about one quarter of a mile and then climb the east face, keeping between two obvious ridges.

Peak 12,320+ (0.5 ESE of Pk. 13,046)

From the large lake just north of the peak ascend a narrow snow chute to the top. Class 3. A snow chute on the northeast side has also been done and is class 2 or 3.

Mt. McDuffie (13,271)

This seldom-visited peak was recently named in honor of Duncan McDuffie, an early Sierra explorer and former Sierra Club president (1943-46).

Route 1. North Ridge. Class 3. From the saddle between Peak 13,046 and McDuffie proceed south along the ridge, keeping about 125 feet below the crest on the west side. When nearing the top of the peak keep left of a wide snow chute. Variations, all more difficult, can be made to the right on the final approach.

Route 2. Southeast Ridge. Class 2. From Ladder Lake ascend to the small lake 0.8 mile to the west-southwest. Gain the southeast ridge and stroll to the top. The ridge can be gained from the west, of course, but few persons ever set foot on that side of the mountain.

Langille Peak (11,991)

The easiest way up this beautifully sculptured mountain is via the west ridge, which can be reached easily from the bowl below Hester Lake. Class 3. A more technical route exists on the southeast side. From Little Pete Meadow the route lies near the left skyline. Slabs, ridges, and chutes make up the route, which is mostly class 4, with one or two class 5 sections. Routefinding is challenging (especially with a description like this!).

The Citadel (11,744)

Route 1. West Side. Class 2 up the ridge from Ladder Lake.
Route 2. Northwest Face. From the east end of Ladder Lake head

to the base of the northwest buttress. Climb a class 4 chute to the summit ridge and turn left for the top.

Route 3. North Face. IV or V, 5.7, A3. This 1,700-foot wall is the single most spectacular cliff in LeConte Canyon. Begin climbing in a dihedral containing several overhangs. The crux lies about 600 feet up, where an overhang is turned via difficult aid climbing. The rest of the route is easier; the upper 500 feet, in fact, is easy class 5.

Route 4. Northeast Face. Gullies and chutes lead up this face to the summit ridge. Follow this past the east peak to the higher western summit.

Peak 12,425 (1 SW of the Citadel)

The east ridge is class 3.

Wheel Mountain (12,781)

This peak was so-named because of the strange summit structure—four steep buttresses radiate symmetrically from the top like spokes of a wheel. From the saddle marked 11,553 on the Mt. Goddard quadrangle, southeast of the mountain, two routes have been done. One can drop down a few hundred feet to the west, head north for a while, and then ascend the southwest side of the peak. The other method is to ascend the southeast ridge from the saddle, keeping to the left when necessary. Both routes are class 3.

Rambaud Peak (11,040+)

Class 2 from the upper reaches of Rambaud Creek.

The Devil's Crags (11,040+ to 12,560+)

At the southern end of the Black Divide is a spectacular group of pinnacles, easily spotted from the Palisade group. Although the John Muir Trail passes within a few miles of the pinnacles, they are seldom visited. The Devil's Crags have a northwest-southeast alignment and are numbered from the northwest, and higher, end. Eleven pinnacles are now numbered, but since several numbering systems have been used, the numbers in the summit registers might not coincide with the present system, in use since 1954.

Crag 1 has three routes. The southeast face route begins from the saddle (marked 11,553 on the map) southeast of Wheel Mountain. Ascend southeast to an easy high point and then descend to the saddle immediately below. A scree slope leads into the basin west of the Devil's Crags. Next, ascend any of several routes which lead into the long, left-diagonaling chute which cuts the southwest face of Crag 1. Ascend this chute all the way to the arete, then turn right and scramble to the summit. Class 4. A somewhat harder variation has been done; this was the route of the first ascent in 1913. Halfway up the diagonal chute, leave it and take a chute which leads up and right to the summit arete.

The second route on Crag 1 starts from the small, white-topped peak northwest of the crag. Follow the class 4 arete to the top.

Another route is found on the northeast face and is also class 4. From the lake at the head of Rambaud Creek walk south-southeast nearly one-half mile to a small saddle under the spectacular north-

The Devil's Crags from the east.

east arete. Rope up here and traverse up and right onto the wide face to the right. Attain a chute in the middle of the face above its overhanging lower portion and then climb to the top.

To climb Crag 2, approach as for the southeast face route on Crag 1. Drop farther down the scree slope and ascend the first chimney and the wall to its right. This leads to a knife-edge arete and the top. Class 4.

Crag 3 also has three routes. From the east climb the 2–3 chute, and from the notch ascend the left side of a broken wall. Traverse up and right on a wide, sloping ledge to the north arete. Climb the left side of this to the northwest arete; the summit is not far beyond. Class 4.

The second route ascends to the 3–4 notch from the west. From here ascend class 5 rock for 100 feet; above this point the route is easier.

The easiest route on Crag 3 is as follows: climb the 2–3 chute from the west and join the first route at the notch. Class 3.

To reach Crag 4 climb to the 3–4 notch from the west (class 3) or the east (class 4). From the notch climb the broken west side of the arete to the top.

Crag 5 has a class 3 route. From the east climb the 4–5 chute, taking the left fork near the top. From the notch traverse right into a shallow chute and follow it to the arete. Continue up this until just before the summit block; then traverse it on the right.

Crag 6 can be reached from Crag 5 via the main arete. Class 3.

Crag 7 is easily reached via a class 3 traverse from Crag 6.

Crag 8 is one of the easiest crags to climb. From the west climb to the 7–8 notch and ascend the class 2 slope to the top.

To climb Crag 9, attain the 8–9 notch from either side. From here climb up and right onto the arete, which is followed nearly to the top. Class 4.

Crag 10 is class 4 from the west. Reach the 9–10 notch and follow the west side of the arete. From the east a class 2 route can be done by climbing to the 10–11 notch and following an easy slope to the summit.

To reach Crag 11 attain the 10–11 notch from the east and then head left up the ridge. Class 4.

Mt. Woodworth (12,219)

Class 2 from the south or southwest. The north ridge, easily reached from the basin to the northwest, is also class 2.

The Sierra from the Air

Photographs by Jim Stuart

1. Looking south toward the Devil's Crags.

2. The east faces of the Mt. Whitney group. Mt. Russell is on the right. Thor Peak lies directly below Whitney.

3. On the left skyline are the summit towers of Mt. Corcoran. In the foreground is the great south face of Lone Pine Peak.

4. The biggest rock wall in Sequoia National Park—the south face of the Angel Wings.

5. A light dusting of October snow accentuates the topography of the east face of Clyde Minaret.

6. Another view of Clyde Minaret shows the south face; a popular Grade IV route lies near the dihedrals on the right.

7. The four major peaks are, from left to right: Mt. Winchell, Mt. Sill, Thunderbolt Peak, and North Palisade.

8. Middle Palisade on the left. On the right is the striking Clyde Peak; Twilight Pillar drops from its summit.

9. The east face of Mt. Brewer. The regular route, from East Lake, ascends the ridge in the left foreground.

10. A view up the east arete of Mt. Clarence King. The standard route goes up the left skyline ridge.

1

3

6

8

9

10

The Palisades

Simply stated, the Palisade group contains the finest alpine climbing in California. The peaks are high and very serrated, and easy routes are in a minority. The western escarpment is much more precipitous than in other parts of the Sierra, and the peaks are often as hard from the west as from the east. The largest glacier in the Sierra blankets the northeast side of the northern Palisade section, and ice-climbing possibilities are varied and numerous. Five of the eleven 14,000-foot peaks of the range are found in an eight-mile section of crest.

South of Bishop Pass the Sierra crest rises abruptly in a broad, talus-covered slope to Mt. Agassiz, the northern sentinel of the Palisades. Then, in rapid succession along the main crest, one finds Mt. Winchell, Thunderbolt Peak, North Palisade, and Mt. Sill; the last three peaks form the highest continuous ridge in the range. A break of two miles occurs southeast of Sill—the peaks are lower and relatively unobtrusive. Then the crest rises abruptly once again, and the southern Palisades, dominated by the beautiful Clyde Peak and the toothed Middle Palisade, come into view. Another break occurs and four miles down the crest is the last 14,000-foot peak of the group, Split Mountain, formerly called the Southeast Palisade.

The Sierra crest, as usual, runs in an almost perfect northwest to southeast course. In the Palisades, this fact confuses those who think of the crest as running north to south and who therefore think that the U-Notch Couloir, for example, is on the east side of the North Pal-Sill massif instead of its north face.

Basically, however, the geography in the region is straightforward. Small spurs depart from the main crest at regular intervals; none are significant. On the western side of the crest of the northern Palisades area, which runs from Bishop Pass to Mt. Sill, are two of the most beautiful lake basins of the Sierra, Dusy and Palisade basins. The minor ridge which divides them contains interesting peaks which offer striking views of the western escarpment of the group. On the northeast side of the Palisades the principal geographical feature is the watershed of Big Pine Creek. This creek forks near the end of the road from Big Pine; the north fork begins in the Big Pine Lakes, which are numbered First through Seventh. The south fork is very short and its branches originate from glaciers which lie beneath the southern Palisade group (which begins with Mt. Jepson and continues to Taboose Pass).

The glaciers in the Palisades, while extraordinary by Sierra standards, offer little hindrance to the mountaineer. Icefalls are unknown, there are no crevasses of any magnitude, and the couloirs above the glaciers rarely exceed 45 degrees. Bergschrunds can present an interesting problem after early August, yet they can nearly always be bypassed. By mid-September the couloirs which rise above the glaciers are generally rock-hard snow in transformation toward blue ice.

Rockfall in the Palisades is common, and the glaciers below the northeast faces often show results of barrages. The traditional mountaineering rules apply to combat this hazard: early mornings are safest, cold mornings are preferable to warm, and the late season is less death-dealing than the early and mid-seasons. In other words, it could be considered foolhardy to attempt the V-Notch Couloir on a warm mid-morning in July; a better time would undoubtedly be a crisp fall dawn.

Several glaciers are not shown on the topo map. The most notable of these is the pocket glacier which lurks below the northeast face of Mt. Agassiz. Climbers have long considered the huge western lobe of the Palisade Glacier as a distinct entity and have applied to it the name Thunderbolt Glacier.

William Brewer and his colleagues of the California Geological Survey were the first to take notice of the Palisades. In 1864, from a long distance, they saw ". . .a range of peaks. . .which we called the 'Palisades.' These were unlike the rest of the crest in outline and color, and were doubtless of volcanic origin; they were very grand and fantastic in shape.'' Brewer was wrong about the volcanic rock; a dark, metamorphic rock had fooled him. The members of the survey team made no attempt to approach the peaks, but they estimated their height as between 13,500 and 14,000 feet.

A few years later members of the Wheeler Survey also saw the peaks and actually measured some of them. They triangulated the height of the "N.W. Palisade" (now North Palisade) as 14,275 feet, remarkably close to the present computation of 14,242 feet. In 1879 Lil Winchell named the mountain after Frank Dusy, a pioneer of the region. Sixteen years later Bolton Coit Brown renamed the high point Mt. Jordan, after the president of his alma mater, Stanford University. Because of the lack of communications in those days, the haphazard naming of remote peaks was quite common. The first reference to the name North Palisade occurs in 1904.

Joseph N. LeConte, then thirty-three, had for some years been desirous of the major Palisade summits and in 1903 traveled to the northern Palisades with James Hutchinson and others. From a timberline camp on Glacier Creek they attempted North Palisade, but after attaining the Sierra crest between their peak and Mt. Sill, were stopped by the great gash now known as the U-Notch. Hutchinson went over to the drop-off and studied the route beyond. LeConte wrote later that ''. . .not a single foothold could be found on the other wall. . .it was clearly 'no go.' We took a long rest, enlivening it somewhat by rolling huge boulders down the precipice on to the glacier.'' Upon completion of this ancient Sierra ritual they trudged up the easy slopes of a mountain which, seven years earlier, LeConte had named Mt. Sill. From the summit they were greatly impressed with the expansive glacier which lay beneath them. It had never been described, but they immediately knew that it was the biggest glacier in the range.

Later that day, after descending from Sill, Hutchinson wandered over to a saddle to reconnoiter the western escarpment of North Pal.

His report at the evening's campfire was discouraging; exploration in that direction appeared to be, in LeConte's words, ". . .a useless venture as well as a rather dangerous one." Nevertheless, the next morning LeConte, Hutchinson, and James Moffitt were laboriously climbing the broad couloir which led to the U-Notch. Realizing that they would be faced with the predicament of the previous day if they continued all the way to the notch, LeConte, by chance, discovered a narrow ledge which exited the couloir to the left. This was to prove the key passage, and many hundreds of climbers have since searched for the identical ledge. Before noon they reached the top, and the "stupendous panorama of precipice, glacier, and desert burst upon us."

After the three high points of the Palisade group—Split Mountain, Mt. Sill, and North Palisade—had been climbed, there was a hiatus of nearly two decades before the next major peak was ascended. By 1919 North Pal had been climbed on five occasions, Sill not since the first ascent, and peaks such as Agassiz, Winchell, Thunderbolt, and Middle Palisade had never seen an attempt. Then, in quick succession, all four fell to determined climbers. Middle Palisade was the first to be ascended, after two attempts had failed. In both of these attempts climbers had tried the wide southwest face, and had mistakingly chosen a chute which led to the top of what was christened Peak Disappointment by the first group. The second team, Francis Farquhar and Ansel Hall, quickly rectified their error by descending 2,000 feet, moving over several chutes, and ascending the correct mountain. Thunderbolt Peak was the last 14,000-foot peak to be climbed in the Sierra. The 1931 team consisted of Robert Underhill, of the Appalachian Mountain Club, and six Sierra Club mountaineers who were being trained by Underhill in the use of the rope in mountaineering.

Although LeConte had written in 1904 that his North Palisade route was the only feasible line up the peak, he had mentioned casually that "an approach from the east might be possible, though very doubtful." Norman Clyde, who was living in the Owens Valley during the late 1920s, was the first to explore the glacier approaches to the Palisade group. Between 1925 and 1934 he was responsible for about fifteen first ascents or new routes on the crest peaks. The summer of 1930 must have been an especially good one for Clyde. In his account of that season's ventures, he called a route on Middle Palisade "one of the best climbs in the Sierra." Less than a month later came an ascent of the northeast face of Mt. Agassiz, which he described as "one of the finest rock-climbs in the Sierra." And of the next day's ascent of the north face of North Palisade, Cyde wrote, "one of the very best climbs in the Sierra." Clyde had a good time in these mountains.

In addition to the peripatetic Clyde, members of the newly formed Sierra Club Rock Climbing Section were quite active in the 1930s, and soon all the major peaks had several routes.

Throughout most of the 1940s and 1950s, few new routes were done. Mountaineers seemed to be content with the many fine alpine routes already established, and the area became known as the ultimate snow- and ice-climbing spot in the range.

Traverses of sections of the main crest have always been popular. In 1938 Jack Riegelhuth and W. K. Davis made the Winchell-North Pal traverse in thirteen hours. Thunderbolt to Sill traverses, and vice versa, are very common, as is the Clyde-Middle Pal traverse. The tortuous course between Bishop and Southfork passes has probably never been done; it will be a multi-day classic.

Winter mountaineering has attracted climbers in increasing numbers ever since Winchell was first climbed in January 1938. North Palisade was climbed via the U-Notch in March 1940. Dave Brower, an early proponent of winter climbing, was a member of both these expeditions.

In the early 1960s the late Larry Williams opened a climbing school at Third Lake. This school, the first mountain-based one in California, soon became popular and hired some noted instructors. These instructors have been largely responsible for the incredible surge of new routes in the last ten years. The late Don Jensen was the leading figure in this group. Most of the new routes are rock climbs of a high standard. Temple Crag, one of the great peaks of the

Sierra, now has twenty routes, many of which are high-level rock climbs done in the past decade.

Approaches to the Palisade group are extremely straightforward. The Bishop Pass trail, which leaves from South Lake, gives ready access to the western side of the northern Palisades. Dusy Basin provides a lovely base for climbs on the west sides of Winchell and Thunderbolt; camping is presently regulated in the basin. Palisade Basin, more difficult to reach, is a common starting point for the southwest route on the North Palisade. The John Muir Trail parallels the main crest in the southern Palisades and provides excellent access to the chain of peaks extending from Middle Palisade to Cardinal Mountain.

Most mountaineers approach the group from the east. A road which departs U.S. Highway 395 at Big Pine ends near the junction of the north and south forks of Big Pine Creek. Good trails lead up both streams to campsites beneath the glaciers. The Palisade Glacier can be reached by a crude trail which leaves the main north fork trail about one-half mile beyond Third Lake. This trail climbs through dense willow groves to Sam Mack Meadow, then wanders due south up rounded ridges to hit the glacier at its northern extension.

Besides Bishop Pass, there are several other knapsackers' passes across the main crest. North to south, these are:

Agassiz Col (13,200+) is the notch between Mts. Agassiz and Winchell. It offers a practical method of crossing from Big Pine Lakes into Dusy Basin. The eastern approach begins at Sam Mack Lake and involves an easy glacier and a short section of class 2 rock. Coming from the west, choose the largest chute which leads to the notch.

Scimitar Pass (13,040+) lies immediately southeast of Mt. Jepson (Peak 13,390) and provides an interesting route from Glacier Creek on the west to the north branch of the south fork of Big Pine Creek. From Lake 11,672 on Glacier Creek climb easy slopes toward the pass, but instead of going directly to the low saddle, head up and right a few hundred feet onto the shoulder of Palisade Crest. The remainder of the crossing is then obvious. Coming from Elinore Lake, head due south onto a prominent ridge. Follow this as it curves westward to the Sierra crest, which it reaches a few hundred feet above the saddle. Class 2.

Southfork Pass (12,560+) is located between Disappointment Peak and the Thumb. The class 2-3 notch provides a popular and convenient way of connecting the Muir Trail with the south fork of Big Pine Creek. The pass is quite easy on its south flanks, but the route from Brainard Lake involves talus, loose moraines, and a small glacier. A tiny pinnacle which lies in the pass can be turned on either side, although the "correct" pass is to its west.

Birch Creek Pass (12,800+) lies one-half mile east of Southfork Pass. An old trail, not shown on the present map, leaves the McMurry Meadows area on Birch Creek at an elevation of 6,400 feet. This trail apparently wanders up to about 10,000 feet. Climb to Birch Lake; then ascend a class 2-3 cliff to the gentle slope which leads to the pass. The south side is easy.

Red Lake Pass (12,640+) is an obscure saddle between Mt. Prater and Split Mountain. From the east hike up the trail along Red Mountain Creek to Red Lake. Head northwest from here to the ridge west of Peak 12,627 and traverse to the Sierra crest. Class 2-3.

Taboose Pass (11,360+) is the one to cross if the peaks in the Split Mountain area are desired. It is an arduous pass, involving as it does a vertical rise of 6,000 feet. The dirt track to the roadhead departs U.S. Highway 395 midway between Big Pine and Independence; follow signs toward the Taboose Creek Campground; then continue up the desert slope on the only significant road.

There are other noteworthy climbers' passes in the region. In general north to south order, these are as follows.

Jigsaw Pass (12,622) crosses the Inconsolable Range near its junction with the main crest and provides a quick route between the Bishop Pass area and the Big Pine Lakes. From the latter, the approach starts at Fifth Lake. Head west into the valley between

Two Eagle Peak and Mt. Robinson and take the north branch of the stream when it forks at 11,300 feet. From the headwaters of this branch ascend large boulderfields to the pass, which is not the low point visible but rather a point a few hundred yards to the left. The approach from the Bishop Pass trail is more complicated. As seen from the trail at an elevation of 11,500 feet, Jigsaw Pass is to the east, a few hundred yards to the right of the low point in the ridge north of Agassiz and just right of a low, angular peaklet. Climb the right-hand chute of two chutes; it's easier than it looks. Class 2.

Glacier Notch (13,040+) separates the Mt. Sill massif from Mt. Gayley and offers a fine high-level crossing between the two forks of Big Pine Creek. A short chute in the cliff above the eastern end of the Palisade Glacier is class 2–3 and involves much loose rock. The east side is easier, but miles of talus will be found.

Contact Pass (11,760+) lies just east of Temple Crag. It is quite easy on both sides. The name derives from the clashing zones of granite which are so obvious from a distance.

Knapsack Pass (11,673) crosses the ridge which separates Dusy and Palisade basins and is class 1.

Thunderbolt Pass (12,320+) also lies on the divide between Dusy and Palisade basins. This class 2 pass lies immediately west-southwest of Thunderbolt Peak and is used by those camping in Dusy for approaches to Thunderbolt and North Pal.

Potluck Pass (12,080+), first visited by James Hutchinson in 1903 on his reconnaissance of North Palisade, crosses a minor ridge 1.1 miles south-southeast of North Pal. The pass is part of a high-level knapsackers' route from Bishop to Mather passes. Class 1 from the west; class 2 on the east.

Cirque Pass (12,000+) lies 0.9 mile southwest of Palisade Crest. This class 2 pass is used by those traveling cross-country between Bishop and Mather passes.

Chimney Pass (12,560+) crosses the same spur as Cirque Pass. It lies 0.3 mile southwest of Palisade Crest and is class 2.

Two topo maps, Mt. Goddard and Big Pine, are needed for the Palisades.

Northern Palisades

Chocolate Peak (11,658)
From Ruwau Lake the southeast side is class 2.

Peak 13,356 (1.1 ENE of Chocolate Pk.)
Class 2 from the north. It is also an easy stroll from nearby Peak 13,501.

"Cloudripper" (Pk. 13,501, 1.1 ESE of Chocolate Pk.)
This peak, the high point of the short Inconsolable Range, is an easy hike from the vicinity of Seventh Lake. The north side is class 2, and the west slopes are class 3.

"Picture Puzzle Peak" (Pk. 13,278, 1.4 SE of Cloudripper)
The north slopes and the northeast couloir are class 3; the southwest face from Bishop Lake is class 4.

Gendarme Peak (Pk. 13,241, 1 N of Mt. Agassiz)
Class 3. The name of this small peak became official in 1969.

Aperture Peak (Pk. 13,200+, 0.4 N of Mt. Agassiz)
Class 3 from Jigsaw Pass. Also class 3 from the southeast. The name became official in 1969.

"Two Eagle Peak" (Pk. 12,880+, 0.5 NE of Pk. 13,241)
This "peak," prominent from Fifth Lake, is actually a spur extending northeast from Gendarme Peak. The peak offers many possibilities for rockclimbing. The standard route ascends the north side of the east ridge and is class 3. One technical route has been reported, on the east side of the south buttress. This buttress is distinguished by a very steep, 800-foot-high face rising out of the valley leading toward Jigsaw Pass. There are minor aretes and gullies to the right of this face. From the valley below the wall, scramble up and right into a class 4 chimney just right of the face.

Climb the left wall of the chimney for about four pitches to the ridge at the top of the buttress; then traverse 150 feet along the flat ridgetop to a large, red tower. Climb this via a chimney on the right. Next, follow the sharp arete to the top. II, 5.6.

"Mt. Robinson" (Pk. 12,800+, 1 NE of Mt. Agassiz)

This convoluted peak, which rises abruptly between Fifth and Sam Mack lakes, contains scores of aretes, chutes, and faces. The summit ridge is serrated and there are many nearly equal high points.

Route 1. The Lichen Arete. II, 5.7. Hike into the valley between Two Eagle and Robinson a short distance; then cut up toward a permanent snowfield under the north face (don't continue around onto the northwest face). On the north face are three couloirs, the right-hand two joining halfway down. Between these two couloirs and the left one is the prow-shaped Lichen Arete. Increasingly difficult climbing leads up the broad face to the beginning of the arete. Start up an easy chimney; then move right to a ledge on the prow. Climb a steep 5.7 open book to a small ledge just left of the arete; then gain a good belay platform a few feet higher. Easier climbing leads upward for several pitches to a notch, on the other side of which is a steep, red tower. Climb this by a delicate traverse up and to the left. Beyond, one more moderate pitch leads to Lichen Summit. The main summit is a long scramble to the southwest. Most parties will probably prefer to descend from Lichen Summit, which is complicated but not particularly hard.

Route 2. Northeast Face. Class 3. One looks directly at this route from near the outlet of Fifth Lake.

Route 3. Southeast Side. Class 3. From the north end of Sam Mack Lake one may pick out numerous possibilities on the rugged slope above.

Route 4. South Face. II, 5.7. Above the tiny tarn just west of Sam Mack Lake is a wall cut by many aretes. This route lies on the second-from-the-right arete. Many variations are possible. The climb ends not far below the true summit of Robinson.

Route 5. Southwest Ridge. Class 3. From the broad saddle between Agassiz and Robinson follow the jagged ridge to the top.

Mt. Agassiz (13,891)

This giant mass, formerly called Agassiz Needle, lies at the northwest end of the Palisade group. The summit offers an excellent view; the ascent is very popular.

Route 1. From Bishop Pass. Class 2.

Route 2. Northeast Side. Class 4. From Fifth Lake hike up the canyon directly to the small glacier (not shown on the map) nestled under the northeast face. From here one can study the route. A Y-shaped couloir will be seen to the right of the center of the face. Start in this couloir and then work out left onto the face. When about halfway to the summit, traverse right to an arete which overlooks the couloir. Follow this arete for a short while; then either work up and right (easier) or head up and left to the summit.

Route 3. East Ridge. From the glacier mentioned in the preceding route, climb the 45-degree left couloir of two prominent snow couloirs which end at a deep notch on the east ridge. From the notch follow the ridge to the top. Most of the route is class 4, but a few easy class 5 sections will be found.

Route 4. Southeast Side. Class 2. From the terminal moraine of the glacier just east of Agassiz Col work up a chute which empties just north of the moraine. Follow this chute to the ridge north of the Col and ascend it to the summit. One can also climb the ridge all the way from Agassiz Col—stay on the right side of the ridgecrest.

Mt. Winchell (13,768)

Route 1. Southeast Side. Class 5. From the Winchell-Thunderbolt notch ascend several hundred feet of class 3 rock to a prominent chute. Three easy class 4 pitches follow, and a broad ledge is reached. Next, climb over a small overhang and head up a crack to a belay alcove beneath another overhang. Turn this on the right via a cleft which leads out onto the east face. Class 4 climbing then leads to the summit.

Route 2. East Arete. This excellent class 3 route is by far the most popular way to reach the top of Winchell. From Sam Mack Lake walk up toward the Thunderbolt Glacier. Keep just to its right; then, when under the east arete, climb its south face. Follow the arete to the steep upper part of the peak. An easy chute leads to the top.

Route 3. North Face. Class 4. Climb the glacier which lies just east of Agassiz Col. From its top climb the sloping north face, keeping between the buttress on the left and the couloir on the right.

Route 4. Northwest Ridge. IV, 5.8. Gain the Agassiz-Winchell ridge just south of Agassiz Col and follow the jagged and long ridge to the summit. At one point a long rappel is necessary to reach the main notch of the ridge—the crux is the steep wall just beyond.

Route 5. West Face. Class 4. In the center of the west face lie two prominent, parallel chutes. A giant talus fan emerges from them. Begin climbing several hundred feet left of the left chute and climb class 3 and 4 rock for about 400 feet until it is feasible to work right and enter the left chute. Follow the class 3 chute upward for about 800 feet; then leave it and climb a steep, yellowish chute on the right. From its top ascend an arete which overlooks enormous gullies on both sides. The summit ridge is soon reached. There are many variations to this route. The right-hand chute from the base is 5.7; the upper part is easy and can be reached from the left chute, about halfway up the peak.

Route 6. Southwest Chute. Class 4. No one knows where this route really lies. It must be to the right of the preceding route; perhaps one diagonals to the right from a point midway up the right chute.

Thunderbolt Peak (14,000+)

This was the last 14,000-foot peak to be climbed in the Sierra. During a wild storm on the first ascent, a bolt of lightning left Jules Eichorn severely shaken; hence the name. The actual summit of Thunderbolt is a steep monolith, and it is quite difficult to climb. A rope can be thrown over it for aid or for a belay. Done free, it is probably 5.8.

Route 1. The Underhill Couloirs. Class 4. From the Palisade Glacier these two couloirs lead to the deep notch between Thunderbolt and the northwest peak of North Palisade. Climb either couloir or the rib between them to the notch. From here climb steep slabs and cracks until it is possible to traverse out left on ledges. These are mainly class 3 and soon lead to the top.

Route 2. East Face. III, 5.5. From the base of the right Underhill Couloir walk right on debris-covered ledges which lead onto the east face. After about 200 feet, climb up and then left to a low-angle dihedral. Work more or less straight up for several pitches (easy class 5, usually) to easier climbing and the top. This route is quite enjoyable and has relatively good rock.

Route 3. East Couloir, Left Side. III, 5.6. A prominent snow couloir can be seen on the east side of the peak. Climb the couloir or its left side for a while; then traverse left. Next, head upward to low-angle rock near several bands of light-colored rock. This section is the crux; above, class 3 and 4 scrambling leads to the top.

Route 4. East Couloir, Right Side. Class 4–5. Start in the couloir; then climb up and right to the summit ridge. It is also possible, apparently, to climb the entire couloir to the notch between the main peak and its northern peak.

Route 5. Northeast Buttress—The Prow. III, 5.6. This great buttress almost divides the Palisade Glacier. In fact, climbers have long called the section of glacier northwest of the buttress the Thunderbolt Glacier. The route begins in a short, steep chimney some 50 feet left of the extreme tip of the buttress. Class 4 and 5 climbing leads up a few hundred feet to the relatively level top of the buttress. Follow this surprisingly long ridge to the top of the peak.

Route 6. North Couloir. Class 4. This route, formerly misnamed the Northeast Buttress Route, begins in the wide ice couloir which rises above the Thunderbolt Glacier. Surmount the bergschrund; then climb the wall on the left of the couloir for a few hundred feet until it is possible to head up and left to the level section of the northeast buttress. Follow this to the top.

Route 7. Northwest Ridge. Class 5. Climb the ridge from the

Winchell-Thunderbolt col. The difficulties occur high on the ridge.

Route 8. West Face. Class 4. Begin climbing in the first chute left of Thunderbolt Pass. Follow the right branch higher up until it ends in an ice-filled chimney; then work right to an arete. Leave this after a while and traverse to the right into the next chute. This leads to spurs, ridges, chutes, drop-offs, aretes, gendarmes, and, finally, the summit.

Route 9. From Thunderbolt Pass. Class 4–5. From the pass climb onto the arete above and follow it upward, weaving around obstacles on both sides, for many hundreds of feet. When an "insurmountable" face bars progress, traverse right and drop into a chute. This leads to the summit ridge.

Route 10. Southwest Chute No. 1. This is probably the easiest route to the top of Thunderbolt and can be done unroped by many climbers. From Thunderbolt Pass enter the first chute to the right. A chimney several hundred feet up can be passed on the right. Above, the chute insists on dividing—always take the right fork. The summit ridge is reached between the north summit and the main peak. A class 3–4 pitch from the notch between the two summits is the final obstacle.

Route 11. Southwest Chute No. 2. Class 4. Ascend the enormous chute which terminates in the notch between Thunderbolt and the northwest peak of North Palisade. From here follow Route 1 to the summit.

North Palisade (14,242)

North Pal, a highly coveted peak, is the highest of the Palisade group and has many fine routes. Its northwest peak, nearly equal in height, has for some years been called Starlight Peak. Routes 6, 7, and 8 lie on the glacier side of Starlight, and Route 9 passes over its summit.

Route 1. Via the U-Notch. Class 4. The U-Notch is the prominent and well-named low point between Polemonium Peak and North Pal. Cross the Palisade Glacier and ascend the 40-degree snow to the notch. By late August ice appears; in October this is a fine ice climb.

From the U-Notch, climb a class 4 chimney on the wall above. This leads to easier climbing and the top.

A variation has been done and is a bit easier. From the U-Notch drop down the opposite side (the southwest chute) for about 120 feet. Climb up cracks and ledges; then traverse left on a ledge which leads around the corner. Ascend a chute to easier scrambling.

Route 2. Northeast Buttress. II, 5.6. From the right side of the bergschrund which guards the U-Notch Couloir, proceed up a great open chimney (with light gray rock) for about 300 feet. When the wall becomes very steep, move right on a vertical section to broken, brown rock. Climb up for a few hundred feet to class 3 slabs which lead to the top.

The largest glacier in the Sierra lies beneath the northern Palisades. This view is from the northeast. Glacier Notch lies on the curving ridge which drops down and left from Mt. Sill. Thunderbolt Peak's protruding northeast buttress divides the Palisade Glacier.

Route 3. The Doors of Perception. III, 5.8. Three strenuous pitches of crack and chimney climbing lead up the very striking open book on the face a few hundred feet to the right of the U-Notch Couloir.

Route 4. North Buttress. II, 5.8, A2. This is the wide, broken buttress immediately left of the Clyde Couloir, the steep snow gully on the northeast face. Start in the center of the buttress and climb a full rope-length to a ledge. Continue up and somewhat right (using some aid) to a small ledge beneath a prominent overhang. A strenuous chimney leads through this overhang to a sloping ledge. From here proceed up and left (one 5.8 section) to the easy slabs below the summit snowfield.

Route 5. Clyde Couloir. Class 4–5. This is the prominent snow gully which leads to the notch between North Pal and its northwest peak. Above the bergschrund climb the right-hand wall for a few hundred feet until the gully narrows. Climb onto an arete on the right and follow it to within a few hundred feet of the summit. Now, cross the couloir and traverse to the summit snowfield. Much rockfall has been reported on this route.

The couloir itself has been followed all the way, but rockfall makes this a potentially hazardous endeavor.

Route 6. Starlight Buttress. III, 5.5? Climb the buttress just right of the Clyde Couloir. Many variations are possible. The route ends atop Starlight Peak, the name climbers have given the northwest peak of North Pal.

Route 7. Starlight Peak—Piper at the Gates of Dawn. III, 5.7 or 5.8. This route lies directly up the northeast face of the peak. Proceed across the glacier to the prominent apron below the main face. Work up and left into a vertical crack in the center of the apron. Follow this crack over a ceiling and continue upward until the crack becomes indistinct. A few pitches of class 4 lead to a point about 10 feet to the right of two great towers which can be seen easily from the glacier. Climb straight up steep flakes and cracks (5.7). The last pitch leads out onto the face and turns an overhang on the right.

Route 8. Starlight Peak—The X. II, 5.7. To the right of the center of the northeast face one will see two long, diagonal crack systems.

These cracks form a gigantic X. This route, containing much loose rock, ascends both right-hand segments of the X. Most of the climbing is class 4 or easy 5, but a few sections near the beginning approach 5.7.

Route 9. Northwest Ridge. Class 4. Follow the ridge from the Thunderbolt-Starlight notch. Most of the first section of ridge (to Starlight) is done on the right side of the arete; later, obstacles are turned on both sides. This is a highly enjoyable and spectacular traverse.

Route 10. West Chute. The location of this route is somewhat vague. From high in Palisade Basin the route probably ascends a chute on the left side of the broad southwest face, intersecting the summit ridge north of the top. Class 4, apparently.

Route 11. West Face. Class 5. Begin climbing left of a black streak at the base of the face. Cross to the right above the streak and enter a wide chute. Follow this until it narrows; then cross right into the next chute via a horizontal white vein. Climb to the top.

Route 12. Southwest Side. Class 3. This is the original, and easiest, route. From Palisade Basin enter the deep chute which heads toward the U-Notch, the prominent gap to the right of the summit. Another way to recognize the correct chute is to locate three white cliffs at the base of the face. These mark the entrance to two chutes—the correct one is the right-hand chute. Ascend the chute to a point about halfway to the U Notch. At the upper end of a bare-bottomed area in the chute, one can follow a narrow ledge which runs around the corner into the next chute left. Climb this until progress is blocked; then cross right into a third chute, often snow-filled. Scramble up this to the summit ridge and head left over large blocks to the exposed summit slabs.

As a variation, one can climb the chute all the way to the U-Notch and follow the class 4 section of Route 1 (or its variation).

"Polemonium Peak" (Pk. 14,000+, 0.15 ESE of North Palisade)

There is some question whether this insignificant peaklet is worth a name or "peak" status. The summit can be reached from the

U-Notch via a class 4 pitch and a little scrambling. The south side, from a small glacier, is class 2 or 3. The spectacular V-Notch Couloir, left of the U-Notch Couloir, rises above the Palisade Glacier and offers excellent 50-degree snow and ice climbing.

Mt. Sill (14,162)

This is the most massive peak of the Palisades and is the goal of many a mountaineer. The view from the top is impressive; Walter Starr, Jr. has written, ". . . it can be said to be the [ultimate] of all Sierra peaks in the extent and quality of the views it offers."

Route 1. East Couloir. Class 3. A couloir just left of the giant east face leads to the first notch southeast of the summit mass. Climb the Sill Glacier; then enter the left branch of the couloir. Higher, follow the main couloir to the notch and ascend the easy southeast ridge.

Route 2. East Face. III, 5.7. The Sill Glacier has done such a good job in undercutting the lower part of this face that there is only one chimney which provides a reasonable starting point in the center of the wall. Climb in or near this chimney (it has several chockstones) for two pitches (5.7). Above, much easier climbing leads up a shallow basin for about four pitches. At this point there are two choices, roughly comparable in difficulty (5.7). Either follow a large chimney system up and slightly left, or climb diagonally up and around a shallow buttress on the right. Enter a chute and then follow a ramp system which leads back left. Either variation ends about 100–200 feet southeast of the summit. This climb is long, interesting, and not highly sustained.

Route 3. Swiss Arete. II, 5.4. This excellent route, formerly called the North Buttress, lies on the arching arete at the right side of the east face. From Glacier Notch traverse up and left into the obvious, snow-filled north couloir. Leave this after a few hundred feet and scramble left onto low-angle ledges at the base of the arete. Stay close to the prow for several pitches until a holdless wall forces one to make an exposed move (5.4) to ledges around to the right. From here climb either of two 5.4 corners to a platform 30 feet above. Continue to the top over large, class 4 blocks.

Route 4. North Couloir. Class 3–4. From Glacier Notch proceed up and left into the snow-filled couloir. Climb this via 35-degree snow or by class 3–4 rocks on the right. The couloir ends at a notch between Sill and a small, pyramidal mass to the north. Traverse up and right for one pitch; then head up steep, broken rock to the summit ridge. The top is a 10-minute scramble from here.

Route 4 is a popular descent route and is a bit tricky to find from above if one is unfamiliar with the route. From the top of Sill head toward North Pal, and, after dropping about 300 vertical feet, leave the ridge at a platform and drop down the steep rock toward the glacier. After a 150-foot descent, traverse down and right to the notch between Sill and its small northern pyramid. If the snow is soft, and if the party is experienced in glissading, this affords a very efficient way off the mountain.

Route 5. Northwest Face. Class 3–4. Many routes can be found on the face to the left of the V-Notch Couloir. The rock in this area is not terribly solid.

Route 6. From the West. Class 4 from the U-Notch.

Route 7. Southwest Slope. Class 2–3. From the foot of the small glacier southwest of Sill either climb the glacier to attain the summit ridge or turn the glacier on the right by means of a steep but easy cliff.

Mt. Gayley (13,510)

Route 1. From Glacier Notch. Class 3. This enjoyable scramble leads to a superb viewpoint.

Route 2. South Side. Several class 3 routes can be found from the basin south of the summit.

Route 3. West Face. Class 3. Ascend a large gully. Variations are possible.

Route 4. North Face. Several class 4 and 5 routes can be found on the face which rises above the eastern end of the Palisade Glacier.

Temple Crag (12,999)

To the rockclimber, the northern aspect of Temple Crag is one of the most stimulating sights in the Sierra. At Third Lake, a lazy and rewarding day can be spent watching the sunlight play across the scores of aretes and gullies. It is a very confusing mountain to describe because of these convolutions. Third Lake is the best viewpoint, and all long-distance descriptions will be from there.

Before describing the many routes, a word will be said about the geography. The north buttress and its sheer, wide right side dominate Third Lake. To the left of the buttress is a fantastic melange of ribs and chutes. Routes 3–10 lie in this region. The north buttress contains two very prominent steps, which are easily discerned from First Lake. The first of these steps is the top of the Lower Buttress. The second step, relatively close to the summit of Temple, is the top of the Upper Buttress (also known as the North Peak). To the right of the north buttress is the rugged northwest face, which extends over to and blends with the Mt. Gayley massif. Unlike the northeast face, the ribs here are generally neither distinct nor continuous. Routes 13–19 lie in this section of cliff.

Route 1. Southeast Face. Class 3. A deep, class 2 chute on the southeast face soon leads to talus fields. The entry to the chute lies a few hundred feet down and southwest of Contact Pass. Climb the talus fields to a point just below and right of the top. A 60-foot, class 3 section leads to the narrow summit ridge; follow this left a hundred feet to the summit.

Route 2. From Contact Pass. Easy class 4. At the very top of the pass face the cliff—a 40-foot crack will be seen near the base. Climb this (class 4); then scramble up and right to talus fields. Join Route 1 near the summit.

Route 3. Eclipsed Arete. 5.3. No one really knows where this route is located. It is an "easterly route" when viewed from Third Lake and is very probably the next arete left of the Venusian Blind Arete. It appears short and subject to myriad variations.

Route 4. Venusian Blind Arete. III, 5.6. Two all-year snowfields emerge from chutes at the base of the northeast face. This route, and the following two, begin from the left-hand snowfield. The section of cliff left of this snowfield is complicated, and, depending on the time of day, details are either easy or impossible to make out. From various aspects the section may be seen to have as many as five parallel ribs or aretes. The base of this section is broad, and most of the ribs begin distinctly when about 400 feet above the talus. The right-hand rib rises steeply (even overhanging at times) from a point immediately next to the snowfield. The second rib starts much lower and merges with the first after about 400 feet. The third and fourth ribs begin much higher up than the second. The third is a shallow and ill-defined arete. The fourth begins with a sweeping slab some 200 feet high. This is the beginning of the Venusian Blind Arete. The fifth and last rib is really only one short, steep tower.

Climb the left-hand snowfield for 150–200 feet until a snow-covered ledge leads horizontally left onto the very prow of a buttress. Scramble up and left about 350 feet to the left side of the base of the 200-foot-high sweeping slab. This slab is the farthest visible to the left; it is not the minor slab which begins the third rib. Climb an open book for 100 feet. The next pitch stays close to the left side of the slab and then moves onto the prow above the slab. Move up through a ceiling; then climb a class 4 pitch. This is followed by a 10-foot notch and a 100-foot tower on the right. From the top of this tower move immediately left onto the major tower of the arete and climb it in three pitches. Above, one long pitch over gendarmes leads to the base of the next pillar. This is 160 feet high. The remainder of the climb is easy and involves notches, gendarmes, and blocks. This section takes one to talus slopes on the east side of Temple Crag.

Route 5. The Moon Goddess Arete. III, 5.6. Ascend the left-hand snowfield as described in the preceding route, and take the snow-ledge exit. From the very prow of the buttress, climb up and left about 200 feet. Move right a few feet and reach the base of the Moon-Goddess Arete, the second rib described in Route 4. Easy and beautiful class 4 and 5 pitches lead upward on the crest of the arete to a large and imposing gendarme. This can be passed by means of an exposed 5.4 traverse on the right. From the notch behind the gendarme proceed upward a pitch toward a major, almost flawless, 200-foot-high tower. Continue up and right around the prow of this tower (5.6) and then make an exposed traverse 80 feet right until cracks are reached that can be followed 150 feet upward to a platform atop the tower. The arete is then followed for two or three pitches over gendarmes and short walls. The talus slopes on the east flank of Temple are soon reached. As a time-saving expedient, one can escape into a class 4 gully on the left when near the base of the flawless tower.

Route 6. The Sun-Ribbon Arete. IV, 5.8. This is an exposed, committing, and difficult route. Climb high into the left-hand snow-field mentioned in Route 4 to near its top; a prominent, 100-foot, left-facing open book will appear to the right. Scramble a few hundred feet over to the base of this book and climb it. From its top ascend class 3 rock for about 200 feet to a small, prominent gen-darme which marks the beginning of the smooth, even rise of the arete above. From the notch behind the gendarme climb directly upward on the prow (five pitches, 5.5–5.7) to an obvious alcove at the top of the prow. Beyond this alcove is a notch which is most easily crossed by lassoing a horn across the gap and making a tyrolean traverse. Next, a moderate traversing pitch to the left past gendarmes brings one to a notch. Drop down about 10 feet to belay. Enter the obvious, left-facing crack above either directly from its base (5.9) or via a delicate traverse (5.8) from the left. Steep and difficult climbing leads upward to easier climbing. Several more pitches lead to a notch. One may climb down into this and ascend the other side (5.4). Pass a smooth, steep wall on the right and regain the crest of the arete. Two moderate pitches and a bit of scrambling lead to the talus east of the summit. It is possible to escape into a gully on the left from the top of the pitch above the tyrolean traverse.

Route 7. Northeast Face. III, 5.4. This route begins near the left side of the right-hand snowfield mentioned in Route 4. Climb a right-facing chimney or open book for about 400 feet to much easier ground. Next, bear up and right many hundreds of feet toward a very prominent notch (this is the notch behind the Upper Buttress). Before reaching the notch, however, head off left and scramble up steep terrain to the summit ridge. Most of this route is class 3.

Route 8. Mendenhall Couloir. III, class 4–5. The right-hand snowfield mentioned in Route 4 emerges from a dark and forbidding slot. Climb steep snow and then the slot (about four feet wide, with chockstones) to reach easier ground. As in the preceding route, climb nearly to the prominent notch and then bear left to the summit ridge.

Route 9. 26th of July Arete. III, 5.8. On the face to the right of the Mendenhall Couloir, but left of the great north buttress, are two buttresses or ribs. The left-hand one is steep and ill-defined at its base and blends into a talus-covered rib higher. The right-hand rib, however, is sharp and continuously steep throughout its length. It is not easily seen from Third Lake, but from Second Lake it is quite striking in the morning sun. Climb the wall to the right of the very steep lower section for two pitches (some 5.8 on the second) to the base of the prominent gully which separates the July Arete from the north buttress. Move immediately to the left onto the arete and climb vertical cracks for 50 feet until under a wide overhang. Move onto a block on the right; then continue 20 feet up a small dihedral. Move out to the left (5.8) onto the very crest of the arete. A bit higher is a 5.7 crack and above this the difficulties ease. Four pleasant pitches lead to the top of the arete. The summit of the Lower Buttress is now about 300 feet above and to the right across a small notch. Most of this distance is scrambling, but a short 5.5 section is obligatory. It is possible, of course, to continue to the top of the mountain via any of several routes. Most parties will prefer to descend from the top of the Lower Buttress via the first part of Route 13. A short rappel will be necessary at the very bottom.

Route 10. Communion Route. III, 5.8. Climb the first few pitches of the preceding route to the prominent gully. Climb the wall on the right side of this gully to the notch atop the Lower Buttress.

Route 11. Dark Star. V, 5.7, A3. This route, the longest in the Palisades, goes directly up the elegant north buttress. Obvious scree ledges lead from the left over to the base of the actual buttress, some 300 feet above the ground. On the very prow of the buttress is a shallow, but prominent, right-facing dihedral. Climb this for one and a half pitches to a ledge on the left. Traverse 20 feet left; then pendulum to an expanding aid crack on the left. The third pitch proceeds straight up corners to small platforms. Move slightly left and then head up to a large belay flake. A short, easy pitch is followed by a moderate pitch to the base of a very deep chimney. Ascend this far back inside to a platform behind chockstones. Four hundred feet of scrambling (and some easy class 5) leads to the top of the Lower Buttress. Routes 9–13 all converge at this point, and it is possible to downclimb and rappel Route 13 if so desired.

Dark Star, however, continues up the massive Upper Buttress. From the ridge which connects the Lower and Upper buttresses traverse left and slightly upward for 75 exposed feet; then proceed directly upward (5.7) for about 50 feet. Next, move slightly right into a recess and climb it for 30 feet or so until it ends in a small ceiling split by an A2 crack. Above this, a short distance of moderate free climbing leads to easy ledges on the summit ridge of the Upper Buttress. Scramble over to the notch separating the Upper Buttress from the summit area; the Mendenhall Couloir comes in at this point but is *not* recommended as a descent route. Either continue up the airy, but not-too-difficult, north ridge or traverse about 100 feet from the notch and then head up and left for 300 fairly easy feet to the east talus slopes of the mountain.

Route 12. Barefoot Bynum. IV, 5.7, A3. Approach as for the preceding route; this climb parallels the lower part of Dark Star. Begin climbing about 40 feet right of the Dark Star dihedral in another shallow, right-facing dihedral. Climb first in the dihedral; then angle right and head for a large, bulging ceiling split by a vertical cleft. This is about 200 feet above the start. Aid over the ceiling leads to a crack-and-chimney system which is followed for about four pitches to its end. This section is predominantly free climbing. Higher, about 400 feet of scrambling (with some clifflets) leads to the top of the Lower Buttress. From here descend Route 13 or continue upward via one of the other routes.

*Temple Crag from Third Lake. The Sun-Ribbon Arete is the right-slanting
ridge which lies above the island in the large snowfield. The sharp formation
just right of the summit is the top of the Upper Buttress. On the prominent
sun-shadow line is the great north buttress.*

Route 13. North Buttress, Right Side. III, 5.5. Although this route is not particularly difficult, it is a long one, and the routefinding problems are significant. Begin at the base of the northwest couloir of Temple (the obvious snow-filled chute to the right of the north buttress), and after a few hundred feet of 35-degree snow climbing a short class 4–5 pitch leads up the left wall of the couloir. There are several ways to go in this area. Class 3 climbing is found above here for a few hundred feet. Soon it is possible to begin diagonaling up and left toward the obvious top of the Lower Buttress. This section is all class 3 and 4 and is a bit loose. From the top of the Lower Buttress a ledge traverses right about 150 feet to a crack system just left of a prominent, left-facing open book easily seen from Third Lake. It is not clear whether the crack system or the book is climbed; either probably goes, and a rating of 5.5 has been given for this area. Three pitches lead to scrambling and the top of the Upper Buttress. Next, follow either of the two ways mentioned in Route 11.

Apparently there is a variation on the lower part of this route: instead of diagonaling all the way over to the top of the Lower Buttress, it is possible to ascend straight toward the open book.

Route 14. Northwest Chimney. III, 5.7. Follow the first part of the preceding route up the snow couloir and the wall to its left. Then, instead of diagonaling left toward the top of the Lower Buttress, continue up the obvious, shallow North Chute. After about 500 feet a spectacular, right-facing dihedral containing a chimney will be seen rising the entire height of the western face of the Upper Buttress. Five long pitches up this chimney system bring one almost to the top of the Upper Buttress. From here follow either of the two ways mentioned in Route 11.

Route 15. North Chute. Class 4. Follow the preceding route and continue up the chute instead of climbing the chimney on its left-hand wall.

Route 16. Northwest Face. Class 3. This is the easiest way up Temple Crag from the north. The deep, snow-filled couloir is very obvious from Third Lake. Not so obvious is the deep chute which lies several hundred feet to the right; this chute diagonals left and joins the snow-filled couloir 800 feet above the talus. Take the chute to the couloir and follow it upward for about 300 feet until a low-angle gully shoots left. Easy scrambling on the left side of this leads upward many hundreds of feet directly toward the summit. When the steep summit headwall is reached, simply bear right and climb class 3 rocks to a prominent notch. A class 3.1 pitch leads to easy romping and the top.

A variation, about 5.5 in difficulty, can be made. Climb the 35 degree northwest couloir to a series of chockstones about 600 feet up. These can be passed on the right. Join the regular route just above the upper chockstone.

Route 17. The Surgicle. 5.7. About halfway up the rib which forms the left side of the deep chute of Route 16 is a prominent pinnacle, the Surgicle. Climb the face east of the spire and then the east face of the pinnacle itself. Rappel the route. Another line has been done on the north ridge of the spire. Three pitches are involved and the climb is rated II, 5.8.

Route 18. The Rabbit Ears. II, 5.5. Several hundred feet to the right of the deep chute of Route 16, and about 150 feet above the talus, is a long, slanting platform easily seen from Third Lake. Above this platform are three indistinct, parallel ribs. On the central rib, about halfway to the skyline, is a large pinnacle with a conspicuous north face split by a large crack. From the platform climb the gully which leads up to the right side of the Rabbit Ears and attain the large crack. This chimney is the crux pitch. Rappel the route.

Route 19. Pillar of the Red Eye. III, 5.9. To the right of the platform mentioned in the preceding route one will immediately discern a dank slot which drains a snowy basin high above. Immediately to the right of the slot is a smooth pillar about 600 feet high; a diagnostic red patch will be seen on the right side of the pillar, about three-quarters of the way to the skyline. Rope up about 50 feet right of the slot and climb upward just left of a prominent, left-facing open book covered by a ceiling. Traverse right into the book after a while to an uncomfortable belay spot. The next pitch continues up cracks in the book and then overcomes the ceiling by a 5.8 crack. Continue up easier rock for four pitches. At this point one has arrived at the base of an immense block with smooth, steep walls on either side. Traverse right about 30 feet to a prominent crack on the right-hand side. Climb this narrow crack (some 5.9) for 80 feet to the top of the block. Easy climbing then leads to the Temple-Gayley ridge. To descend, traverse the ridge toward Gayley for a short distance; then diagonal down ledges toward the snowfields north of Gayley

Route 20, Temple-Gayley Traverse. Class 4–5. This long and sometimes exposed ridge is infrequently climbed, and the main problem seems to be one of length, not difficulty.

Mt. Alice (11,360)
Class 2 and 3 from all directions. This is one of the ugliest mountains in the Sierra—a veritable pile of rubble.

Kid Mountain (11,896)
Class 1 or 2 from the north.

Isosceles Peak (12,240+)
This well-named peak is a striking sight from some parts of Dusy Basin. The northwest face is class 3.

Columbine Peak (12,652)
Class 2 from Knapsack Pass. A fine view of the Palisades is obtained from the top. One can also climb the class 2 northeast ridge.

Giraud Peak (12,585)
This peak has a very distinctive north face. The east arete is easy.

Peak 13,920+ (0.5 ESE of North Palisade)
Class 2–3 from the north or the east.

Southern Palisades

Mt. Jepson (Pk. 13,390, 1.5 S of Temple Crag)

This recently named peak commemorates Willis Linn Jepson, the noted botanist. Class 2 from the south. A technical route, rated III, 5.8, has been done on the steep northeastern face. On the center of this face are two chimneys. The route begins about 40 feet to the right of the left chimney. Climb one pitch (5.7); then enter the chimney. The angle eases for a while, but the wall steepens again for the fifth pitch. Above this lead, continue up the chimney into an immense cave. Awkward and difficult chimney climbing leads out under the lip of the cave. The summit is one short, moderate pitch above.

Palisade Crest (13,440+)

III, 5.5. The traverse of the eleven pinnacles which make up this serrated ridge takes a long time, but it is not particularly difficult. Some of the northeast faces of the crags have been climbed, but the routes are short and not too interesting.

"Clyde Peak" (Pk. 13,920+, 0.4 NW of Middle Palisade)

This striking peak of monolithic granite was one of Norman Clyde's favorite peaks and is unofficially named for him. The significant features of the peak can be seen from near the start of the South Fork trail. Of the two high points visible, the left summit is the higher. The prominent, steep column leading straight down from the summit is Twilight Pillar. A route has been done on this and also on the face to each side. The northeast ridge and the north face lie near the right-hand skyline.

Route 1. Southeast Ridge. Class 4. Climb the jagged and exposed ridge from Middle Palisade.

Route 2. Thunderbird Wall. III, 5.7. To the left of the earlier-mentioned Twilight Pillar is a wall with a conspicuous crack and chimney system. The start of the serious difficulties can be reached either from ledges on the left or from the base of Twilight Pillar. Four pitches in the crack system lead to the ridge about 200 feet southeast of the summit.

Route 3. Twilight Pillar. III, 5.8. Start either directly below the buttress (one 5.7 pitch from the Middle Palisade Glacier) or from the upper left-hand corner of a large, all-year snowpatch part way up the face. Above and left of this snowfield the buttress steepens abruptly. Climb the face left of a right-facing open book for 175 feet to a platform. Continue up a shallow dihedral for about 80 feet; then make a delicate traverse around a corner to the right. The next three or four pitches are less intimidating and follow the crest directly to the summit.

Route 4. Eagle Face. II, 5.4. From the upper left-hand edge of the snowfield mentioned in Route 3, enter a chimney about 100 feet right of Twilight Pillar. After 80 feet in this, move out right onto the slabby face and follow it upward for several easy, pleasant pitches. Then cross a rotten area to a small snowpatch on the left and climb the steep wall above for two or three left-diagonaling pitches. Care must be taken to follow the easiest way—variations are considerably more difficult and offer inadequate protection.

Route 5. North-Northeast Ridge. Class 4. This long, clean-looking ridge leads to the lower, western summit of Clyde. Attain the ridge from the Clyde Glacier (north of the mountain) and follow it to the top. If one stays on the exact crest of the ridge, there is some 5.9 climbing.

Route 6. North Face. Class 3–4. From the Clyde Glacier, climb the left-hand couloir of the north face to the west ridge; then follow it left to the top. This route is the normal descent from Clyde. One can also traverse across the north face to the northeast ridge and then drop down the easy terrain below the Eagle Face.

Route 7. South Side. Class 3–4 from the John Muir Trail .

Middle Palisade (14,040)

Route 1. Southeast Ridge. Class 4 from Disappointment Peak. Stay mostly on the right side of the ridge.

Route 2. East Face. Class 3. Several class 4 routes have been done on the face above the glacier. An easier route follows the shallow chute directly below the summit and directly above the moraine that divides the glacier. From the top of this moraine climb onto the left-hand segment of the glacier; then leave it when a ledge leads up the buttress on the right. Enter a broad couloir, leave it at a conspicuous patch of white rock, and traverse right into the next couloir. Take the left branch higher up; this leads to the summit ridge.

Route 3. Northeast Side. Class 4. From the moraine which divides the Middle Palisade Glacier, climb up the right-hand segment. Several routes can be found on the face above.

Route 4. Northwest Ridge. Class 4 from Clyde Peak.

Route 5. Southwest Chute. Class 4. The southwest side of the Middle Palisade massif is somewhat featureless, and many persons have become disoriented, climbing the well-named Disappointment Peak by mistake. Take the third chute left of the junction of the main wall and the southwest spur of the massif. The chute which lies in the junction is the first chute. The routefinding is a bit tricky near the top; when three-quarters of the way up, leave the chute and ascend the face on its left. This eventually brings one to the summit ridge.

Disappointment Peak (13,917)

Just southeast of Middle Palisade, and at about the same elevation, are three distinct peaklets. The central one is the highest and has been called Disappointment Peak since 1919, when the first ascenders, who had intended to climb the unclimbed Middle Palisade, found themselves separated from it by class 4 gaps.

Route 1. East Ridge. Climb to the crest from the north side and follow the class 3 ridge to the top.

Route 2. Northeast Couloir. Class 4. Climb the right-hand couloir of two couloirs on the face.

Route 3. Southwest Chute. Class 3. Climb up the first chute left of the junction of the main Middle Palisade massif with its prominent southwest spur.

The Thumb (13,388)

Route 1. Southwest Slopes. Class 2–3. Approach this route from Birch Lake; the main difficulty is a short wall at 12,000 feet. One can also reach the southwest slopes from the west by means of a class 2 pass a bit east of Southfork Pass.

Route 2. Northeast Side. Class 4–5. From the west one can see a deep couloir leading up the northeast side of the peak to the northeast ridge. It can be recognized by the fact that it is the couloir closest to the Thumb which actually reaches the ridgetop. Climb the couloir until near its top; then exit right onto a sharp arete and climb to the main ridge. Higher, a steep step is turned on the left and is the last obstacle before the summit. There is a lot of loose rock on this route, especially in the lower couloir.

Route 3. Northwest Face. Class 4. Climb a couloir on this face and then circle right to the easy south side of the peak.

Route 4. Northwest Corner. III, 5.7. The upper portion of the northwest side of the Thumb has two prominent faces at right angles to one another. Each of these faces is marked with black dikes which may be mistaken for chimneys. This route more or less follows the corner between the two faces.

Peak 13,520+ (1 SE of the Thumb)

Class 3 from Birch Lake. It is also class 3 from Lake 11,767 to the west. The north ridge also seems to be class 3.

Birch Mountain (13,665)

The western and southern sides of this great hulk are class 2. The north face has been climbed via one of many ribs and chutes and is class 3.

Mt. Bolton Brown (13,538)

The northwest ridge and the north slopes are both class 2. The southwest side of the peak is a bit more difficult.

Mt. Prater (13,329)

The southeast ridge is quite easy once it is gained from the west.

The north ridge has been climbed: from the cirque north of Lake 11,599 ascend to the ridge via the largest chute right of the pinnacles between Bolton Brown and Prater. Cross over to the east plateau and head south to the north peak—a class 3 notch separates it from the higher south peak.

Peak 13,040+ (1 W of Mt. Prater)
Class 2 from Mather Pass. The south summit is higher.

Mt. Tinemaha (12,561)
Class 2 and 3 from all sides.

Split Mountain (14,058)
Route 1. West Side. Class 3–4 up ribs and chutes.
Route 2. Northwest Shoulder. Class 2.
Route 3. North Side. From Lake 11,599 (northwest of the peak) climb to the saddle between Prater and Split; then ascend class 2 talus to the summit.
Route 4. From the East. Class 3. From Red Lake walk northwest to the ridge between the two northern glaciers shown on the topo map. Follow this ridge to the saddle north of the peak. Then follow Route 3.
Route 5. Southeast Side. From a point high in the cirque east of Peak 13,803 climb the slope to the south summit of Split. A class 3 descent is made into the notch between the peaks—the north summit is an easy walk from here.

Peak 13,803 (0.5 SSW of Split Mtn.)
A steep class 3–4 couloir lies on the southeast wall.

Cardinal Mountain (13,397)
From Taboose Pass climb either the southwest spur or a chute to its right. Class 2.

Peak 12,851 (1 SW of Cardinal Mtn.)
The ascent from Taboose Pass is very easy.

The Kings River Region

Three great forks of the Kings River dominate a 500-square-mile section of the western Sierra. These vast watersheds formed important avenues for early explorers of the range. Although the scenery is often splendid, mountaineers will find less of interest in this area than in others. Only at the very headwaters of the streams will one find the rugged peaks characteristic of the High Sierra. Rockclimbers, however, will find a few excellent areas at the lower elevations.

The North Fork of the Kings is the shortest, and will be of limited interest to the climber except for the peaks around its headwaters in Blackcap Basin. Most of the lower portion of the river flows through gentle, forested country better suited for hunters than for climbers.

The Middle Fork originates at 12,000 feet near the junction of the Goddard Divide with the Sierra crest. The fine peaks around the headwaters have already been described in the Evolution chapter. East of the Black Divide, the river flows through the incredible LeConte Canyon, turns the divide, and then runs twenty miles in a nearly straight southwest direction to its junction with the South Fork. Midway along this twenty-mile stretch is the remote Tehipite Valley. Overlooking the valley on the north is the largest dome in the Sierra, Tehipite Dome. Overlooking the valley on the south is a wall with a fabulous array of pinnacles, cliffs, and hanging valleys. Foremost among the last is the Gorge of Despair, which contains several impressive and monolithic turrets.

The South Fork has its headwaters in the barren Upper Basin, a few miles south of Middle Palisade. The peaks close to the Sierra crest have been described in the Palisades chapter. The stream flows southwest through the seldom-visited valley below the Muro Blanco, past Paradise Valley, and finally turns west as it enters the second most famous canyon of the Sierra, the canyon that gave a

221

national park its name. Though often compared with Yosemite Valley, Kings Canyon is not nearly as grand as Yosemite, lacking as it does those fine meadows, high waterfalls, and monolithic walls which have made the Valley a worldwide attraction. Nevertheless, Kings Canyon is a noteworthy place and contains much to hold the visitor. A few miles downstream from the canyon the river passes through a curious region of limestone and soon joins the Middle Fork of the Kings River.

This chapter has been divided into four sections, the first of which covers the peaks north of the Middle Fork as far upstream as Goddard Creek, which is the border between the Kings River and Evolution regions. Most of the peaks in this section lie on or near a twenty-mile-long ridge which is known in its northern half as the LeConte Divide (which separates the North Fork of the Kings from the South Fork of the San Joaquin) and in the southern half as the White Divide (which separates the North Fork from Goddard Creek, a tributary of the Middle Fork). At the end of the first section, the rock climbs around Tehipite Dome are described.

The second and third sections describe the wealth of rock climbs in the Gorge of Despair and Kings Canyon, respectively.

The fourth section covers the Monarch Divide, Cirque Crest, and the peaks south of Palisade Creek.

While traveling through the Central Valley of California in 1805, the Spaniards came across a great river and, as was their wont, gave it a name suggested by the church calendar: *el rio de los Santos Reyes*, the river of the Holy Kings—that is, the Three Wise Men. Although the Spaniards knew of the existence of the snowy range of mountains to the east, they made no recorded attempt to reach them. Forty years later, Lieutenant John Frémont and sixteen soldiers tried to cross this part of the Sierra in December. Reaching 11,000 feet on the North Fork of the Kings, probably near Blackcap Basin, they encountered sub-zero temperatures and terrific gales; snow blindness was also a problem. Frémont was impressed with the beauty of the area and later wrote: "If we could be free from the many anxieties that oppress us, even now we would be delighted here; but our provisions are getting fearfully scant.''

By the late 1850s Owens Valley Indians were guiding prospectors across what is now Kearsarge Pass and very probably through Kings Canyon, but it was not until 1864, that key year in the history of the Sierra, that the area was first described. William Brewer, several other members of the California Geological Survey, and a group of soldiers entered the great canyon of the South Fork. Brewer wrote of their campsite, ''It was a very picturesque camp, granite precipices rising on both sides to immense height. The river swarmed with trout; I never saw them thicker. Next to Yosemite, this is the grandest canyon I have ever seen.'' The party started north toward the Middle Fork but soon found that the descent from the Monarch Divide would be too taxing for their pack animals. James Gardiner and Charles Hoffmann climbed a peak above Granite Basin, probably Goat Mountain. It was from here, or nearby, that the Palisades and Mt. Goddard were first seen and named. Stymied in their attempt to head north into unknown country, the party chose instead to follow the well-known prospectors' route from the South Fork, up Bubbs and Charlotte creeks to Kearsarge Pass and thence into Owens Valley.

Within a very few years the Kings Canyon region became familiar to more and more adventurers. Judge Elisha Winchell visited the area in 1868 and a few years later wrote a long-winded account of his trip. He claimed that ''many a deep and dreadful abyss lies hidden in that Andean region.'' John Muir decided in 1873 that he should see the new wonder; he was impressed. He made at least three trips into Kings Canyon and felt that ''the destructable beauty of this remote yosemite is doomed to perish'' because of the effects of the sheep and cattle which were being taken up the canyons during the summers.

Less was known of the Middle Fork. During the 1870s Frank Dusy, a stockman, explored the river to its source and possibly was first to obtain a good look at the Palisade Glacier. Lilbourne Winchell, son of the judge, accompanied Dusy on an 1879 trip and witnessed him taking the first photographs of the towering Tehipite Dome. Winchell spent that summer exploring the Middle Fork. He named the Gorge of Despair, visited the Palisades, and in late September made the first climb of Mt. Goddard, with Louis Davis.

Following the ascent of Goat Mountain, there were few recorded ascents for many years. Joseph N. LeConte first visited the region in 1890; during the next twelve years he explored a large section of the Kings River country. In 1898 he crossed the divide which now bears his name at Hell-for-Sure Pass and climbed Red Mountain. Later, on a reconnaissance of the Palisades, he climbed Observation and Marion peaks.

There was remarkably little mountaineering done in the region for the first half of the twentieth century; it was not until the 1950s that most of the peaks of the LeConte and White divides were climbed. During the same time rockclimbers were discovering the Gorge of Despair and the cliffs of Kings Canyon. The two big-wall climbs of Kings Canyon, the faces of North Dome and Grand Sentinel, were done in the late 1960s by climbers who had learned their techniques in the other great valley, eighty miles to the north.

The Kings River area can be approached in a multitude of ways. Most mountaineers will prefer to come in from the west; from north to south, these approaches are as follows.

From Florence Lake a trail along the South Fork of the San Joaquin River leads to the northern outposts of the LeConte Divide. The central section of the divide is best reached via the seventeen-mile-long trail which begins at the Courtright Reservoir and crosses the divide at Hell-for-Sure Pass. The southern part of the divide and the White Divide are best approached from the Wishon Reservoir.

Since there is no trail up the rugged lower section of the Middle Fork, the Tehipite Dome area is difficult to reach. The approaches to this region are mentioned in the Tehipite Dome description.

The Gorge of Despair has a steep, arduous approach; while only twelve miles in length, a vertical rise of 6,300 feet is involved in crossing the Monarch Divide. The topo map is extremely unreliable regarding the trail systems in the area, and much of the route is either trailless or on poor, hard-to-locate paths. Ascend the trail up Deer Cove Creek (a few miles west of Cedar Grove on the Kings Canyon Highway) toward Wildman Meadow. Between this meadow and Frypan Meadow follow faint tracks up the gentle divide which marks the national park boundary. After a short while a fairly good path is reached; follow it upward as it traverses steeply left below a rocky hill (Point 9,675). From a saddle one-half mile south southeast of Grizzly Lakes the path cuts east and climbs across a hill to the East Fork of Grizzly Creek. From here head over to the lakes and ascend to the 10,640-foot saddle northeast of Mt. Harrington. The Gorge of Despair is just below and northwest. A drop of 2,500 feet takes one to benches on the creek near the turrets. Variations on this approach can (and will) be found. The Lewis Creek trail seems a better approach to some; the standard route is met near Frypan Meadow. Also, the pass just west of Hogback Peak can be used—a class 2–3 traverse to the west across slabs is necessary to reach the top of the Gorge.

The rock climbs of Kings Canyon are easily accessible from the main highway.

The peaks of the Monarch Divide can be approached via three trails which leave the Kings Canyon Highway; all these trails involve horrendous vertical rises.

Cirque Crest peaks can be reached most easily via the long, hot trail which leaves the Middle Fork at Simpson Meadow. The eastern peaks of this group are easily approached from Lake Basin, on the Cartridge Pass Trail.

The group of peaks west of Upper Basin can be approached via the trails along the four streams which surround the area. This is the one section of the Kings River area which is best approached from the east side of the main crest. Southfork and Taboose passes, described in the preceding chapter, provide a long one-day approach to these peaks.

There are only a few climbers' passes in the region, and these are all found in the vicinity of Lake Basin.

Red Pass (11,600+) lies 0.7 mile north-northwest of Marion Peak and connects Lake Basin with the South Fork of Cartridge Creek. Class 2.

Upper Basin Pass (12,320+) is found just south of Vennacher Needle and offers a very efficient method of crossing from the Muir Trail to Lake Basin. Class 2.

Dumbbell Pass (11,680+) lies 1.6 miles north of Marion Lake and provides a quick class 2 crossing from Lake Basin into the basin containing Dumbbell Lakes.

Cataract Creek Pass (11,520+) is located 0.4 mile east-southeast of Observation Peak. It connects Amphitheater Lake with Dumbbell Lakes and is class 2.

A number of topo maps are needed to cover the Kings River region: Big Pine, Blackcap Mountain, Mt. Goddard, Marion Peak, Mt. Pinchot, and Tehipite Dome.

North of the Middle Fork

Mt. Henry (12,196)

The nicest route yet done on this peak appears to be the class 3 north ridge. Follow the arete which leads from the next peak north and bypass large blocks and notches on the east. Easier routes have been made. The northeast ridge from Goddard Canyon has been climbed and is class 2. The west and southwest slopes are also class 2.

Red Mountain (11,951)

This uninteresting peak is class 1 from all directions; the shortest approach is from Hell-for-Sure Pass.

Peak 11,998 (1.7 S of Red Mtn.)

Class 1 from the southwest. A 600-foot-long technical route, rated II, 5.7, A2, has been done on the north face. Climb a crack system just to the right of a pillar which splits the face. Most of the route is free.

Peak 12,265 (3.2 SE of Hell-for-Sure Pass)
The west ridge is a class 3 knife edge.

Blackcap Mountain (11,559)
Class 1 and 2 routes can be found on the southern and eastern flanks of this peak.

Mt. Reinstein (12,604)
The southeast ridge is class 3. From Blackcap Basin a class 2 route has been done up the south side.

Peak 12,479 (0.7 S of Mt. Reinstein)
Several chutes on the southwest face lead nearly to the summit of this peak. Climb the left-hand chute until very near its top; then exit left onto the south ridge. Class 3.

Peak 12,209 (1.4 SSE of Mt. Reinstein)
Climb the class 3 east ridge. The easiest way to turn the steep lower part of the ridge is to pass behind a huge boulder; then head upward.

Peak 12,309 (1.8 S of Mt. Reinstein)
From the lower eastern summit (easily reached via class 2 routes) traverse the ridge to the south for a while; then drop down a chute leading west. Descend this; then traverse right toward a notch. Cross a sandy chute and climb onto the ridge leading to the higher, western summit. Class 3.

Finger Peak (12,404)
Class 3 via the northwest ridge, and class 2 from the southeast and southwest.

Blue Canyon Peak (11,849)
    Class 2 from the east.

Peak 11,969 (1.2 SE of Blue Canyon Pk.)
    A class 3 route has been done on the west ridge, and it was
reported to be the best climb in the area.

Peak 12,081 (0.9 S of Blue Canyon Pk.)
    The northwest ridge is class 3; the northeast ridge is a bit easier.

Tunemah Peak (11,894)
    Class 2 from the west and south.

Kettle Dome (9,446)
    This dome lies several miles north of Tehipite Dome. The north-
east slope is class 3. A technical route, rated II, 5.7, has been done
on the west face. Climb three pitches up the center of a shallow bowl
to a ledge at the base of the summit headwall. Traverse right to the
crest of the southwest buttress and follow it to the top.

Tehipite Dome (7,708)
    A boring 18-mile approach is likely to limit the popularity of the
Sierra's largest dome. Leave the road south of the Wishon Reservoir
and follow the Tunemah trail past Cliff Bridge and Crown Valley to
the base of Kettle Dome. Leave the trail here and thrash through
brush and forest to the class 3 ridge which leads out to the summit.
This is the original route and is basically the approach for the
following two routes. Although a trail goes along the Middle Fork,
below the dome, this approach is not recommended because of
length, rattlesnakes, brush, and debilitating heat. From near the top
of the dome, climb down steep slopes along the eastern side of the
rock. This 2,500-foot descent involves steep brush, traverses, rappels, and moderate rockclimbing.
    Route 1. South Face, Right. V, 5.8, A3. Begin climbing a crack
behind a 200-foot pillar which leans against the wall; then follow a

steep and exposed crack system which lies only a few feet right of the nose that forms the center of the dome. Stay close to this nose for hundreds of feet of difficult aid climbing and awkward free climbing. Next, a tension-traverse left leads into a chimney. Aid, up a loose and offset crack, brings one to a hard, unprotected ramp which ends in a shallow chimney. A few hundred feet higher one attains a huge, brush-covered ledge. It is possible to escape from here· follow the ledge west into the forest.

From the ledge work up the left side of an immense tower. Above this, proceed more or less straight up into a dihedral system which becomes the route line. Some aid is required in this section. Soon the angle decreases and knobs begin to appear. Enjoyable free climbing leads up for many pitches to the top of the dome. Ten bolts have been placed on the seventeen pitches which comprise this Sierra classic.

Route 2. South Face, Left. VI, 5.9, A4. Begin climbing several hundred feet below and left of the preceding route. Mixed free and aid climbing leads up crack systems to the huge, brush-covered ledge described in Route 1. Follow this route to the top.

Obelisk (9,700)

Four miles west of Tehipite Dome, and at the westernmost point of Kings Canyon National Park, is a solitary, pointed monolith. Noted for its excellent rock, the Obelisk has four fine routes, although, like Tehipite, the long approach will probably deter most climbers. From the road just below the Wishon Reservoir take the trail which leads generally southeast past Cliff Bridge, Statum Meadow, and Spanish Lake to Geraldine Lakes. From here a short bit of cross-country travel east brings one to the Obelisk.

Route 1. South Face. II, 5.6. Climb a long, broken chimney on the south side of the rock to a steep, 100-foot wall. This is the crux; above here the remainder of the route is obvious and easy.

Route 2. North Face and West Arete. Rating unknown. Begin climbing on a short, 45-degree ridge near the center of the face. Ascend this for about 100 feet to its end; then traverse right on small, exposed ledges to the west arete. Follow this to the top.

Route 3. West Face. II, 5.7. Seven steep and interesting pitches lead to the top.

Route 4. East Face. II, 5.5? About 200 feet down the hill from the notch behind the Obelisk lies the start of this route. A short bit of class 3 leads to a depression. A 100-foot pitch leads to a 100-foot traverse along easy ledges. From here wander up the face almost anywhere for three or four more pitches.

Spanish Mountain (10,051)

This peak, located a few miles west of the Obelisk, is an easy climb from Geraldine Lakes or the trail north of the peak. The southwest side of the peak falls away 8,000 feet into the Kings River in a horizontal distance of only four and a half miles.

The Gorge of Despair

"Silver Turret" (9,913)

As the climber drops below the 10,000-foot level in the Gorge, the towers which have proved so arduous to reach begin to come into view. First to strike the eye is Silver Turret, a Bugaboo Spire-like formation on the west edge of the valley. The southeast ridge, which is the left skyline, affords a pleasant class 4 route.

A route on the north buttress has been done and is the longest and hardest route yet done in the Gorge. Ascend an ever-steepening slab for several pitches; then work into a chimney and follow it to the top of an inconspicuous, greenish wall. Continue up and left to easier chimneys; then surmount the final overhang directly and climb several class 4 pitches to the summit. A tension-traverse on the first pitch is used to pass a blank spot; this is the only aid on the route. III or IV, 5.8, A1.

"Fang Turret"

Just south of Silver Turret lies this 90-foot pinnacle. From the notch southeast of the spire the 5.7 route is obvious.

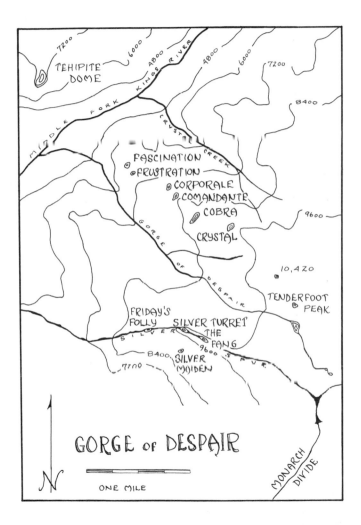

7200
6000
4800
KINGS RIVER
4800
6000
7200

TEHIPITE
DOME

MIDDLE FORK

CRYSTAL CREEK

8400

FASCINATION
FRUSTRATION
CORPORALE
COMANDANTE
COBRA
CRYSTAL

GORGE OF DESPAIR

9600

10,420

TENDERFOOT
PEAK

FRIDAY'S
FOLLY

SILVER TURRET
THE FANG
9600

SILVER SPUR

8400
7200
SILVER
MAIDEN

GORGE of DESPAIR

N

ONE MILE

MONARCH DIVIDE

"The Python"
This is the next high point up the ridge from Fang Turret and is class 4.

"Friday's Folly" *(9,388)*
Below and southwest of Silver Turret is a large, wedge-shaped mass. The 5.3 route ascends an overlapping flake formation midway along the eastern face.

"Silver Maiden"
About 500 feet below the Fang-Silver Turret notch, and southeast of it, is a large tower. Begin climbing on the northeast side; after 30 feet a sharp arete is reached. A traverse on the north side of this arete leads to a belay platform. From here descend south to a prominent rib and climb this to an alcove underneath a large block. Belay here. Next, ascend a chimney which tapers into a classic, steep lieback. Above this a shoulder is reached; the summit is class 4 from here. The rating for this climb is unknown, although some aid was used on the first ascent.

"Tenderfoot Peak" *(10,621)*
Rising north of the large lake at 10,000 feet in the Gorge is a peak with an impressive southwest face. The easiest route is via the talus slopes to the right of this face. Class 2. A giant open book on the face has been done and is rated II, 5.6. Climb the book for 80 feet and then traverse right into a gully. Follow this for a pitch and a half; then traverse left and proceed to the top.

"Crystal Turret" *(9,520+)*
Three routes have been made on this beautiful crag, which is the highest on the eastern rim of the Gorge. The original route is the easiest: walk up brush-covered slopes to the right of the spire until just below the drop-off into Crystal Creek. Above, on the south face, one will see a large window just below gigantic, overhanging blocks. Rope up about 50 feet left of the window and ascend a

lieback crack. Traverse right from here; then climb a very steep jamcrack. Pass through the window and proceed up an obvious slab to a huge ledge just below the top. Walk far out on a ledge to the south and ascend an easy friction arete to the summit. The route is 5.6.

For the second route, walk up to the actual drop-off mentioned above. Just left of the east buttress is a 15-foot-wide dike of dark rock which contrasts sharply with the surrounding granite. Climb this dike for 50 feet to its end and then move right and ascend the prow of the buttress to the huge ledge below the summit. 5.7.

The southwest face, prominent from the Gorge, has also been climbed. The 5.8 route ascends the most conspicuous chimney which diagonals up the wall. The route is quite clear and, for the most part, very enjoyable class 4. A 5.8 move or two is found at the start of a flared chimney above a big ledge.

"Cobra Turret" (9,040+)

This is the wide, bulky formation down the ridge from Crystal Turret. One route has been done: from near the highest point of the forest on the northwest side of the rock, scramble up low-angle rock to a large tree 75 feet above the ground. Climb up and right from here, passing two small ledges, to an open book. Ascend this, pass an overhang on the right, and belay a bit higher. The next pitches can follow either the crack or the knobby face above the belayer.

"El Comandante Turret" (8,530)

Down the ridge from Cobra Turret is a large white formation with a deep chimney on its south side. The original route on El Comandante ascends the rounded prow just left of the chimney. After a few hundred feet a broad, sloping ledge is reached. This ledge is followed upward until it ends abruptly at a notch overlooking the impressive north face. From the notch climb upward just right of the arete 150 feet to the top. A short 5.7 friction traverse is necessary about 40 feet below the top.

An easier route is as follows: climb the chimney mentioned earlier to the broad, sloping ledge. Turn right and enter another chimney which shoots upward. When this ends, follow a thin crack to the top. 5.4

A third route has been done; it lies on the southwest face—a wide, fairly low-angle wall. At the lower right side of this wall is a small, orange dike which diagonals up and left toward a slot 175 feet above the ground. Ascend the dike and the face to its left to the slot. Exit upward and left from the top of the slot and follow a left-diagonaling crack-ledge under an overhang. Cut back to the right above this overhang; then traverse up and right until a sloping belay spot directly above the belayer is reached. A long, easy pitch, with many fine knobs, leads to the notch mentioned in the first route. The climbing on the lower portion of the route is not well protected, and the belay anchors leave something to be desired. II, 5.7.

"El Corporale Turret" (8,400+)

This is the small satellite which clings to the north side of El Comandante. An obvious gully on the south face is class 3–4; the rounded rib just left of the gully is a more interesting route and is class 4.

"Frustration Turret" (7,280+)

About one-half mile below El Corporale lie the two final formations of the eastern rim of the Gorge. Frustration is the higher of the two and the most massive. From the notch which separates the formation from the hillside, walk down along the east face for 100 feet until below and left of a small, solitary pine which is visible some 60 feet above. A tricky pitch leads to this tree; 20 feet higher is a ledge which can be traversed easily to the right for 100 feet. This ends at a broken area on the northeast side of the pinnacle. From here climb to a sloping ledge, ascend it to its upper end, and climb a crack to a steep slab on the northwest corner of the rock. Climb up via one of several variations to a ledge 100 feet below the summit. A few aid placements may be necessary to overcome a short wall. Higher, bear up and left. A traverse around the south side of the summit block leads to easy climbing and the top. II, 5.7, A1.

"Fascination Point" (7,120+)

This is the final formation; its north face falls 3,000 feet into the Middle Fork of the Kings River. From the eastern base of Frustration Turret walk down the steep talus gully for about 300 feet; then contour north to the second gully (the first ends in a drop-off). Ascend this gully to the notch between Fascination and the mass to its south. Class 3 climbing leads to the top.

A tiny pinnacle located between Fascination and Frustration has been climbed, and a few aid placements are used.

The South Fork Rock Climbs

The Grand Dike (ca. 8,000)

Five miles northwest of Cedar Grove (on the Kings Canyon Highway) lies a short, jagged ridge containing impressive towers. The easiest approach is to ascend the Deer Cove trail from the South Fork of the Kings River. The towers have been numbered, starting from their lower end.

Tower ½. This is the small tower attached to the south side of the first main pinnacle. Two routes have been done. A 5.3 route begins from the notch between ½ and Tower 1. Scramble via an intricate route to a short chimney on the northwest face. Climb this chimney, passing a small chockstone, to class 4 rock and the top. The other route begins from the same place as the first and ascends the easy class 5 east face.

Tower 1. Class 4. Climb the east face of Tower 2 for about 70 feet to a broad ledge. Follow this left to the 1–2 notch and then circle around the west side of 1 and scramble to the top. The 1–2 notch can be reached more easily from the 2–3 notch by following an easy ledge.

Tower 2. Class 4. This is the small, truncated block between the larger Towers 1 and 3. From the broad ledge mentioned earlier a short chimney continues up the east face. A class 3–4 route has been done from the 2–3 notch: climb a chimney on the northwest face to the top.

Tower 3. From the 2–3 notch traverse around the southeast face until progress becomes difficult. From here climb up and back to the right to a large ledge. The next pitch heads to the left and generally follows the northwest corner of the pinnacle. This pitch leads to the crux, a 5.5, 70-degree face with a paucity of holds. Work up and slightly right; from the top of the pitch the summit is easily reached. Another route has been done and is about 5.4 in difficulty. Continue the traverse at the start of the preceding route until reaching a tree on a platform on the northwest face. Using this tree, climb upward to some bushes; then traverse right around a corner and join the other route.

Tower 4. The 5.3 route begins in a large chimney on the north-west face. Climb this about 30 feet and then exit right onto small holds. Ascend to small belay ledges. Continue upward and then bear slightly left to a large, partially detached flake. Above this is a small ledge. Climb the face to a shoulder and scramble to the top.

Tower 5. A class 3 or 4 route lies on the broken southeast face above the 4–5 notch. The class 3 north face offers another way to the top.

Tower 6. From the notch between Towers 5 and 6 drop down to the left about 30 feet and, using a tree, surmount the overhang which runs along the base of Tower 6. Above this, scramble to the top. The route is easy except for the overhang at the base. A class 3 route has been done on the north side.

Towers 7 and 8. Class 2 and 3 routes can be found on these towers.

"Kings Tower" (ca. 3,600)

This small but spectacular pinnacle is located just above the

Kings Canyon Highway, 2.9 miles east of the bridge over Ten-Mile Creek and 3.6 miles west of the main highway bridge at Boyden Cave. The approach is via a brushy gully on the right. From the notch separating the spire from the hillside climb a lieback above an alcove to a secure platform. Climb the left side of the south face to a narrow ledge which leads right. The final part of the route lies on the east face. To descend, make a 75-foot rappel off the south face.

"Windy Bluff"

A prominent limestone arete lies just north of the main highway bridge at Boyden Cave. Ascend the gully on the east of the arete until it is possible to make an easy traverse left onto the prow. Several pitches of class 4 and 5 climbing up the left side of the arete lead to the top. Descend class 3 to the east. 5.5.

Boyden Rock (4,480+)

A 5.5 route has been made on the east side of this rock, a giant limestone monolith. The route lies just left of the big northern escarpment. Follow the Cave trail around the corner; then bushwhack up toward a not-so-obvious buttress. Several hundred feet of moderate climbing leads to the summit. To descend, rappel toward the southeast; then head to class 3 pinnacles on the southeast. The watercourse northeast of the rock can also be used for descending.

"Bulldog Rock" (ca. 5,200)

From the Lewis Creek bridge several pinnacles will be seen on a granite ridge across the river. Bulldog Rock is the lower of the two most conspicuous formations. From the notch above Bulldog walk around east on an easy ledge to the north face. From a block climb up to a narrow ledge which heads up and right. At its upper end ascend to the sloping west face and climb it to the top. 5.6, A1.

"Hathaway's Delight" (ca. 5,400)

This is the higher of the towers mentioned in the preceding description. Approach from the west to a high-angle gully below the upper south notch. Several pitches up this deceptive gully lead to the notch. Next, traverse east to a platform and follow a high-angle trough to the top. 5.4.

"Spook Spire" *(ca. 6,800)*

One-quarter mile east of the turnoff into Cedar Grove's Camp 4 is a paved loop turnout on the north side of the road. This is a good vantage point. Very high on the wooded rim to the south is a squarish cliff which extends farther down into the forest than do the other cliffs in the area. At the left edge of this cliff is a thin, spectacular pinnacle. It does not quite reach the skyline and is hard to see unless the lighting is such that it throws a telltale shadow. A few pitches of class 4–5 climbing are necessary to reach the notch behind the pinnacle. From here, climb out onto a ledge on the east face; then make a long reach to a crack. This leads up and left; some aid has been used in this section. The summit is soon reached. II, 5.6, A2.

Roaring River Falls

Three short routes have been established on the walls both to the left and to the right of the falls.

The first route begins about 150 yards right of the falls. A large gully with a white block halfway up its right side will be seen above. Begin climbing about 100 feet left of this gully and follow an obvious line. II, 5.4.

On the east side of the falls is a clean, low-angle apron. A route begins at a small pine midway across the apron. Ascend via face climbing to a large, jutting block; turn this on the right. Continue straight up to a tree. Traverse left, turn an overhang on the left, and proceed up to a belay tree. Traverse left; then follow easier climbing to the top. II, 5.6.

The last route begins several hundred feet to the right of the preceding climb. Rope up just right of a right-facing open book and climb two pitches to a prominent ledge system. Traverse left from the high point of the ledges; then proceed straight up over an overhang. Next, head upward for several pitches toward the center of a black bowl. Exit this to the right; the top is just above. II, 5.6.

North Dome (8,717)

Near the end of the Kings Canyon Highway is a fine-looking dome on the north side of the road. The "back side" is easy, but the south face is very precipitous. At the center of this face is a long, left-leaning dihedral which ends just left of the conspicuous summit ceiling. The route follows this dihedral and for the most part is quite obvious. The difficulties involve passing overhangs on the right-hand wall of the dihedral. IV, 5.8, A4.

A four-pitch route has been established on the lower section of the south face. This route is rated III, 5.7, A2. To the left of the preceding route is a prominent, Roman-arch-shaped apron. The first pitch ascends the left side of this apron; the remainder of the route proceeds up and left over steps to a tree on a sloping ledge. This is the top of the route.

Grand Sentinel (8,504)

Rising 3,500 feet above Zumwalt Meadows is an impressive, pointed peak with a sheer northern escarpment. The summit can be reached easily from the south; the trail up Sphinx Creek is the best access. Several routes have been done on the north side of the formation. An obvious Y-shaped talus gully next to the upper face has been climbed via its right arm and is class 4 in places. On the right side of the face two steps will be seen in profile. A class 5 route leads to the top of the second step; the actual summit lies far beyond. The hardest route to date lies on the steepest section of the upper north face, where a greenish, 800-foot-high open book will be seen. Seven difficult pitches lead up into this book. Five pitches in the book, involving a fair amount of aid climbing, take one eventually to easier climbing and the top. V, 5.9 or 5.10, A2.

The Sphinx (9,146)

This seldom-climbed pinnacle was the first rock climb done in the Kings Canyon region. The Sphinx can be seen from the end of the Kings Canyon Highway as the double-summited formation far back on the canyon wall to the southeast. Hike up the Bubbs Creek trail to the Sphinx Creek trail and follow this to a point just south of Peak 9,721. Contour around left to the steep wooded ridge which leads down toward the Sphinx. Massive firs obscure the view of the rock, but soon a granite mass looms ahead. This is the higher summit; climb it (class 3) and then drop down the other side to the notch between the summits. From here ascend a short, narrow ledge which diagonals left. After 15 feet hand-traverse up and right to a small pedestal. The remainder of the route lies on the south side and is obvious. 5.2.

A route has been done on the long, smooth buttress on the north side of the Sphinx. From above the higher summit head down the slope to the west until it is possible to make a reasonable entry onto the buttress. Two class 5 pitches take one to the crest; from here work upward (5.6) to the summit tower. Turn this on the northern flank and climb to the top. II, 5.7.

The Monarch Divide
and the Upper South Fork

Mt. Harrington (11,005)

The top 300 feet of this peak, which overlooks the Gorge of Despair, is a spectacular pyramid and can be seen from many points in the central Sierra. The north ridge provides a short but enjoyable class 3 route. The south arete is class 4, and the west face is class 3.

Hogback Peak (11,077)

Class 2 from the saddle to the west. The 1954 climber's guide described the peak thus: "An ascent would involve hours of drudgery for rather dubious rewards."

Slide Peak (10,915)
The east slope is easy.

Kennedy Mountain (11,433)
An easy ascent from nearby Kennedy Pass.

Comb Spur (11,618)
Class 2 routes can be found on the seven peaklets of this three-mile-long ridge which extends southeast from Kennedy Pass.

Mt. Hutchings (10,785)
A trail northeast of this peak makes the ascent a simple one.

Goat Mountain (12,207)
Class 2 from the vicinity of Grouse Lake.

Goat Crest (12,059)
There are several easy peaklets on this small spur.

Kid Peak (11,458)
Class 2 from Paradise Valley.

Dougherty Peak (12,244)
Class 2 from Slate Lakes.

Slate Peak (12,620)
The western ridge is class 2–3. The ascent from the lakes south and southeast of the peak is class 2.

Marion Peak (12,719)
From Marion Lake a class 2 route can be made by ascending to

the saddle between Marion and the peaklet to the northeast and following the ridge to the top. The long northwest ridge is a nice class 3 route.

Red Point (11,840+)

Class 1 via the south ridge.

Windy Cliff (11,132)

The east side of this amorphous mass has been climbed and is class 2.

Mt. Shakspere (12,151)

Not much is known about this peak, but it appears easy from most directions.

Observation Peak (12,322)

Class 2 from the south. The northwest ridge has been done. The east ridge is class 2 from the saddle south of Amphitheater Lake.

Peak 12,860 (1.6 SE of Observation Pk.)

From the lake one-half mile southeast of the peak ascend a class 2 or 3 couloir on the southeast face. Class 3 climbing is encountered near the summit.

Vennacher Needle (12,996)

This peak, one of the most ill-named in the Sierra, is class 2 from anywhere on its southern side.

"Saddlehorn" (Pk. 12,080+, 1.2 SE of Vennacher Needle)

Viewed from Taboose Pass, this is a spectacular peak. The east side, a rounded ridge, is class 4 via steep slabs. A short 5.8 route has been made up cracks on the south face.

Mt. Ruskin (12,920)

From Cartridge Pass climb the ridge which eventually curves

right to the top. Class 3. The southwest slope and the east ridge are also class 3.

The Kearsarge Pass Area

Elegant peaks and well-trammeled lake basins are encountered in the twenty-five mile stretch of mountains between the southern Palisades and the northern Whitney group. Such well-known campsites as Bench Lake, Rae Lakes, Bullfrog Lake, and Vidette Meadow have pleased so many generations of hikers, fishermen, and mountaineers that severe regulations now apply regarding camping in these lovely places. Much of this traffic results from the pass for which this chapter is named; Kearsarge Pass provides a quick, efficient method of reaching the back country. Rising above some of the campsites mentioned earlier are beautiful, isolated mountains. Mt. Clarence King and its satellite peaks are the principal mountaineering attractions in the northern part of the region. And, farther south, peaks such as East Vidette and Center Peak engage the interest.

The crest of the Sierra in the northern part of the region is relatively low and very colorful. It is not terribly appealing for the climber, for though the peaks are sometimes pleasing in shape, they are usually composed of monstrous piles of talus, often at a gentle angle. Those who desire peaks with more challenging routes must turn to the sub-ranges to the west. Below Kearsarge Pass the peaks begin their rise toward the Whitney group, but the mountains are still unspectacular, especially on their west sides.

The Kings-Kern Divide is by far the most significant east-west spur in the region; it leaves the main crest at Junction Peak, about six miles south of Kearsarge Pass, and for six miles presents a formidable barrier until it joins the Great Western Divide. This barrier stymied Muir Trail-builders until 1932, when Forester Pass was opened. Previously, travelers had to cross the main crest twice to bypass the obstacle. The divide marks the boundary between Kings Canyon and Sequoia national parks and forms the cross bar in a giant letter H; the Great Western Divide is the left-hand segment, the main crest the other. As the name implies, the divide separates two watersheds. These two rivers dominate the entire southern Sierra.

Two major creeks are found in the northern part of the region; both are tributaries of the South Fork of the Kings River. Woods Creek drains the area between Pinchot Pass and the Rae Lakes, while Bubbs Creek, long a favorite of Sierra travelers, begins under the northern escarpment of the Kings-Kern Divide and flows north for a few miles before curving westward for its journey into Kings Canyon.

Indians, sheepherders, and prospectors were using Kearsarge Pass, Bubbs Creek, and Kings Canyon as a trans-Sierra route by the mid-1850s, and it is entirely possible that some of them were the region's first climbers. However, it seems that they had better things to do than write accounts of their mountaineering. The first description of the region occurred in 1864 when members of the California Geological Survey went over Kearsarge Pass—they did no mountaineering in the area. On this journey Charles Hoffmann made a fine sketch of what is now called Charlotte Dome. William Brewer described it as ". . . a grand smooth granite rock . . . about three thousand feet, smooth and bare. . . ." One can forgive Brewer his redundancies and curious lack of skill at estimating height, for he had discovered one of the most beautiful Sierra domes. Its thousand-foot face wasn't climbed for over a century.

John Muir visited the region in 1873; he hiked alone up Bubbs Creek and climbed a peak which he thought was Mt. Tyndall, although it was much more likely a mountain closer to Center Basin, perhaps Mt. Keith. Typically, Muir barely mentioned the climb, being much more attuned to the ecology of the area.

Gentle Mt. Gould, just north of Kearsarge Pass, was the first recorded ascent in the area. Joseph N. LeConte and three others made the ascent in 1890. A few years later many of the most prominent mountains were climbed. LeConte was one of the two most conspicuous figures of this era; the other was Bolton Coit Brown.

Brown, a professor of fine arts, made two noteworthy ventures into the region. In 1895, after climbing a few peaks farther north, he made a solo attempt on the area's outstanding feature—the pyramid of Mt. Clarence King. Named thirty-two years earlier for the first great Sierra mountaineer, the remote peak had no record of attempts. Brown failed close to the summit; he encountered massive slabs of granite. A year later he returned and, in one long day (a day which involved a trail-less 6,700-foot elevation gain), made the first ascent.

This solo adventure was the finest Sierra climb of the nineteenth century. Two rockclimbing techniques were used for the first time in North American mountaineering. One was the use of artificial chockstones and the other was the use of a rope sling for direct aid. Brown wrote that he "tied a big knot in the rope-end, threw it repeatedly until this caught in a crack, when I climbed the rope." At the monolithic summit block Brown used the other technique: "I finally looped the rope over an all-too-slight projection . . . and compelled myself to put one foot in it and lift myself, so to stand, dangling in that precarious sling, until I could get my arms over the top." Once safely on top, Brown noted that "if you fall off one side, you will be killed in the vicinity; if you fall off any of the other sides, you will be pulverized in the remote nadir beneath."

During the same summer, near the top of Mt. Gardiner, Brown was surprised to encounter a party led by Joseph N. LeConte; he had met LeConte a few days earlier but had no idea that he also coveted the peak. They joined forces, and two of the greatest figures of California mountaineering accomplished their only common first ascent. LeConte also made the first ascent of a mountain which he called University Peak (at that time *the* university was the University of California).

The Kings-Kern Divide had been crossed near Mt. Jordan in 1864 by Clarence King and Richard Cotter on their epic journey toward Mt. Tyndall. Many years went by before the forbidding peaks of the divide were climbed. A man named Gregory climbed a high pile of talus in 1894 and built a large cairn that soon became known as Gregory's Monument. In 1896 Bolton Coit Brown took his wife, Lucy, on her first trip to the mountains, into the Kings-Kern region. On August 1 they made the first crossing of Lucy's Foot Pass, climbed and named Mt. Ericsson (for the inventor of the *Monitor*), and went up Gregory's Monument. Lucy Brown remained here while her husband traversed an exposed knife edge to the actual summit. He had long desired a worthy peak to name after *his* university and so this peak became Mt. Stanford. Three years later the president of Stanford University, David Starr Jordan, stood on the summit and thought that he had "never seen a more magnificent mountain panorama."

The next major figure to enter the Kearsarge scene was George Davis, a topographer for the U.S. Geological Survey. In 1905 he climbed at least five major peaks in his quest for a perfect survey job. His Mt. Goddard quadrangle, published in 1915, was long held to be one of the finest examples of the cartographer's art.

Norman Clyde was not as active in this region as in some others; between 1922 and 1935 he made "only" fifteen or twenty first ascents, mostly of minor peaks. Independence Peak, south of Onion Valley, was a favorite of Clyde's, and he climbed it five times in 1926 and 1927.

Relatively few technical climbs have been done in the region, and the climbing history of the last few decades has been mostly class 3 and 4 routes on low-angle faces and ridges. The two major faces of the northern region, those on Mt. Clarence King and Mt. Cotter, were climbed in the early 1970s. The "big wall" of the Kings-Kern Divide, the face of the outer Ericsson Crag, was ascended in 1972.

There are many approaches into the Kearsarge Pass region, and most of these are from the east. From the west there are only two feasible approaches. Both western approaches begin from the end of the Kings Canyon Highway. Shortly after the trail starts, one comes to a major junction. If one chooses to continue up the South Fork of the Kings, and later Woods Creek, the peaks of the northern section of this chapter will be within striking distance. The other choice, the Bubbs Creek trail, leads into the heart of the Kearsarge area. From the roadhead to Vidette Meadow is thirteen miles.

From the east there are many possible routes over the Sierra crest. Excepting Taboose Pass, mentioned in the Palisades chapter, these routes are listed here in north to south order.

Sawmill Pass (11,347) connects the Woods Lake environs with Sawmill Creek on the east. To approach from the east, leave U.S. Highway 395 about ten miles north of Independence at the turnoff to the Division Creek Powerhouse. Shortly beyond the powerhouse is the trailhead. The elevation gain to the pass is 6,700 feet, and the ten-mile hike is an unmitigated horror of steep, dry terrain.

Baxter Pass (12,320+) is another strenuous route, involving an elevation gain of 6,300 feet in nine miles. Leave U.S. Highway 395 a few miles north of Independence and follow signs for the campground on Oak Creek. The roadhead is not far beyond. The trail leads to Baxter Lakes, just above the John Muir Trail.

North Dragon Pass (12,400+) lies 0.3 mile north-northeast of Dragon Peak and offers a one-day route from the Kearsarge roadhead to Rae Lakes. From the east follow the trail which ends at the lakes east of Dragon Peak and proceed toward the col right of the mountain. When part way to this col, traverse to the right around a square-topped peaklet north of the col. Cross the ridge which runs east of this peaklet near the point where it rises from the ridge. Continue to the right on the east side of the main crest for a while; then cross it and drop down toward Dragon Lake. Class 2–3.

Gould Pass (12,800+) is located about one-half mile north of Mt. Gould. From Golden Trout Lake the route is clear. Class 2. The pass can also be approached from Kearsarge Pass by ascending to the Rixford-Gould crest and then following the ridge northeast toward Dragon Peak. The descent to the lakes south of Dragon Lake is easy. Coming from these lakes to the pass, take the right-hand talus slope to the col.

Kearsarge Pass (11,760+) is by far the most popular entry into the region. The 9,200-foot-high roadhead is reached via a good highway from the town of Independence. The pass is about four or five miles from Onion Valley. The upper part of the trail is so well graded and obviously designed for pack animals that hikers have made major shortcuts. This "ecologically unsound" practice is quite obviously the common man's reaction to horse trails.

University Pass (12,640+) lies one-half mile southeast of University Peak. The northeast side, reached from Onion Valley via the Robinson Lake trail, often contains snow until late season, and an ice axe is helpful. The southwest side, which drops into Center Basin, is composed of steep talus. Although this pass provides a one-day route to the Kings-Kern Divide, it should not be used as an alternate to Kearsarge Pass unless the traveler is competent on rough, steep, and loose terrain.

Junction Pass (13,200+) was the route of the John Muir Trail until 1932, but the trail has not been maintained since. The class 2 pass affords a good cross-country route between the Shepherd Pass trail and Center Basin.

Shepherd Pass (12,000+) is one of the more dreadful east-side approaches in the range. The ascent from desert to alpine zone is an interminable ordeal of dryness and steepness. A 500-foot descent midway is a classic destroyer of morale, regardless of the direction one is traveling. The pass provides a direct way of reaching the southern portion of the Kings-Kern Divide, as well as the northern Whitney area and the Great Western Divide.

Other passes abound in the region; most are easy and can be traversed by backpackers as well as climbers. North to south, these are as follows.

Arrow Pass (11,600+) lies 0.75 mile southeast of Arrow Peak and connects the Bench Lake area with the lake at the head of Arrow Creek. Class 2.

Explorer Pass (12,080+) is located 0.6 mile north-northeast of Pyramid Peak, and just northwest of the second-to-last lake on the creek east of the mountain. A class 3 chute, often snow-filled, is found on the northwest side.

Baxter Col (12,480+) separates Mt. Baxter and Acrodectes Peak and offers a class 3 route between Woods Lake and the Baxter Lakes.

Basin Notch (10,800+) is the best way to reach Sixty Lakes Basin from the northern Rae Lakes. The class 1 route passes through a slot on the ridge one mile north of Fin Dome. Leave the Muir Trail at the pond between the two northernmost Rae Lakes.

Sixty Lake Col (11,680+) connects Gardiner and Sixty Lake basins. The class 1–2 pass lies one mile south of Mt. Cotter.

Rae Col (11,680+) lies 0.6 mile north-northwest of Glen Pass. It affords an easy, talus-covered route between the Glen Pass area and Sixty Lake Basin.

Gardiner Pass (11,200+) once had a trail, but it is no longer in prime condition. The traveler, however, will have little difficulty in crossing from Charlotte Creek into lower Gardiner Creek.

Deerhorn Saddle (12,560+) lies between Deerhorn Mountain and Mt. Stanford. The pass provides a class 2 route between Vidette Creek and the Harrison Pass area.

Andy's Foot Pass (13,600) is located immediately southeast of Gregory's Monument. It offers a high, class 2–3 crossing of the Kings-Kern Divide. Carry an ice axe until early August.

Harrison Pass (12,720+), once a well-used route, has not been maintained for many decades and traces of the trail are infrequently found. The south side is class 1; the north side, for the upper 300 feet, is a steep, miserable scree slope in late season. In early and mid-season the slope is composed of dangerously hard snow.

Ericsson Pass (12,560+) lies 0.4 mile northeast of Mt. Ericsson. In early season this pass is preferable to nearby Harrison Pass since there is less snow and the slope is not as steep. Class 2–3 climbing is encountered in the upper 200 feet on the north side.

Lucy's Foot Pass (12,400+) is an excellent method of connecting the East Lake area with the headwaters of the Kern River. The pass, located just west of Mt. Ericsson, is class 2 or 3. A cliff near the top on the north side can be turned on the west.

Milly's Foot Pass (12,240+) is northeast of Mt. Genevra. The

class 3 pass offers a convenient way of crossing the divide from
Lake Reflection. A diagonal ramp on the west side of the pass leads
to a short section of climbing at the very top. The other side is
easier.

Thunder Pass (12,720+) crosses the Kings-Kern Divide just east
of Thunder Mountain. Class 2.

Two topographical maps, Mt. Pinchot and Mt. Whitney, cover
the Kearsarge Pass region, though the Marion Peak quadrangle is
useful if approaching from Kings Canyon.

Pinchot Pass Area

Arrow Peak (12,958)

The northeast spur provides an enjoyable class 3 route; a few
knife-edge ridges must be traversed en route. The southeast slope
has been climbed: from the false summit to the south climb a
knife-edge ridge to the true summit. Another route begins from
Bench Lake and ascends to the saddle 0.4 mile east of the top. A
talus slope leads upward from here.

Arrow Ridge (12,188)

Class 1 from Arrow Peak.

Peak 12,000+ (0.5 SE of Bench Lake)

A low-angle apron on the northwest side of this peak has many
technical-climbing possibilities. One route, called Bench Lake
Boogie, has been done so far. Start climbing in a deceptively
easy-looking, left-facing open book and follow it for two pitches. A
few more pitches lead to the unroping point. III, 5.9.

Pyramid Peak (12,777)

The southeast ridge is class 3. Easier routes probably exist on the west side of the peak.

Peak 12,160+ (0.55 SSE of Pyramid Pk.)

Class 3 via the southeast face.

Peak 12,350 (1.1 ESE of Pyramid Pk.)

Class 2 or 3 from the west or via the south ridge.

Window Peak (12,085)

Class 3 via the east face. The broken ridge leading over from Castle Domes has been climbed, as has the ridge which leads toward Pyramid Peak.

Castle Domes (11,360+)

The highest dome is an easy climb from the lake east of Window Peak. The second most prominent dome is easy from the east.

Peak 12,285 (0.75 NW of Goodale Mtn.)

From the lake a mile southeast of Taboose Pass climb the class 3 west slope.

Goodale Mountain (12,790)

The class 3 summit rocks of this peak can be reached via the east slope (class 1) or from the saddle to the west (class 2).

Striped Mountain (13,120+)

The northeast and east slopes, reached from Taboose Pass, are class 2. The west ridge is class 2.

Peak 12,720+ (1 SW of Striped Mtn.)

Both the northwest ridge and the southeast ridge have been climbed; the latter is class 3.

Peak 13,259 (0.6 S of Striped Mtn.)

The south slopes and east ridge combination is class 2. The north face has been done and is class 3.

Mt. Pinchot (13,495)

Class 1 and 2 routes can be found on all sides of this mountain.

Mt. Wynne (13,179)

The traverse from nearby Mt. Pinchot is apparently class 3; easier routes can be made on the remaining sides of the peak.

Mt. Ickes (12,968)

The northeast and west ridges are class 2.

Crater Mountain (12,874)

Class 2 from almost any direction. Don't expect to find a crater on the top.

Mt. Perkins (12,591)

Class 2 via the west slope. The peak has been done from the east: from the end of the road in Armstrong Canyon hike up the canyon to about the 10,200-foot level; then head due north for about one-half mile to a ridge which runs east-northeast from a peaklet 0.6 mile north of Perkins. Follow the ridge to the peaklet; then go south over class 2 slopes to the top.

Colosseum Mountain (12,473)

The west ridge and the southwest slope are both class 1. From a chain of tiny lakes northwest of the peak, climb a class 2 chute. The north ridge is apparently class 4.

Mt. Cedric Wright (12,372)

This recently named peak commemorates the noted Sierra photographer. Class 1 from the lake to the southeast. A class 3 route has been made from the saddle between this peak and Colosseum Mountain.

Mt. Baxter (13,125)

Route 1. West Ridge. Climb to the saddle between Acrodectes

and Baxter from the north (class 3) or the south (class 2); then walk up the class 2 west ridge.

Route 2. Southwest Slopes. Class 2. Ascend a loose talus chute which rises above a tiny lake southwest of the mountain.

Route 3. South Ridge. Class 3. From the largest Baxter Lake climb to the notch in the summit ridge one mile south of the top. Follow the east side of the ridge to the summit, keeping as close to the ridgecrest as possible.

Route 4. Southeast Slopes. Class 2.

Route 5. North-Northeast Face. Class 3. Climb a wide chute which leads to the summit plateau, some 300 yards east of the top.

Route 6. North Ridge. Class 2. This ridge can be reached from either Stocking Lake or the headwaters of Sawmill Creek.

Acrodectes Peak (13,183)
Class 2 via either the west or east ridge. The south side of the peak is also a long talus trudge.

Peak 12,852 (0.95 W of Acrodectes Pk.)
The north ridge is class 2. A chute on the south face leads to the southwest ridge and is class 3.

Peak 12,804 (1.05 NW of Acrodectes Pk.)
The southeast ridge is class 3. Another route has been done: from Woods Lake head southwest to the ridge which leads to a plateau just west of the northwest glacier; then ascend the west slope to the top. Class 2.

Kearsarge Pass Region

Peak 12,160+ (1.1 N of Mt. Clarence King)
The two summits of this peak at the north end of the King Spur have been climbed and "require a rope."

Mt. Clarence King (12,905)

Route 1. Regular Route. 5.4. The saddle just south of the summit of this classic-shaped peak can be reached very easily from the west, or with a bit more difficulty (class 2–3) from Sixty Lake Basin. From the saddle ascend steep talus and sand slopes to the final rocks. Stay very close to the east drop-off and work upward over class 4 cracks and ledges. The difficulties increase about 150 feet below the top. A tiny hole under a conspicuous overhanging block can be used, or a steep jamcrack (5.0) and squeeze chimney around the corner to the left can be climbed. Either route brings one to the monolithic summit boulders. A short 5.4 pitch on the south side leads to the register. Protection is not necessary—the configuration of the rock provides enough safety—and the climbing is not easy; many persons have been defeated.

Route 2. Southeast Face. III, 5.8. Climb this clean, 800-foot-high wall directly in line with the summit. Two 5.8 cracks are encountered.

A chimney system a few hundred feet to the right of this route has been climbed, but nothing is known about the route.

Route 3. East Ridge. Class 4, except for the 5.4 summit block. The last several hundred feet of the ridge provide some airy and intricate class 4 climbing.

Route 4. Northwest Face. IV, 5.7. Begin climbing at the left side of the face, at the point where the wall joins the spur which runs out to the north. A class 4 ramp leads up 200 feet to this junction. Next, climb a 5.7 pitch in the main corner; then leave the corner and diagonal right for one lead. The next half-dozen or so pitches alternate horizontal traverses with diagonal sections, always keeping to the right. When feasible, climb upward about five pitches to the west ridge, some 300 feet west of the top. Climb the ridge to the summit boulders.

Mt. Cotter (12,721)

The south side of this peak offers numerous possibilities for class 2 and 3 ascents.

The north peak of Cotter has been climbed by at least two routes.

The north ridge is class 4. The smooth-appearing, 70-degree east face has been climbed: start climbing somewhat right of the center of the wall. On the second pitch make a giant rope-traverse or pendulum to the left into a new crack system. Only two aid points were used on the first ascent. IV, 5.9, A1.

Mt. Gardiner (12,907)

From the south ascend easy slopes to the lower, southern summit. A short, class 4, knife-edge ridge leads across to the main summit. The southeast ridge is quite easy and leads to the lower summit. The glacier on the northeast side of the peak has been used as a route.

Glacier Monument (11,165)

This peak, located west of Gardiner Pass, is easily climbed from the pass.

"Charlotte Dome" (Pk. 10,690, 2.05 SW of Mt. Gardiner)

The southern escarpment of this striking formation is one of the most beautiful pieces of granite in the High Sierra. The north side of the dome is class 3 and can be approached from Gardiner Pass. Two technical routes have been established. The south face is rated IV, 5.8 and begins in a deep recess at the left side of the face. Ten pitches of cracks, dihedrals, and chickenhead knobs lead to the summit. Another enjoyable route has been made on the southwest arete. This eleven-pitch route is rated IV, 5.9.

Mt. Bago (11,869)

Class 1 from the vicinity of Charlotte Lake. The south face, which rises above Junction Meadow, is very convoluted and impressive. At least one technical route has been done: from the meadow one will notice a very orange buttress split by a huge dihedral. The route ascends the right-hand skyline for 1,000 feet on excellent rock. IV, 5.7.

Peak 11,360+ (1 ESE of Mt. Bago)

Easy, except for the class 3 summit block.

Fin Dome (11,693)

This popular peaklet is very familiar to travelers in the Rae Lakes region. The regular route, class 3–4 in difficulty, lies on the west face. From the slopes just south of the dome, traverse upward diagonally to the north. After reaching the approximate center of the west face, begin zigzagging back and forth between ledges, ramps, and short cracks. If care is taken, a class 3–4 route can be followed, but it is very easy to get onto somewhat harder terrain.

The south side of the formation has been climbed by several routes, varying from class 4 to 5.6 in difficulty. The east face has also been done—two pitches, 5.7.

Peak 13,070 (0.6 N of Diamond Pk.)

Class 3 from Baxter Pass and class 2 from Diamond Peak.

Diamond Peak (13,126)

The west slope offers a long and arduous talus trudge. The ridge from Black Mountain has been traversed and is class 2. On the northeast side of the peak are two snow couloirs—the left one is class 3. The couloirs are easily approached from the Baxter Pass trail.

Mt. Mary Austin (13,040+)

This recently named peak is class 2 via the southeast slopes.

Black Mountain (13,289)

Class 2 from Dragon Lake. Also class 2 from the north. From Parker Lakes the east ridge can be climbed and is class 2.

Dragon Peak (12,995)

From the lakes to the east climb to the col just south of the peak. Follow the ridgecrest north; then work around onto the west face and climb to the class 3 summit pinnacle. The peak has also been reached via a class 3 traverse from Mt. Gould. The easiest way up the peak is from the lake basin to the southwest.

Mt. Gould (13,005)

This peak is an easy talus walk from Kearsarge Pass or Golden Trout Lake, but the summit rocks are class 3.

Peak 12,800+ (0.4 E of Mt. Rixford)

This good-looking peak is class 3 from all directions except the north, where a steep, loose cliff bars the way.

Mt. Rixford (12,890)

This uninteresting peak is a walk-up from Bullfrog Lake. One can also climb it from Mt. Gould; keeping below the ridgecrest makes this a class 2 venture. The northeast side of the mountain has been descended, but there is a lot of loose rock in this area.

Painted Lady (12,126)

Class 2 from the lakes just north of Glen Pass.

Kearsarge Peak (12,598)

Mining trails on the southeast side of the mountain lead almost to the top. More interesting routes have been done on the south side.

Kearsarge Pinnacles (11,680+ to 12,000+)

South of the Kearsarge Lakes is a row of jagged, unaesthetic pinnacles. These have been numbered from southeast to northwest. Since several numbering systems have been used, one should not be surprised to find that the summit register numbers differ from the present numeration. The pinnacles are generally climbed from the notches between them. Easy-to-reach notches from the north are: 3–4, 5–6, and 9–10. Notches 4–5 and 8–9 are more difficult to reach.

Class 3 and 4 routes can be discovered on Pinnacles 1 through 5. Pinnacle 6 can be climbed via a class 3 route from the 5–6 notch. An easy class 5 route has been made on the west face: from the 6–7 notch traverse east into a gully. Climb over an overhang and follow cracks and ledges upward to a prominent open book. Leave this halfway up, traverse right, and climb to a shoulder south of the top.

Pinnacle 7 is easy and popular. Pinnacle 8 can be climbed from the 7–8 notch and is class 5. Pinnacle 9 is easy class 4 from the 8–9 notch and also from the 9–10 notch.

Pinnacles 10, 11, and 12 are relatively easy and can be ascended from the 9–10 notch, from the north, or from Bullfrog Lake.

The Kearsarge Pinnacles from the north.

"Nameless Pyramid" (Pk. 11,920+, 0.5 SSE of Kearsarge Pass)

This peaklet, clearly visible from the Owens Valley, can be reached from Kearsarge Pass via the class 3 north ridge. A short, enjoyable, technical route has been done on the east face. From Heart Lake one can see the route, a long crack system which diagonals up and right to a notch just right of the summit. Opinions vary about the difficulty of this route; it is probably 5.7. Variations exist on the lower part; there may be entirely separate routes.

Peak 12,160+ (1.3 SSE of Kearsarge Pass)

The south arete is class 3.

University Peak (13,632)

Route 1. Northwest Side. Class 2. From the upper Kearsarge Lake proceed southeast and climb to the low gap west of the peak. Next, either climb the west ridge to the summit (class 2–3) or walk around a bit onto the easier southwest slope.

Route 2. South Slopes. Class 1–2. Ascend from Center Basin.

Route 3. Southeast Ridge. Class 2 from University Pass. Stay on the left side of the ridge if the easiest route is desired.

Route 4. East Side. From the end of the stream above Robinson Lake climb class 3 rock to the top.

Route 5. Northeast Ridge. From Robinson Lake climb the class 3–4 ridge.

Route 6. Northeast Face. III, 5.7. From Slim Lake walk to the base of the wall and climb easy gullies on the lower part of the face. After 800 feet of class 3 climbing, the steeper, slabby, upper 600-foot section is reached. This leads to the northeast summit.

Route 7. North Face. Class 3 via an inconspicuous route.

Independence Peak (11,744)

The north ridge is class 3; the mountain is easier from the northwest and west.

Center Basin Crags (12,480+)

These sharp pinnacles on the main Sierra crest have been numbered from north to south. Crag 1 is class 5 via its south arete. Crags 2, 3, and 4 have been traversed and are class 4. Crag 5 is an easy scramble from the north.

Mt. Bradley (13,289)

Class 2–3 from Center Basin via chutes. Class 2 from Pinyon Creek on the north. Also class 2 via the east slopes. The ridge from Center Basin Crags is class 3–4.

Kings-Kern Divide and Environs

East Vidette (12,350)

The east ridge is class 3. Class 4 routes can be found on the north and northwest sides of the peak. The west face has been climbed by means of a steep, shallow chute which ends about 300 yards south of the summit. Class 4.

East Spur (12,735)
Not much is known concerning the route or the rating.

West Vidette (12,560+)
From Lake 10,820 to the east climb to the saddle south of the peak and follow the ridge upward. Class 2.

West Spur (12,640+)
This peak, one-half mile south of West Vidette, has been climbed from East Lake. Another route has been done from Lake 10,820 to the northeast. Climb to the saddle north of the mountain and follow the ridge south. Class 1–2.

The Minster (12,240+)
This ragged ridge has been traversed from east to west.

Deerhorn Mountain (13,265)
This spectacular landmark has twin summits. The southeast summit is a bit higher than the other.

Route 1. Southwest Chute. Class 3 or 4. Climb to the notch between the twin summits; then climb the main peak via the arete or the face to its left.

Route 2. Southwest Face. Class 3 or 4. From the creek to the southwest, climb the face, aiming for a spot west of, and 300 feet below, the lower northwest summit. From here work around to the left and attain the northwest summit. The higher summit is but a scramble from here.

Route 3. West Side. Class 3. From either the north or the south, climb to a point a bit east of the low point between the Minster and Deerhorn. Climb the west ridge, staying mostly on its left side.

Route 4. Northwest Peak, Northeast Buttress. Class 3. From the upper reaches of Vidette Creek climb the buttress which leads directly to the lower summit.

Route 5. Southeast Peak, Northeast Ridge. Class 4. From near the bottom of the snow chute which drops down between the twin summits, climb up to the northeast ridge of the main peak, attaining the ridgecrest about halfway up. Follow the ridge until about 60 feet below the top; then ascend a class 4 pitch to the summit block.

Southeast of Deerhorn are two sharp satellite peaks. The southeast one has been climbed and is class 4–5 via a chute on the southwest side.

Center Peak (12,760)

The easiest route is via the east slopes and is class 2. Two other routes have been established. One goes up the impressive north side. Three chutes disgorge talus fans into Center Basin. Ascend the central chute until well inside it; then exit right into a chute which leads toward the northwest buttress. Ascend the buttress to a saddle; then wander back and forth to the summit. The third route lies to the right of the preceding route and about 100 yards right of the steepest section of the face. Climb directly up the class 3 face to a tunnel at its top. From here follow ledges to the summit.

Peak 13,280+ (0.75 NE of Mt. Keith)

The class 5 summit block can be reached easily either from Center Basin or from Anvil Camp on the Shepherd Pass trail.

Mt. Keith (13,977)

The northwest side of the peak is class 2, as are the southeast and northeast sides. The ridge from Junction Pass has been used as a route and is class 3.

Junction Peak (13,888)

Route 1. South Ridge. Class 3. Ascend Diamond Mesa and follow a knife-edge ridge to the top.

Route 2. West Ridge. From Forester Pass follow the west ridge, passing a subsidiary peak en route. Once on the main peak, stay a bit right and use various chutes as needed. Class 3.

As a variation, one can climb the steep snow (or ice) gully which leads to the col between the main and subsidiary peaks from the north.

Route 3. North Buttress. III, 5.7. This is the impressive left skyline of Junction Peak when observed from the John Muir Trail north of Forester Pass. Stay mostly on the right side of the crest of the buttress. Loose rock on this route makes two pitches real "horror problems."

Route 4. East Face. Class 3 or 4. Climb the right-hand couloir of two couloirs on the face.

Route 5. Southeast Ridge. Class 4. Ascend the ridge which leads to Junction from Shepherd Pass.

Peak 13,680+ (0.8 NW of Junction Pk.)

Class 2 from nearby Forester Pass.

Peak 13,760+ (1.1 NW of Junction Pk.)

From the lake south of the peak, climb to the ridge between Mt. Stanford and this peak. Follow the west ridge to the top. Class 3.

Mt. Stanford (13,963)

This high peak, lying just north of the Kings-Kern Divide, has several interesting routes, none of them trivial.

Route 1. South Ridge. Class 3. From the vicinity of Harrison Pass, climb up easy talus slopes to Stanford's south summit (Gregory's Monument). Exposed climbing then leads over to the true summit. Most of the short traverse is done on the east side of the classic knife-edge ridge.

Route 2. West Face, Right Side. Class 3–4. This route begins more or less directly below Stanford's south summit. Climb up and left along a steep ramp/gully. After a few hundred feet a watercourse is reached. Follow this upward for about 500 feet to a narrow, talus-filled chute. From the notch atop the chute, the summit is a five-minute scramble.

Route 3. West Face, Left Side. This class 3 route ascends the face to a ridge north of the summit. A short scramble leads to the top.

Route 4. North Ridge. Class 3. From the saddle between Stanford and Deerhorn, head east to the north ridge and wander up to the top. The north ridge has also been reached from the east by means of an arete which extends east from a point just south of Peak 13,414. This variation is also class 3.

Route 5. East Face. Class 3. Climb either a snow chute which lies directly below the summit or the face to its left.

Peak 13,414 (0.6 N of Mt. Stanford)

Class 2 from the northwest and from the southwest.

Caltech Peak (13,832)

The east ridge is class 3, as is the west face. The easiest route, however, is found on the southeast side.

Peak 13,030 (1.1 SSW of Caltech Pk.)

Class 3 from the southwest; all other sides of the peaklet are much easier.

Mt. Ericsson (13,608)

Route 1. South Ridge. This long, involved class 3 climb turns gendarmes and false summits on both the west and the east.

Route 2. West Flanks. From Lucy's Foot Pass follow the easy slopes to the class 3 summit rocks.

Route 3. Northwest Couloir. Class 4. From the talus slopes north of Lucy's Foot Pass climb the chute which ends at a notch between Ericsson and the first crag to the north. When about 100 feet below the notch, turn right and climb an icy couloir which leads to the ridgecrest a bit west of the summit. From here it is a walk.

Route 4. Northeast Ridge. Class 3 from Ericsson Pass.

Ericsson Crags (13,040+ to 13,120+)

North of Mt. Ericsson is a jumbled mass of rock cut by deep gullies, highlighted by airy ridges, and capped by several major crags and many minor ones. As seen from the vicinity of Harrison Pass, there are four major summits. Closest to Ericsson, and the most spectacular, is Crag 1A. The highest of the lot, Crag 1, is next. Then comes Crag 2, a pyramid-shaped mass, and Crag 3, with its impressive north face. On a spur running west of Crag 1 is the formidable-looking Crag 1W, about which nothing is known.

Crag 1A. Not much is known about this crag either, except that it can be climbed from near the upper reaches of Crag 1.

Crag 1. The class 4 route lies on the southeast face. From the west ascend the chute which ends in the notch between Crags 1 and 1A. Two-thirds of the way up this chute is a branch; head up the left fork and climb to a broad shoulder just south of the top. From here attain an open chimney on the southeast face and follow this chimney.

Crag 2. From the west ascend the chute leading to the 2–3 notch until it is possible to leave it and enter the next-to-highest subsidiary chute on the right. This leads to the northwest face of Crag 2. Take the right-hand branch of this subsidiary chute; then exit left, class 4, just before reaching some caves. From here it is easy going to the top.

Crag 3. From the west ascend a chute leading to the 2–3 notch. When nearly to the top of this chute, traverse left into the next chute. Exit this new chute by means of a delicate chimney which leads to the south ridge of Crag 3. Follow this ridge for a while; then wander up to the top. Class 4. A fine route has been done on the 1,300-foot north face of the crag. Begin climbing just right of a prominent buttress near the middle of the face. IV, 5.7.

Mt. Genevra (13,055)

The summit rocks of this peak are class 3. Class 2 routes lead to these rocks from the east, from Milly's Foot Pass, and from the southwest. A class 3 route has been made on the north face: climb a snow chute which leads to the summit ridge, just west of the top. A snow chute on the south side has been descended.

Mt. Jordan (13,344)

This peak has two summits; the southern is the higher and is a short class 4 scramble. From the east climb to the saddle between the two summits and follow the class 3 ridge to the summit pinnacle. The north face of the north summit has been done and is class 3. The west side of the peak is class 2, although the summit block, as noted, is class 4.

Peak 12,070 (0.8 NNE of Mt. Jordan)

Class 3 from the south saddle. This peak was called Crag Reflection by David Starr Jordan on his 1899 map.

Peak 12,513 (1 SE of Mt. Jordan)

Class 3 from the south.

Peak 13,090 (0.4 SW of Mt. Jordan)

A class 2–3 chute on the east face leads to the ridge just south of the top. A chute on the south side of the peak is class 3. The north summit, by the way, is the higher.

Peak 13,231 (1.2 SW of Mt. Jordan)

The southwest face is class 2; the summit rocks are more difficult. The east face has also been climbed.

The Great Western Divide

Many who have stood atop Mt. Whitney have wondered about the serrated ridges and rocky pyramids to the west, but few of them have ever visited the Great Western Divide. Forty-five miles in length, the divide is the most conspicuous sub-range in the Sierra. Only one road approaches anywhere near the remote ridge. Although mountaineers have been attracted to the major peaks for over a century, the summit registers reflect the fact that climbing is not as popular here as in other parts of the range, and the signature of Norman Clyde is still to be marveled at in many of these historic books—for a while at least. Over half the entries in many registers have been made in the 1970s by climbers who use pages of the valuable books to record sketches, poems, furious messages to previous guidebook authors, advice to future ascenders, and unacclimated paeans to the Chap even higher who created such a beautiful, desolate landscape.

The Great Western Divide begins near the confluence of Bubbs Creek and the South Fork of the Kings River and rises almost immediately to the Mt. Brewer group, with its impressive collection of east faces. Just south of this point the Kings-Kern Divide shoots across from pointed Thunder Mountain toward the main crest. Immediately below this junction lies the easily recognized Table Mountain; its summit plateau is the biggest in the Sierra and is a favorite landing spot for government helicopters. A few miles farther down the divide is one of its most distinguishing landmarks, the tower of Milestone Mountain. The divide next makes a short excursion to the southwest, and Triple Divide Peak is soon seen; this marks the watershed boundary between the Kings, Kern, and Kaweah rivers. Leaving the divide at this point is its most significant spur, the Kaweah Peaks Ridge. This is one of the most jagged and remote places in the range, and its forbidding northern sentinel, Black Kaweah, is one of the Sierra's most awesome peaks. The volcanic rock of the region changes radically from black to red in a few thousand feet; this rock is so loose and friable that the area has proved a death zone for the unwary.

The main divide continues south to Kaweah Gap. West of this pass is a stunning array of granite cliffs and towers—the Hamilton Lakes region. Continuing south, the ridge soon rises to its final cluster of rocky summits, near Mineral King.

Although the Great Western Divide continues south for another fifteen miles or so, the peaks quickly become low, forested, and of litttle interest to the mountaineer. An exception to this is the Needles, a recently developed rockclimbing area twenty-five miles south of Mineral King. This area, and a few others scattered around the Giant Forest in western Sequoia National Park, are covered in the "Peripheral Climbing Areas" section. While not truly in the High Sierra, the boundaries do not need to be stretched unduly to include these popular sites.

The familiar figure of William Brewer dominates the exploratory period of the northern Great Western Divide. When he and fellow members of the California Geological Survey were in the Kings Canyon area in 1864, they climbed Mt. Silliman and descended into the watershed of Roaring River. From here they saw a rocky pyramid to the east; Brewer and Charles Hoffmann climbed it on July 2. Other members of the Survey later gave it the name of their field leader, Brewer. From the top the pair had a marvelous panorama of the Sierra, and dominating the view to the east was a great chain of high peaks. One they named Mt. Tyndall and another became Mt. Williamson. Fourteen miles away was "the culminating peak of the Sierra," which they named after their leader, Josiah Whitney. This remote peak was immediately coveted by Clarence King, and on July 4 he and Richard Cotter obtained permission from Brewer and set out on their famous attempt on Whitney, which resulted in the first ascent of Tyndall instead.

Only a few peaks were climbed in the nineteenth century. Sheepherders were in the upper Kings and Kern watersheds during the 1860s and undoubtedly climbed a few peaks, but an ascent of Sawtooth Peak in 1871 by a deer hunter is the earliest recorded ascent in the southern part of the divide.

During the 1870s a prospector named William Wallace searched for riches in the high country of the Great Western Divide and in 1881 went across the Chagoopa Plateau and the Kern trench to make an early ascent of Mt. Whitney. On the return trip Wallace and two compatriots, Wales and Wright, made the first ascent of the highest point of the Kaweah Peaks Ridge. A high, isolated mass, Mt. Kaweah is located at the extreme south end of the ridge. Unlike its spectacular neighbors, Mt. Kaweah is a very gentle peak. For many years it was thought that the Kaweah Ridge was part of the main divide, but in 1897 William Dudley, another noteworthy pioneer of the region, proved otherwise. He showed that the Kaweah River was misnamed: it originated not in the Kaweahs, but west of the main divide.

In the summer of 1912 Charles Michael, who has been mentioned earlier as a Sierra explorer who delighted in class 3+ solo climbing, made the first ascent of the pinnacle on the Kaweah Ridge which now bears his name. During the same summer Francis Farquhar, William Colby, and Robert Price climbed Milestone and Midway mountains. Their register on the latter peak was still intact in 1970 and was unquestionably the oldest existing record on a Sierra peak.

Although Michael had climbed a pinnacle on the jagged Kaweah Ridge, the distinctive summit nipple of the Black Kaweah awaited its first footsteps. Farquhar had studied the peak and reported that the west ridge would be the best bet. James Hutchinson, who since 1899 had made such classic first ascents as Matterhorn Peak, Mt. Abbot, Mt. Humphreys, and North Palisade, came into the Kaweahs with several companions in 1920. He too studied the peak, and of the proposed west ridge route later wrote, "It looked pretty fair, but I must confess there were some deep, ugly gashes in it, which did not appeal to me greatly." Nevertheless, the fifty-three-year-old Hutchinson, Duncan McDuffie, and a packer with the curious biblical name of Onis Imus Brown set out at dawn, carrying "an emergency fifty feet of rope." Part way up, the route "was absolutely appalling—the knife-edge running up to the peak, and the peak itself [was] seamed, cracked, scarred, and broken by weathering as on no other mountain we had ever climbed; the whole ridge appeared to be disintegrating rapidly . . . . Our footsteps followed a most uncertain zigzag course, and had they been plotted would have indicated anything but a temperance movement. The way those ragged rocks were broken, splintered, massed, and piled together, helter-skelter, would have rejoiced the heart of a cubist artist. Again and again I was reminded of. . . 'The Nude Descending the Stairs.' "

At a notch 600 feet below the summit the situation was "hopeless and desperate." Nonetheless, the intrepid team persevered and, on top by 2 P.M., "spontaneously set up a mighty shout of joy . . . . The only sign of life having been there before was an eagle's feather on the extreme summit. This we carried away as a trophy."

Approaches to the Great Western Divide are numerous; only the standard ones will be mentioned here. The Mt. Brewer group can be approached from Kings Canyon in either of two ways. A ten-mile trail leads to Sphinx Lakes, under the northwest shadow of the group. A fourteen-mile trail goes up Bubbs Creek and then East Creek to East Lake, an adequate base for routes on the east side of the group. East Lake can also be reached via the sixteen-mile trail over Kearsarge Pass.

The Milestone Mountain group is best reached via the long, arduous trail over Shepherd Pass. Allow two days for this grind. The west side of the group can be reached via the twenty-six-mile-long hike from Kings Canyon, using the Sphinx Creek and Cloud Canyon trails.

The fine rockclimbing area at Hamilton Lake is reached via the High Sierra Trail, which originates at Crescent Meadow, in the Giant Forest. Sixteen miles of up and down walking lead to Valhalla.

The Kaweahs can be reached easily from Mineral King via Glacier and Cyclamen Lake passes. Any other approach will involve at least two days of steady marching.

The peaks in the southern part of the Great Western Divide are very easily attained from the roadhead at Mineral King via any of a half-dozen trails

Many passes can be used by the climber in this region; most are simply talus trudges and can be done with heavy loads. North to south, some of these passes are:

Brewer Creek Pass (12,640+) crosses the Great Western Divide 0.45 mile southeast of Mt. Brewer and connects Brewer Creek with Ouzel Creek. Class 2.

Longley Pass (12,400+) lies just southeast of South Guard and is very easy.

Milestone Pass (12,960+), located immediately southeast of Milestone Mountain, affords a high crossing of the Kern Ridge. It is the route of choice to connect the Colby Pass area with the upper Kern Basin. Class 2.

Triple Divide Pass (12,160+) is located just northeast of Triple Divide Peak. It offers a class 2 crossing from Cloud Canyon to the Kern-Kaweah River.

Lion Lake Pass (11,600+) is a class 2 saddle one-half mile west of Triple Divide Peak. It crosses the divide which separates the Kings and Kaweah rivers.

Miner's Pass (11,920+), also called Coppermine Pass, crosses Glacier Ridge about 0.3 mile north of its junction with the Kings-Kaweah divide and is an excellent high route between Deadman and Cloud canyons. Class 2.

Lion Rock Pass (11,680+) lies one-half mile east of Lion Rock. Combined with Lion Lake Pass, this class 2 saddle allows the climber quick and easy traveling between Cloud Canyon and the Kaweahs.

Pants Pass (12,000+) crosses the Kaweah Peaks Ridge just

northwest of Peak 12,415. From Lake 10,730 in Nine Lakes Basin climb rough talus to the pass. Coming the other direction, proceed to the tarn just north of Lake 11,380 near the headwaters of the Kern-Kaweah River. A steep avalanche chute leads to the obvious pass. Class 2–3.

Pyra-Queen Col (12,800+) is located 0.55 mile northeast of Black Kaweah. This class 2 pass is an excellent route to take across the Kaweah Peaks Ridge between Nine Lakes and Kaweah basins.

Kaweah Pass (12,320+) is found immediately northeast of Mt. Kaweah on the broad saddle which contains Lake 12,328. This pass allows the traveler to cross from the High Sierra Trail to the Kern-Kaweah River. Class 2.

Glacier Pass (11,040+) lies 0.6 mile east-southeast of Empire Mountain and can be reached very easily from the final switchbacks of the Sawtooth Pass trail. Class 2–3; carry an ice axe until late August.

Cyclamen Lake Pass (11,040+) crosses the Great Western Divide one-half mile northeast of Cyclamen Lake. The pass separates the Cliff Creek watershed from Big Five Lakes and is an integral part of the Mineral King–Kaweah Ridge route. Class 3.

Three topographical maps are necessary to cover this area: Mineral King, Triple Divide Peak, and Mt. Whitney.

North of Kaweah Gap

Cross Mountain (12,185)
Class 2 from most directions, but a class 3 route has been done on the northwest face.

Peak 12,893 (0.95 NNE of North Guard)
It is rather odd that this beautiful, very prominent peak is unnamed. Class 4 via the northwest ridge; class 3 from the saddle to

the south. A technical route has been done on the northeast face: follow a corner to an obvious, diagonal, ice-covered ledge midway up the wall. Traverse left on the ledge to a prow which leads directly to the summit. The route is rated IV, 5.8.

Peak 12,600 (0.65 NNE of North Guard)

This bump on a ridge is easy class 3 via the northeast side.

North Guard (13,327)

The south slopes and southeast ridge of this fine peak are class 3. Another, harder, route has been made on the northeast side. From the north forks of Ouzel Creek ascend the northeast flank of the peak to a shoulder or col north-northeast of the summit. From the shoulder climb a short crack on the prow to a platform; then head right on the broken rock of the north face. Another class 4 crack leads to easy ground and the top.

Mt. Brewer (13,570)

This symmetrical peak dominates the northern part of the Great Western Divide.

Route 1. Southwest Side. Class 1–2. From Brewer Creek climb to the notch just south of the peak and follow the ridge to the top.

Route 2. Northwest Slopes. Easy from the north fork of Brewer Creek.

Route 3. Northeast Couloir. Class 2 or 3. To the right of the impressive northeast face is a short couloir usually filled with snow. Climb this to the north ridge, which is followed to the summit.

Route 4. Northeast Face. III, 5.7. A large rib runs directly up the face to the summit. Begin climbing in the first chimney right of the overhangs at the base of this rib and ascend for about 200 feet. From here traverse right into the next chimney and proceed up it until it opens out. A short section up and right leads to several class 4 pitches. Aim now for the higher of two notches which may be seen right of the summit. Attain the summit ridge between the two notches.

Route 5. East Side. Class 2. This is the most popular route on

Brewer and is seen easily from East Lake. Ascend the long, gentle ridge which lies between the middle and south forks of Ouzel Creek. The ridge terminates just left of the summit pyramid. Pass through a small notch to reach the south ridge and follow this to the top.

Peak 12,960+ (0.9 ESE of Mt. Brewer)

From the south fork of Ouzel Creek, the sharp, loose northeast ridge can be climbed and is class 3. Both the north and south faces have also been climbed and are class 2 or 3.

Peak 11,520+ (1.9 ENE of Mt. Brewer)

This "peak" is actually a three-quarter-mile-long ridge which overlooks East Lake. The north and south faces have been done; the latter is class 3. The southwest ridge offers a nice class 3 route involving towers, blocks, and knife-edge ridges.

South Guard (13,224)

Class 2 from Longley Pass or from the Brewer-South Guard saddle.

Thunder Mountain (13,588)

From Lake 12,280 to the east, climb up onto the east ridge, reaching it at a point just right of the apparent high point. Drop down a short distance on the other side of the ridge and head toward the mountain. Cross a square block in the notch between the south and middle summits; then traverse up across the east face of the middle summit to the notch between it and the north summit. A class 3–4 jamcrack on the southwest side of the north summit leads to the high point. The east ridge can also be reached from the lake basin northeast of the peak.

Peak 12,560+ (1.35 W of Thunder Mtn.)

Class 2 from Table Creek. The following class 3–4 route has been established: climb the north face to the west ridge and follow the ridge to the top.

Table Mountain (13,630)

Route 1. Northeast Face. Class 3–4. From Lake 12,280 climb into the obvious, steep snow couloir which ends on the plateau only a few hundred feet southeast of the top.

Route 2. East Side. Class 3. From the tiny lake about one-half mile to the southeast of the summit, climb up the short, broken face to the plateau.

Route 3. South Side. From the lake one mile south-southeast of the top, climb toward the wide southern escarpment of the peak. A distinct brown ledge will be seen diagonaling across the central part of the face toward the upper right. There are several direct routes to this ledge—class 3–4. It also can be reached via class 3 ledges on the extreme left. The brown ledge and the sections above are easy scrambling. The summit cairn is at the far end of the plateau.

Route 4. West Ridge. From Table Creek ascend a chute on the south side of the ridge, near the east corner, to the southwest edge of the summit plateau. Class 3.

Route 5. Southwest summit. This jagged peaklet, virtually identical in height with the main peak, lies just southwest of the southern part of the summit plateau. Class 3 from the top of Route 3, or from the lake at the start of the same route.

Midway Mountain (13,666)

This peak is distinguished only by the fact of its being the high point of the Great Western Divide. A class 2 route can be found on the ridge which falls into Milestone Creek. It is equally easy from the west.

Milestone Mountain (13,641)

The striking summit pinnacle is a familiar landmark to many Sierra travelers. From the east the last few hundred feet appear to be a serious undertaking. The view of the Kaweahs from the top is one of the greatest Sierra sights.

Route 1. From the East. From Milestone Creek climb toward a steep talus fan which leads up alongside the summit tower. At the head of the talus, climb to a notch at the upper left; then work around onto the classic class 3 west ridge.

Route 2. Northwest Side. From Lake 11,523 west of the peak, climb up the northwest flank to the west ridge and follow it to the top. Class 3.

Route 3. From the South. From Milestone Bowl climb loose rock to the west ridge and follow it to the top.

Route 4. From the Southeast. From Milestone Pass (between the peak and Peak 13,520+) climb over gendarmes to the summit tower. This is a short but hard route.

Peak 13,255 (0.6 SW of Milestone Mtn.)
Class 1 or 2 from Colby Pass. The east side of the south ridge is class 3.

Peak 13,520+ (0.6 SE of Milestone Mtn.)
This multi-acre summit can be reached, class 3, from Milestone Pass. It is easier from the south.

Peak 13,186 (1.5 SE of Milestone Mtn.)
This peak on the Kern Ridge is class 2 via the upper west slopes.

Kern Point (12,789)
Class 2 from the west or southwest.

Peak 12,600 (0.4 SW of Colby Pass)
Class 3 from Colby Pass, and class 2 from the southwest.

Whaleback (11,726)
Nothing is known about either the route or the difficulty of this fine-looking peak.

Peak 12,237 (1.8 NW of Whaleback)
This peak, near the northern end of Glacier Ridge, is class 2 or 3.

Peak 12,416 (1.8 SW of Whaleback)
This striking peak, the high point of Glacier Ridge, was one of the

last Sierra mountains to be ascended. The south side is class 2–3; the summit block is class 4. A technical route, rated II, 5.7, has been done on the north face. Five pitches of climbing up a diagonal crack system constitute the route.

Peak 12,640+ (0.7 NE of Triple Divide Pk.)

Class 3 via the southwest slopes.

Triple Divide Peak (12,634)

This peak is the watershed division between the Kern, Kings, and Kaweah rivers. From the saddle north of Lion Lake ascend the class 3 west ridge. Another route wanders up and around gendarmes on the south ridge—class 3. The east ridge is the easiest route—class 2.

Lion Rock (12,320+)

Class 2 from Tamarack Lake. A chute on the east or northeast side of the formation provides an interesting class 3 route. The south ridge has been done also and is easy.

Mt. Stewart (12,205)

Class 2 from Kaweah Gap. The southeast slope from Nine Lakes Basin is equally easy. A technical route, rated III, 5.6, has been established on the 1,200-foot-high north face. Begin climbing on the large, snow-covered platform which is seen below two parallel buttresses. Stay a bit left of the left buttress.

"Angel Wings" (Pk. 10,252, 1.7 W of Mt. Stewart)

The southern escarpment of the Angel Wings is the highest, steepest, and most spectacular rock wall in Sequoia National Park. The actual summit was not reached until 1971, though two technical routes were done earlier.

Route 1. West Side. Class 2 and 3 routes can be done from Lone Pine Creek, but the summit rocks are definitely class 4.

Route 2. South Face. V, 5.8, A4. High on the right-hand portion of the most massive part of the face one will easily spot a huge chimney or dihedral gouged into the rock. This steep feature is the route in the upper half of this climb. Begin climbing on the monolithic wall below the chimney/dihedral and, after a few pitches, reach a prominent chimney/crack. Above this, proceed to the Upper Bearpaw Meadow, a patch of 45-degree grass. One now enters the chimney/dihedral. A few pitches up this is the notorious House of Cards, a section requiring some caution. The climbing remains continuously hard and time-consuming all the way up the chimney. Only the last bit is easier.

Route 3. South Arete. V, 5.9, A3. About one-quarter mile east of the preceding route is a spectacular arete which curves upward to the main summit tower of the Angel Wings. Climb 500 feet of jumbled, mostly class 4 rock to a headwall which requires aid and strenuous jamming. Above, use aid to surmount a prominent, black ceiling. Just above this, move right over difficult rock and then head up toward a conspicuous chimney system. Several pitches up this lead to somewhat easier climbing and eventually the top.

Peak 11,598 (1.8 NW of Elizabeth Pass)

The west slope is class 2. A route rated III, 5.8 has been done on the 800-foot-high northeast face. Climb into a dihedral system slightly left of the center of the face and follow it to the top.

Peak 11,830 (0.55 NW of Elizabeth Pass)

Class 2 from the trail west of Elizabeth Pass. A route has been done on the spectacular northeast arete. After one straightforward pitch, climb three pitches of tricky cracks and chimneys. III, 5.8.

The Kaweahs

Peak 13,140 (0.6 NW of Kaweah Queen)

Class 2 from the southwest.

Kaweah Queen (13,360+)

Class 2 from Peak 13,140 or via the slopes on the west.

Peak 13,232 (0.4 E of Kaweah Queen)

A chute on the south face is class 3 or 4. The northeast ridge is easier.

Black Kaweah (13,765)

Route 1. West-Northwest Ridge. Class 3. Gain the ridge from the south and follow it, keeping on its right side, until just below the top. Enter a wide chute and follow it back to the ridge and scramble to the top.

Route 2. Southwest Face. Class 4. From the lake southwest of the peak, climb loose, high-angle rock to the base of the actual face. Two chutes will be seen above: climb the right-hand one for about 100 feet; then cross to the left-hand one and follow it almost to the summit. Snow lingers in this chute until late season.

Route 3. Southwest Ridge. Class 4. Follow the long, conspicuous ridge to the summit.

Route 4. South Face. IV, 5.7. Begin climbing just left of a huge, prominent dihedral. Angle up and left and wander upward for fourteen pitches, following the safest path. Some of the face-climbing pitches are hard to protect, and most are 5.5 or harder.

Route 5. East Ridge. From the basin southeast of the peak head toward the small notch which lies between Pyramidal Pinnacle and

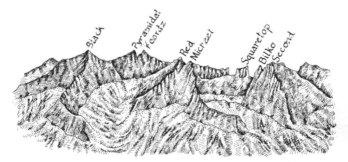

The Kaweah Peaks Ridge as seen from the southwest.

Koontz Pinnacle. Before reaching the notch, however, work up and left, under Pyramidal, to the low point of the main ridge. Follow the ridge toward Black Kaweah, avoiding the many gendarmes. Later, cross several couloirs to a sloping ledge and climb a chute to the summit. Class 4.

One can also reach the east ridge from Lake 11,705 to the north via a class 4 face.

"Pyramidal Pinnacle" (Pk. 13,600+, 0.4 E of Black Kaweah)

From the lake basin south of Black Kaweah climb to the low point mentioned in Route 4 of Black Kaweah. The pinnacle can be reached from here via class 4 rock.

"Koontz Pinnacle" (Pk. 13,600+, 0.5 E of Black Kaweah)

From the lake basin south of Black Kaweah climb the first chute right of the one which leads to the Pyramidal-Koontz notch. Near the top of the chute traverse over to the notch and scramble to the summit. Class 4.

Red Kaweah (13,760+)

Class 3 from Lake 11,825 on the west.

"Michael's Pinnacle" (Pk. 13,680+, 0.1 SE of Red Kaweah)

From the southwest, climb to the southeast ridge of the pinnacle; then wander along an intricate route to the top. Class 4.

"Squaretop" (Pk. 13,520+, 1.3 NW of Mt. Kaweah)

From the southwest ascend to the col between Squaretop and the next pinnacle to the southeast. From the col climb the exposed southeast face for two pitches to a broad ledge. Take a chute on the right to another series of ledges; then work up and left to the summit ridge. Class 4. The northwest face has also been climbed and can be reached from a chute north of the peak. Also class 4.

"Bilko Pinnacle" (Pk. 13,360+, 1.2 NW of Mt. Kaweah)
This is the pinnacle immediately southeast of Squaretop. It is a class 3 ascent from the Squaretop-Bilko col. Another route is found on the southwest side, where a steep chute leads to the southwest ridge. One class 4 pitch is encountered.

"Second Kaweah" (Pk. 13,680+, 1.05 NW of Mt. Kaweah)
Class 2 via the south slope. Three pinnacles on this peak's northwest ridge have also been climbed.

Mt. Kaweah (13,802)
This huge, but unspectacular, mass is the highest peak of the southwestern High Sierra. The slopes from the Chagoopa Plateau are trivial but long. The more interesting route up the ridge from Kaweah Basin is class 4.

Peak 13,285 (1.4 ENE of Mt. Kaweah)
Class 2 from the south.

Red Spur (13,183)
Class 3 via the southwest ridge.

Picket Guard Peak (12,302)
The north ridge is class 3; the south side of the mountain is easy.

South of Kaweah Gap

"Hamilton Dome" (Pk. 9,770, 1.9 WNW of Eagle Scout Pk.)
This beautifully shaped formation was not climbed until recently. Two routes have been put up. A gully on the east side provides a short 5.6 route. The longer north ridge offers seven pitches of excellent climbing. II, 5.7.

"Hamilton Towers" (ca. 10,000, ca. 1.4 WNW of Eagle Scout Pk.)

On the ridge between Hamilton and Eagle Scout creeks is a row of towers. Several have been climbed via class 4 and 5 routes. The third tower from the east has a 5.8 route on its east ridge.

Eagle Scout Peak (12,040)

Class 2 from the east.

Lippincott Mountain (12,260)

The east ridge and the southeast slopes are class 2; the northwest ridge is class 3.

Peak 11,760+ (0.75 S of Lippincott Mtn.)

Class 4 by the northeast ridge.

Mt. Eisen (12,160)

The west slope is easy, as is the southeast ridge from Black Rock Pass. A class 3 route can be worked out from the small lake with an island, northeast of Eisen.

Empire Mountain (11,509)

Class 2 from the Sawtooth Pass trail.

Peak 11,440+ (1 E of Empire Mtn.)

The south slopes are class 2. The north face, which rises above Spring Lake, is nearly a thousand feet high, and contains a technical route rated IV, 5.9. Climb into a dihedral slightly right of the center of a buttress. All of the nine pitches are 5.7 or harder, and four of the first five leads are 5.9. Another route has been done, probably to the left of the biggest face. Follow a direct crack and dihedral system— III, 5.6.

Sawtooth Peak (12,343)

Class 2 from Sawtooth Pass. The face and buttress above Columbine Lake offers a nice route. Climb either a rib or the face to the right. The rib peters out after a while and the climbing becomes serious. Traverse to the left; then climb more or less straight up to the summit. III, 5.8, A1. There are several variations on this route which appear to be about the same difficulty.

Mineral Peak (11,550)
Class 2 from Monarch Lake.

Needham Mountain (12,467)
Class 2 from the south or southeast. A class 3 couloir on the north side of the peak leads to the easy east ridge. Another route proceeds from Lost Canyon to the saddle between Needham and Sawtooth; follow the easy west ridge from here. Class 3. A route rated IV, 5.7 has been done on the northwest face.

Peak 11,861 (1.55 NE of Needham Mtn.)
The northeast ridge is class 3.

Peak 11,680+ (1.3 NE of Needham Mtn.)
Class 3 from the north. Easy scree slopes are found on the south side of the peak, but the two summit "fingers" are class 3.

Peak 11,772 (1.2 NNW of Needham Mtn.)
Easy from the south, but the summit rocks are class 3.

Peak 12,320+ (0.8 ESE of Needham Mtn.)
The south ridge is class 3. A technical route has been done on the north side of the mountain. It lies on the obvious buttress seen on the map 0.4 mile north-northwest of the summit. The route follows the most obvious line; this slants up and left to an obvious arete. Continue up the arete to the top. III, 5.9.

Rainbow Mountain (12,000+)
Class 2 from either Franklin Pass or Franklin Lake.

Peak 11,680+ (1 ESE of Rainbow Mtn.)
  A chimney on the north side of the peak provides a class 3 route.

Florence Peak (12,432)
  Route 1. From Franklin Pass. Follow the class 2 northeast ridge.
  Route 2. East Side. Class 4 from the Rattlesnake Creek region.
  Route 3. Direct Northwest Face. This route heads directly up the 1,000-foot face above the Franklin Lakes. Rope up in the center of the face and climb upward left of a small pedestal. After four pitches a huge ledge is reached. Two pitches higher is another ledge; walk to the right on this for about 100 feet and climb a crack which diagonals up and right to the summit area. The climbing on this route is quite sustained. III, 5.8.
  Route 4. The Great Chimney. III, 5.6. A large chimney will be seen on the northwest face. Ascend the right-hand wall of the chimney for three pitches; then, just beneath huge blocks, exit right to easier ground. Scramble to a headwall where two pitches lead to scrambling and the summit.
  Route 5. The Ramp. Left of the Great Chimney on the northwest face is a long ramp which angles up and right. Climb this until well up the face; then work left to the north-northwest ridge and climb to the top. II, 5.1.

Vandever Mountain (11,947)
  Easy from Farewell Gap. A route has been done in the northwest couloir: from an all-year snowfield, climb in the corner between Vandever and the wall which leads to a saddle north of the peak. II, 5.0. The schist ridge just right of the northwest couloir can also be climbed and is class 3.

Peripheral Climbing Areas

"The Watchtower"
  The Watchtower is a spectacular, 1,000-foot-high formation located near the head of Tokopah Valley, a few miles east of the

General's Highway. The blade-like rock lies about one-half mile southwest of Tokopah Falls. The back side is almost reached by the trail west of Heather Lake. A technical route, rated V, 5.8, A4, lies on the northeast prow. Begin climbing just left of an enormous right-facing open book on the lower face. Intricate aid climbing up discontinuous cracks forms much of the lower difficulties. Higher, the route is mainly free climbing.

Moro Rock

Moro Rock, a prominent and monolithic dome, is located in the Giant Forest region of western Sequoia National Park. A trail, involving a section of stairs, leads up the north side.

Route 1. West Side. Class 4–5. This route begins part way down the western face of the rock and finishes on the trail near the top.

Route 2. South Face. III, 5.7(?). Start climbing on the lower side of the main southern prow of the dome where it rises above a wooded ridge. Two class 4 pitches lead to a long, steep chimney. Several more pitches above this lead to the summit. Difficult climbing and routefinding are found in the middle section.

Route 3. East Side. II, 5.6(?), A2. Descend east from the base of the steps and traverse about 100 yards south along the base of the east face. Scramble up to a crack; this is the only difficult pitch. Keep the steps out of reach by bearing left on the upper 300 feet.

"Castle Rock Spire"

This spectacular pinnacle is the finest in the Sierra, outside of Yosemite Valley. The south side is about 300 feet high; the down-hill side approaches 1,000 feet in height. The spire can be seen easily from Moro Rock in certain lighting. The giant wall of the Fin lies just to the east. The pinnacle is located one-eighth of an inch left of the C in Castle Rocks, in the lower left corner of the Triple Divide Peak quadrangle.

The best approach begins at the Buckeye Flat Campground, near Hospital Rock on the General's Highway. Follow the Paradise Creek trail for one and a half miles until the trail makes a definite and final departure from the stream. After 150 yards or so the trail passes through an area of huge, dead logs. Near this point an old, faint path cuts sharply left. Follow this track for three or four miles as it ascends east toward Dome Creek. Leave the trail at the second rocky gully (the first usually has water until August) and follow it upward. This gully is the one which separates the Fin from the spire. The approach involves an elevation gain of about 4,000 feet.

Route 1. Regular Route. III, 5.8, A2. From the notch behind the spire traverse out onto the east face. Two horizontal class 4 pitches lead to a crack; this later turns into a gully which leads up behind a large flake. Pass through the corridor near the top of the flake; then drop down about 50 feet to a flared corner. Direct aid climbing leads up this for 50 feet or so to an overhang. This is turned on the left via two bolts. Climb a crack to a belay alcove below another overhang. The next pitch is the crux and the routefinding is a bit devious. Traverse up and right about 40 feet to an inconspicuous corner; then traverse straight left to a crack which slants leftward. Follow this to a belay alcove. Climb over another overhang and enter an easy chimney. Belay at its top. An aid pitch leads up and left toward a notch; belay on small ledges. The summit pitch is easy except for a few aid placements in a corner. Rappel the route to the end of the traverse; from here a 150-foot rappel ends in the main approach gully.

Route 2. Northeast Face. V, 5.7, A4. This long route ascends the decomposed corner which rises above the approach gully. Two pitches of rotten, difficult aid climbing start the route. Above, mixed free and aid climbing brings one eventually to the flared corner low on Route 1.

Route 3. West Face. IV, 5.9, A4. A single crack system splits the west face, but it doesn't start until 250 feet above the ground. The routefinding is therefore a bit tricky on this lower section; pendulums, bolts, and hard aid climbing are necessary to reach somewhat easier going. Above a nasty section of manzanita the route is largely free climbing.

"Amphitheater Dome"

This is Peak 9,180, the high point of the Castle Rocks, just south of Castle Rock Spire. The southeast side is class 3–4. A route rated II, 5.8, A2 has been done on the north buttress. Two pitches of free climbing lead to the crux: an overhanging aid problem followed by a hard section of free climbing.

The Needles

A few miles below the southern termination of the Great Western Divide is a cluster of monolithic pinnacles and domes known as the Needles. Lying less than two miles from the Kern River, the highest formation rises to 8,245 feet. The most feasible approach is via the new paved road which parallels the Kern. This road begins about one mile north of Johnsondale. From a campground at Needlerock Creek game trails can be followed to the rocks.

From the campground one can pick out three major groups. On the left is a rounded dome with a lookout station—this is called the Magician. To the right is a group of pinnacles. Farther right is a rounded mass called Voodoo Dome. The group of pinnacles can be sub-divided; a deep notch separates the sharp pinnacle called Sorcerer Needle on the left from the impressive mass of Warlock Needle on the right.

Since the Needles run from northwest to southeast, there has been some confusion regarding directions—e.g., whether or not a certain climb is on the southeast side or the east. The lack of definitive facets accentuates the problem.

Two routes have been made up the southwest spine of the *Magician,* but little is known about the routes or the difficulty.

Sorcerer Needle has three routes. The Southwest Face Route, rated III, 5.7, A2, ascends the deep indentation between the pinnacle and Wizard Needle, a massive satellite to the southwest. Climb to the notch; then follow surprisingly easy chimneys and blocks to the top.

A route has been done on the northwest face and is rated II, 5.7,

A2. From the notch behind the pinnacle (reached from the east via a few loose pitches) move out west and climb a series of parallel cracks to the top.

The East Face Route ascends a 450-foot crack system uphill from the Southwest Face Route. Mixed free and aid climbing is encountered in this III, 5.7, A3 route.

Charlatan Needle is a 40-foot block lying on a larger formation a bit uphill and northwest of Sorcerer. A tricky 5.7 crack on the northwest side offers a nice route.

Wizard Needle is the pinnacle attached to the southwest side of Sorcerer. From the main gully on the north traverse into a prominent chimney on the west face. From a bushy ledge above this, use aid up a curving, 80-foot dihedral which leads to a ledge beneath an overhang. Move right to the prow and climb nubbins to the top. II, 5.7, A1.

Witch Needle is located just northwest of the prominent Warlock Needle. A 5.5 route is found on the "back" side. The west face has a route rated III, 5.9. Begin about 100 yards down from the notch behind the formation at a short pillar. The first pitch leads up a crack which ends with a fingertip jamcrack. Several more fine, difficult pitches involving face climbing on nubbins and thin jamcracks lead to the summit ridge just south of the pointed tip. This is a classic route.

Warlock Needle is the finest-looking pinnacle of the region. Three routes have been established. The South Face Route, rated III, 5.8, A1, ascends the face prominent from the road. Hike up the pine-filled gully southeast of the rock until it is possible to ascend a short gully on the left. From its top a tricky move allows the climber entrance into a chute which leads toward a huge tree. Above this a crack and a right-facing open book lead to a belay pedestal. Move left into a deep, hard chimney which leads to a spacious alcove near a giant platform visible from afar. Climb up and right from here; then use aid to enter an intimidating crack, narrow at the start. Higher, continue upward in a chimney/groove until it is possible to exit right onto a ramp with a jamcrack above. Continue onward to slabs beneath the summit towers. Wander down and right to a large platform below the twin summits. Climb a 5.7 crack to the notch between the summits; the right tower is the higher and is surmounted via a few aid bolts.

The East Face Route lies far uphill from the preceding route. Climb to a large ledge with pines and from its left end ascend blocks 40 feet to a wide platform. Step across to the main face and climb a sinuous crack system for 120 feet. A short aid crack then leads to a belay ledge. Climb a ramp above here; then ascend giant steps via a jamcrack to the platform beneath the summit notch. II, 5.7, A1.

The East Face Traverse Route begins from the notch between Witch and Warlock needles. Traverse out on the east face to the large platform below the summit notch. The traverse is apparently middle class 5.

Voodoo Dome has a 900-foot south face. Start climbing on a rounded buttress just right of a gigantic alcove on the left side of the face. The first pitch is mostly artificial and ends in a hanging belay. Next, climb a greenish, left-leaning dihedral to a chimney. Climb this to a tree and from here climb up and left to a bolt. Hard climbing follows and eventually leads upward and right to a slanting ledge with a huge block. From here use aid under a flake; then continue right into an open book. Use more aid until it is possible to free climb to a large platform. Wander left and climb a groove which lies just above the gigantic alcove. From a sandy ledge thus attained friction up and right toward two parallel cracks. Climb the right-hand one to easier slabs and the top. IV, 5.9, A3.

A second route ascends the gigantic alcove. Climb mixed free and aid pitches up its right side. Pass through the roof of the alcove via a bottomless chimney and join the upper pitches of the preceding route. IV, 5.8, A3.

The Mt. Whitney Area

As if to state emphatically that the High Sierra can put forth one last splendid set of peaks, the Mt. Whitney group thrusts six summits above the 14,000 foot level before dying suddenly in the netherlands to the south. Mt. Whitney itself is not a particularly attractive peak, but its summit has long been known as the highest in the land, and consequently it is often climbed. Yet for every hundred people who laboriously follow the trail to the top, only one is to be found on the much more beautiful summit of Mt. Russell, a scant mile to the north.

Huge rock walls abound in the area, and in the last decade the Whitney group has earned the reputation of being the premier rockclimbing area in the High Sierra. Most famous of these walls is the east face of Whitney itself, a feature plainly visible from the Owens Valley, twelve miles distant and 10,000 feet below. This face was not climbed until 1959, although the so-called East Face Route, a climb which studiously avoids the lower two-thirds of the wall, was climbed in the early 1930s.

Only ten miles separate the two 14,000-foot outposts of the group, Mt. Tyndall and Mt. Langley. The Sierra crest rises immediately from Shepherd Pass to Tyndall, bypasses giant Mt. Williamson, and heads south through barren country to the Sierra's highest body of water, Tulainyo Lake. Immediately south of this lake is the Whitney group itself, which contains as its highest summits Mts. Russell, Whitney, and Muir. Whitney's great height, curving summit plateau, and furrowed west flank make it an easily recognized landmark. East of this massif lie five branches of Lone Pine Creek; the ridges which intervene between these watersheds are sometimes quite spectacular and contain some excellent rock climbs.

South of Mt. Muir the crest makes a 45-degree change of direc-

tion and heads off toward Mt. Langley. Some very fascinating and
rugged country is found in this stretch. South of Langley, Sequoia
National Park ends, the gentle forest begins, and hunters far out-
number mountaineers.

The first exploration of the Whitney group took place in 1864,
when Clarence King and Richard Cotter, of the California Geological Survey, left their base camp west of Mt. Brewer and began their
historic trek toward Mt. Whitney. Relaxing in the evening of their
first day out, at a desolate campsite far above timberline, King
thought that "after such fatiguing exercises the mind has an almost
abnormal clearness: whether this is wholly from within, or due to
the intensely vitalizing mountain air, I am not sure; probably both
contribute to the state of exaltation in which all alpine climbers find
themselves." This exaltation undoubtedly diminished in the wee
hours when their thermometer showed two degrees above zero:
"How I loved Cotter! How I hugged him and got warm, while our
backs gradually petrified, till we whirled over and thawed them out
together."

The next day they crossed the Kings-Kern Divide; this took most
of a day, and some dramatic episodes later found their way into
King's book. The packs were hauled up many a "sheer cliff," and
"smooth precipices" and "thin blades" were surmounted by
death-defying techniques. Once King lassoed a projection with a
rope that he trusted because "I had seen more than one Spanish bull
throw his whole weight against it without parting a strand." That
night, to their vast relief, the pair established a campsite among
trees, where they built a huge fire (it lasted twenty-four hours), ate
chunks of venison, and slept on a bed of pine needles.

On July 6 the two men left camp before dawn and, after toiling for
many hours up gentle slopes fraught with every imaginable peril,
reached the top at noon. King struck his hammer upon the topmost
rock and christened the peak Mt. Tyndall. Tyndall? Wasn't it
Whitney they were supposed to be climbing? "To our surprise,
upon sweeping the horizon with my level, there appeared two peaks

equal in height with us, and two rising even higher." One of these peaks, the one with the gently curving summit plateau, was Mt. Whitney.

Too low on food to attempt Whitney, the pair struggled back toward their base camp. Cotter's shoes soon fell apart and he left bloody footprints in the snowfields. They crossed the Kings-Kern Divide at a different place, hoping it would be easier, but they got into deep trouble almost immediately. At one point Cotter was in the lead and yelled down to King that he could come up the rope. King decided to do without if possible, and when, after some desperate climbing, he arrived at Cotter's stance he found him sitting on a smooth, sloping ledge where "the least little pull would have dragged him over the brink." They raced into camp at the end of their fifth day to find Brewer composing a letter to King's family which began, "It becomes my painful duty to inform you. . . ."

King found Brewer with an ulcerated tooth and attempted to remove it with a bullet mold; failing, they fled into the Central Valley toward a dentist. After the extraction Brewer was in such an expansive mood that King asked if he could leave the Survey and head back into the mountains for another crack at the real Whitney. Brewer not only gave his permission, but also two weeks leave, a hundred dollars, and a two-man military escort. A few days later, however, King made some bad routefinding errors and failed close to his goal. Francis Farquhar has written: "If King's discernment of mountain-climbing routes had been equal to his physical qualifications as a mountaineer, he might have been, in 1864, the first to stand upon the loftiest peak in the United States."

In 1871 King returned again to his nemesis. This time he chose the eastern approach. Clouds obscured much of the range and King once again chose the wrong mountain. A few days later he and his companion emerged onto a high, misty plateau, and King knew he had finally done it. The mists parted for a moment and to the north King saw the "rocky tower of Mt. Tyndall." Poor King—it was Mt. Whitney itself he saw. He stood atop Mt. Langley.

It was two years before his mistake was discovered. A man

named Goodyear climbed Langley, saw a higher peak to the north, and published his findings. King read about his error while on the East Coast and quickly hurried west to rectify it. But he was too late: when he finally arrived on the summit of his dreams in late September, he found a cairn and the names of three parties who had climbed it in the preceding thirty days.

John Muir came to Whitney a month later, made the ascent by the then-standard West Face Route and then headed down to the Owens Valley. A few days later he left Independence on foot to climb the peak from the east. On October 21 he ascended a long, narrow couloir which lay just to the right of the great eastern escarpment—the route now called the Mountaineer's Route. Muir thought it was a fine, strenuous climb, but warned that "soft, succulent people should go the mule way." He repeated this route in 1875; the third ascent by this route was made fifty-five years later by Clyde and Farquhar.

In 1881 scientists became interested in the summit of Whitney as a site for solar heat observations and, as one effect of this study, the summit was for twenty years one of America's most unique military reservations. The Smithsonian Institution built a hut on the summit in 1909 to provide shelter for astronomers who were planning to study the possibility of water vapor on Mars during a propitious viewing time in late summer. Heavy storms almost ruined the project.

Meanwhile, other summits had not been neglected. Mts. Young and Hitchcock were climbed in 1881 by the same team which was to climb Mt. Kaweah a few days later: Wallace, Wales, and Wright. Mt. Williamson was climbed a few years later by the long east-side route. Mt. Muir was probably climbed early, though no records exist, and so by the 1920s only one 14,000-foot peak remained unclimbed. This was the inconspicuous, but very lovely, Mt. Russell. Norman Clyde found a way to its summit in 1926; in the next ten years seven more routes were done.

Rockclimbers knew early about the fantastic walls of the Whitney region. In the summer of 1931 Robert Underhill, who was teaching the ropes to unsophisticated California climbers, climbed the upper right side of Whitney's east face with Clyde, Jules Eichorn, and Glen Dawson. The latter two had never set eyes on the peak, but they were hot young climbers and deemed ready for the ascent. Three hours and fifteen minutes after leaving Iceberg Lake, the foursome was on the summit; only a few pitches had proved at all difficult.

Only in the last decade have rockclimbers discovered the full potential of the region. Two men, Galen Rowell and Fred Beckey, have been responsible for opening up many new areas. Rowell has found some remote and superb back-country routes; Beckey has concentrated his efforts in the immediate Whitney Portal area and has put up some significant routes on the smooth granite buttresses which overlook the road's end.

Approaches to the Whitney area are few in number and are invariably made from the east. The Shepherd Pass trail, mentioned in the Kearsarge Pass chapter, is the route to take if Mts. Tyndall and Williamson are desired. Arduous and trail-less approaches can be made up both Bairs and George creeks; these involve enormous elevation gains. The Mt. Whitney Trail, of course, is the most popular trail in the region and leads into the heart of the mountains. The southern Whitney region can be reached from the Whitney Trail by means of Arc Pass; another approach is via the Meysan Lakes trail. Mt. Langley is quickly reached via the Cottonwood Creek trail, which leads over New Army Pass.

The east face routes of the Whitney massif can be reached from Whitney Portal by following a devious route up the north fork of Lone Pine Creek: leave the main trail about one-quarter of a mile above the parking lot and head over into the gorge on the right. Follow the south side of the creek for nearly one-half mile; then cross the stream near a Matterhorn-shaped talus block and ascend 100 feet up the opposite wall of the canyon. Work downstream on a ledge until near its end, climb up a bit, and then traverse back upstream on a series of ramps known as the Ebersbacher Ledges.

This route, not that hard to find, bypasses the willow-choked stream bed. Continue upstream to Clyde Meadow, take the left fork where the stream branches, and ascend talus to Iceberg Lake—a fine, woodless campsite. An alternate approach is apparently equally fast: from the junction of the horse and foot trails walk north on the former, cross the stream, and ascend a long, easy gully which parallels the stream on the north. This gully eventually leads to benches and slabs which can be traversed to Lower Boy Scout Lake.

At least nine climbers' passes cross the Sierra crest in the Whitney region. North to south, these are as follows.

Tyndall Col (12,960+) lies between Mts. Tyndall and Versteeg and is class 2.

Vacation Pass (12,640+) is located just east of Wallace Lake. Cross the crest a bit north of the lowest point. Class 2–3.

Cleaver Col (12,960+) lies immediately northeast of Mt. Carillon and connects Tulainyo Lake with the northern branch of the north fork of Lone Pine Creek.

Russell Pass (13,280+) provides an excellent route for those traveling between Lone Pine Creek and Wallace Lakes. The high pass is located between Mts. Russell and Carillon. Coming from the east, leave Clyde Meadow in a northwest direction and ascend a steep slope which leads to a plateau under the col. Class 2.

Whitney-Russell Pass (13,040+) provides a good class 2 route between Iceberg and Arctic lakes.

Discovery Pass (ca 13,500) is not really a pass, but a ridge crossing. It allows the traveler access to the Crabtree Lakes from the Mt. Whitney Trail, which is left very close to Trail Crest.

Arc Pass (12,880+) can be reached from Consultation Lake on the Mt. Whitney Trail. It offers class 1–2 passage into the basins at the head of Rock Creek.

Tuttle Pass (12,880+) lies between Mts. Corcoran and Langley. The approach from the east involves a 6,000-foot, trail-less elevation gain. Class 2.

New Army Pass (12,160+) is reached via the trail up Cottonwood

Creek, and is a good approach for the easy south side of Mt. Langley.

Two other passes are found in the region. *Crabtree Pass* (12,560+) lies just west of Mt. McAdie and connects the headwaters of Crabtree and Rock creeks. Class 2. *Pinnacle Pass* (12,240+) crosses Pinnacle Ridge just west of Thor Peak. From Mirror Lake ascend northwest until lodges on the right lead over to the pass, which is just right of a small pinnacle. Class 3 rock is found on the north side of the col.

The Mt. Whitney and Lone Pine quadrangles are the only maps one needs.

Mt. Williamson and Environs

Peak 13,040+ (0.6 E of Shepherd Pass)
The approach is easy from all sides, but the summit rocks require a bit of scrambling.

Peak 12,480+ (1.4 ENE of Shepherd Pass)
Class 2 from the lakes south of the peak.

Mt. Tyndall (14,018)
One of the finest Sierra peaks when viewed from the east; one of the most inconsequential when viewed from the west.

Route 1. Southwest Slopes. Class 2 from Lake 11,952.

Route 2. Northwest Ridge. From a point about one-half mile west of Shepherd Pass follow the class 2 ridge to the summit.

Route 3. North Side. The Sierra crest, at this point an inconspicuous, talus-covered rib, affords an excellent method of reaching the summit ridge. Class 2–3.

Route 4. Northeast Side. Class 4. The original description for this climb is extremely vague: ''climb the first prominent chute on the east face of the north ridge.'' If the ''north ridge'' refers to the obvious northwest ridge, then this route is to the right of Route 3. If the ''north ridge'' refers to the rib of Route 3, then the route probably lies in the trough immediately left of the rib.

Route 5. East Chimney. IV, 5.8. This route ascends the spectacular eastern escarpment. Just to the left of the summit pyramid is a long, not-too-distinct chimney system. Turn the initial overhangs on the right and then follow the chimney for many rope-lengths to the top.

Route 6. East Couloir. III, 5.8. A deep couloir splits the eastern escarpment and leads to a prominent notch a short distance south of the summit. The final rotten headwall is the crux.

Route 7. Southeast Side. Class 4. This route lies on the east side of the peak, well away from the main summit mass. Climb the left wall of the third couloir left of the steep east face for about 500 feet to the easy southern talus slopes.

Peak 13,540 (0.85 WSW of Mt. Tyndall)
Class 2 from the Wright Lakes. The sculpted northwest face is class 3 in places.

Mt. Williamson (14,375)
California's second highest peak is also one of its most massive. The mountain, standing a mile east of the Sierra crest, overshadows all its neighbors and can be seen easily from a 50-mile section of U.S. Highway 395. A half mile northeast of the main summit lie two subsidiary peaklets, Point 14,160+ and Point 14,125.

Route 1. West Side. From Shepherd Pass walk over the saddle northeast of Mt. Tyndall and then drop down talus onto an obvious ridge which runs southeast through the ''Bowl'' toward the west face. The standard route ascends the right side of the wide face to a very obvious black water stain on a small rock band. From here, head up into a large talus gully which can be followed for over a thousand vertical feet. At the top of the gully is an overlook of the north face. A few feet to the right is a 75-foot cleft which leads to the summit plateau. This cleft is the only class 3 portion of the route. The summit lies to the south and is a 10-minute boulder hop.

Many variations have been done. A popular one goes up and right from the black water stain to a talus notch. From here, cross into a chute and wander up to the summit plateau. Routes farther left on the face than the standard route have been done. These have involved class 4 climbing, and much routefinding skill.

Route 2. Northwest Buttress. Easy class 3. From the base of the west face work up and left to a notch behind a prominent tower at approximately 13,100 feet. Then stay on the prow of the buttress to the summit.

Route 3. North Face. Class 4 or 5. Couloirs, ribs, and short faces are found in profusion on this face. It is not known exactly where the route lies, but it ascends to the plateau between Point 14,160+ and the summit.

Route 4. North Rib. IV, 5.7. Coming down the north face from Point 14,160+ is a long, twisted rib which is fairly low-angle at its bottom. The North Rib Route lies on the next major rib to the right. The first two-thirds of the rib is low-angle and fairly easy; the upper section is comprised of ten pitches of 5.5–5.7 climbing. The route comes up to the summit plateau just to the right of Point 14,160+.

Route 5. Northeast Ridge. Class 4. From timberline on Williamson Creek climb a chute up onto the ridge and follow it to the summit. This route is arduous and dry.

Route 6. Southeast Slopes. Class 2. This is the easiest way to the summit, but the approach is long and the route can hardly be called popular. From timberline on the north fork of George Creek climb north up onto the gentle southeast slopes of the peak. A slight barrier at about 13,800 feet is class 2; above, the summit plateau is soon reached. A variation has been done; from the main fork of Bairs Creek climb up a chute to the gentle southeast slopes. Class 3.

Route 7. Point 14,160+. One can reach the notch between the summit plateau of Williamson and Point 14,160+ by several methods: drop down directly from the plateau (class 4); scramble down a ledge leading southeast and then climb back up to the notch;

or, most easily, stay 150 feet below the plateau for quite a way in advance of the drop-off to the notch. From the notch climb up and left about 40 feet to another notch; then descend down and right on the northwest side of the peaklet for one class 4 pitch. Easier climbing soon leads to the top. There are several variations on this route, but all of them avoid the sharp, prominent arete.

Route 8. Point 14,125. This peaklet has been reached by at least three ways. Route 5 leads over the top from the northeast. This is class 3. It can be reached from the top of Williamson by first traversing Point 14,160+. The final climb lies on the class 3 west face. A long route has been done on the northern side. From the 10,000-foot elevation on Williamson Creek one will see, high on the face above, two prominent, dry waterfalls. Wander up a reddish buttress to the left of these waterfalls, pass a cliff on the left, and climb up and left via an obvious chute. Head up and left from the top of this to a saddle. Now traverse over to a broad chute which leads up to easy slopes and the top. Class 2–3.

Mt. Versteeg (13,470)

Class 2 or 3 from most directions.

Trojan Peak (13,950)

This recently named mountain commemorates the nickname of the athletic teams of the University of Southern California. Class 2 or 3 from the Williamson-Trojan saddle, class 3 from the west, and class 2 from the south.

Mt. Barnard (13,990)

Formerly one of California's 14,000-foot peaks, this is now the highest 13,000-footer in the range. A lot of peakbaggers were unhappy when the Geological Survey announced the new elevation. The peak is class 2 from all sides.

Peak 13,680+ (0.65 ESE of Mt. Barnard)

Class 2 from all directions except the east. A IV, 5.9 route has

been done on the stunning pillar on the 1,100-foot-high east face.
Two pitches lead to a horizontal snowfield. Climb to a ceiling; then
traverse left to the base of a dihedral. Follow this for many excellent
free-climbing pitches. The final lead has a 5.9 bulge. A giant
pinnacle named Shaw Spire has been climbed; it lies nestled against
the east face, some 0.4 mile east-northeast of the top. The seven-
pitch, III, 5.8 route lies on the southeast arete.

Peak 12,723 (1.6 ESE of Mt. Barnard)

Class 2 from the south; class 4 from the north.

Tawny Point (12,332)

Class 1 and 2 routes can be found anywhere.

Peak 13,211 (1.75 SE of Mt. Barnard)

This is the good-looking peak just southeast of Vacation Pass. It
is an easy climb from the west. The east-northeast ridge is class 3
and super-enjoyable. Another route, class 4 in difficulty, ascends a
steep gully on the north side and then follows the northwest ridge to
the top.

"Tulainyo Tower" (Pk. 12,800+, 0.25 SSE of Pk. 13,211)

This is a prominent crag on the Peak 13,211–Tunnabora Peak
cirque wall. On the steep east face is a single, 1,000-foot crack. The
lower section is all free climbing; the upper part requires small
amounts of aid. IV, 5.8, A3. The original route climbed the
difficult lower section and then, at the base of a steep, 6-inch crack,
pendulumed right to somewhat easier climbing. This route is rated
IV, 5.9, with one aid placement. The several pinnacles in this
vicinity have been traversed from northwest to southeast—class 4.

Tunnabora Peak (13,565)

Easy from Tulainyo Lake. A route has been established on the
northwest side of the peak. Climb a chute which hits the west ridge
just below the top. Class 2 or 3.

Mt. Whitney Region

Peak 13,355 (0.35 NE of Mt. Carillon)

Class 2 via the northwest ridge. The sharp southwest ridge, if one stays directly on it, is mostly class 4, although one 5.6 section seems mandatory.

Mt. Carillon (13,552)

Route 1. South Slopes. Class 2 from the stream above Upper Boy Scout Lake.

Route 2. West-Southwest Ridge. Class 2 from the Russell-Carillon saddle.

Route 3. North-Northeast Ridge. From the saddle between Peak 13,355 and Carillon, climb the class 2 or 3 ridge to the top.

Route 4. East Face. III, 5.8. This route lies on the face just west of the small lake at the 11,800-foot level in the northernmost branch of the north fork of Lone Pine Creek. The route lies between a gully on the left and a deep cleft on the right. Work up and left via slabs to an open book which slants up and right. Follow this book to a slab which gives access to a narrow crack. Above, climb a chimney/corner and a jamcrack to a point where it is possible to traverse left to a cave in orange rock. Another pitch leads up to one of Carillon's southeast summits.

Route 5. The Impala, Original Route. II, 5.7. The Impala is the sloping pyramid at the base of the long southeast spur of Carillon. Its summit, at 12,080+ feet, lies about one-half mile northwest of Lower Boy Scout Lake. In the middle of the south face is a prominent chimney. Follow this for two rope-lengths, cross a diagonal chimney system, and continue more or less straight up to the false summit. The top is easily reached from here.

Route 6. The Impala, Diagonal Route. II, 5.7. This route begins to the left of the preceding route. Follow the obvious diagonal chimney which runs from the lower left side of the south face to the upper right side. After crossing Route 5, gain the southeast face and climb to the false summit.

Route 7. The Winged Horse. III, 5.8, A3. This formation lies just east of the Impala. Rope up near a fat tree at the base of the south face. A friction pitch leads to a belay ledge. From here climb up and left for a bit; then, using aid, attain a ledge at the base of a groove. Mixed climbing leads up this groove for a pitch. Next, climb up to chickenheads, traverse left, and ascend chimneys to the summit.

Peak 12,960+ (0.65 ENE of Mt. Carillon)

Class 2 or 3 via the southwest slopes.

Mt. Russell (14,086)

This beautiful peak's proximity to Mt. Whitney has resulted in many routes and variations, and on such a complicated mountain these are hard to describe. The south face, in particular, is a convoluted mass of buttresses and couloirs. As seen from the top of Whitney, the peak has twin summits; the west peak is the higher. Dropping down from this summit are two very prominent ribs or buttresses. The one on the left, or west, will be referred to as the Southwest Buttress. The other, for obvious reasons, will be called the Curved Arete. Midway between the two summits, another rib, much smaller than the others, drops down into the talus. This rib divides the south face. These landmarks should be an aid to identifying Routes 3 through 6.

Route 1. East Arete. Class 3. From the saddle between Russell and Carillon (reached easily from either side) follow the arete to the eastern summit. It seems easiest to stay a bit below the crest of the arete on the north side.

Route 2. Southeast Ridge. II, 5.7. Climb the serrated ridge which rises from the Whitney-Russell saddle. One can escape this ridge at many spots by traversing or rappelling into the talus gully on the left.

Route 3. South Face, Right Side. Class 3–4. Easy slopes lead up the face to a rib which drops down from the midpoint of the summit ridge. Take the slope on the right of this rib and climb to the upper headwall. This can be surmounted in several ways. There are several obvious, class 4 routes; easier ways will require careful routefinding.

Route 4. South Face, Left Side. Class 4. Ascend talus as in the preceding description, but stay left of the rib. At the top of the gully, exit up and right to the summit ridge.

Route 5. Curved Arete. III, 5.8. Stay close to the very prow of the arete for its entire length.

Route 6. Direct Southwest Buttress. III, 5.8. On the south face are found steep dihedrals and cracks. Two particularly horrifying crack systems are conspicuous—climb the left-hand one. Four hard pitches lead to easier climbing and the top.

Route 7. West Face. IV, 5.10. Hidden from popular viewpoints, this steep, 800-foot wall is the most striking feature of Russell. The face lies south of the long west arete and is seen easily on the map as a right-angled, heavy contour line. Climb a straight crack system near the center of the face. A square belay platform about 150 feet up is a diagnostic landmark.

Route 8. West Couloir. Class 4. Crammed between the west face and the west arete is a deep couloir, often snow-filled. Ascend the couloir to the arete and scramble over to the summit.

Route 9. West Arete. Class 3.

Route 10. North Face. Class 3 or 4. From the tiny lake under the north side of the mountain, climb the left side of the face over class 2 rock. Reach a ledge which heads out to the right and follow it to the middle of the face. Climb upward to the midpoint of the summit ridge.

Route 11. North Arete. Class 3. From the west side of Tulainyo Lake climb onto the ridge and follow it to the top. Keep to the right when faced with problems.

Route 12. Northeast Face. Class 5. The true northeast face is monolithic and slabby. This route ascends steep snow and slabs to the right of the main face.

Peak 13,920+ (0.6 W of Mt. Russell)

Class 3 from Mt. Russell. The northeast slopes are also class 3.

Mt. Hale (13,440+)

Class 1 or 2 from the south. A technical route has been established on the steep northeast face. Approaching the 1,200-foot face from the northeast, one will notice that the left side of the face is higher than the right side, which rises above a snowfield (seasonal) or a broad ledge. The route begins in the center of the tallest face and initially ascends a right-slanting crack system. The first half of the route is continuous and difficult; the easier-appearing upper section has many short but hard segments. V, 5.9, A3.

Two pinnacles on the ridge southeast of the summit have been climbed. The northerly one is 5.8; the other is 5.6.

Mt. Young (13,177)

Easy from the John Muir Trail.

Mt. Whitney (14,494)

Because this is the highest peak in the contiguous United States, it is the most frequented mountain in the Sierra. At least twenty-five persons will be found on the summit plateau on a summer afternoon and a toilet has been installed for their convenience. In the off season, however, the peak once again resembles the ideal Sierra mountain—clean, windswept, and remote.

Route 1. The Trail. Requiring nothing but patience and stamina, the 10.6-mile path winds upward from Whitney Portal. Most persons take two days for the ascent, but a one-day round trip is hardly out of the question for the climber who is in shape.

Route 2. West Flank. Class 2. This is the original route. Leave the Muir Trail near the 11,800-foot level and scramble up any of several available talus chutes.

Route 3. North Side. Class 2–3. Climb the left side of the north face; then work up and right via shallow chutes to the summit plateau.

Route 4. Cardiovascular Seizure. III, 5.10. This, the first of the east-side routes, lies far to the right of the main east face of the peak and terminates at the 13,700-foot level on the northeast ridge of Whitney. A prominent buttress or pillar will be seen to the left of the

Whitney-Russell saddle. This route begins about 75 feet to the right of a very obvious chimney on this pillar. An easy pitch leads to the beginning of the difficulties. Of the remaining six pitches, none are easier than 5.8. Descent can be made via the very loose couloir to the south.

Route 5. The Rotten Chimney. III, 5.8. This is the chimney mentioned in Route 4. Like that route, this one goes nowhere near the summit of Whitney. Five pitches of extremely unenjoyable climbing lead to the top of the ridge.

Route 6. Mountaineer's Route. Class 2–3. This is the standard descent route for climbers who have done an east face route. As an ascent route it tends to be a bit unpleasant because of the loose talus. From the outlet of Iceberg Lake climb a long, deep gully to the right of the enormous east face. At the 14,000-foot level a notch is reached. From here climb upward over steep blocks to the plateau. There is often ice in this stretch, but it generally can be bypassed. When descending via this route, make sure that you walk about 500 feet west along the edge of the drop-off before descending the north face to the notch. A premature descent will land you in big trouble.

Route 7. East Buttress. Class 5. From Iceberg Lake climb a talus slope toward the rock wall left of the gully of the Mountaineer's Route. After about 500 vertical feet have been gained, head over easy rock to the notch between the First and Second Towers, two obvious landmarks. Rope up at this notch and climb the face of Second Tower until nearly at its top; then turn right and traverse around into the notch behind the tower. A class 5 pitch, the only one of the route, lies above. Continue ascending the prow of the buttress to the Peewee, a giant perched block. Climb past this on the right and ascend easier rock to the summit area.

Route 8. East Face. III, 5.4. This is one of the classic routes of the Sierra, partly because of its spectacular location and partly because it was the first really big wall to be climbed in the range. Much of the route is class 3, but one should plan on encountering several class 4 pitches and one class 5 lead. Climb talus above Iceberg Lake to the notch behind First Tower, some 500 feet above the lake shore. From here an exposed upward traverse brings one to the Washboard, a well-named series of steps. Scramble up to its top; then climb to a short but steep wall on the left. Surmount this (class 4), and then drop down and traverse on a ledge toward the main wall. A few feet higher is the crux section. At least three alternatives exist. The regular route, called the Fresh-Air Traverse, heads out to the left and goes around a block. The exposure assumes serious proportions as one climbs up a short, broken chimney, but after this is overcome, the climber gains the security of big ledges at the base of the Giant Staircase. Proceed up this for a few hundred feet to an apparent impasse; a squeeze chimney on the left is the key. After this the difficulties ease and the summit is only a 15-minute scramble away.

There are several variations above the Giant Staircase, but all are relatively easy. Down below, at the Fresh-Air Traverse, there are two well-known variations. The Shaky-Leg Crack heads upward from near the beginning of the traverse and is easy class 5. The Direct Crack lies a bit farther to the right and involves a short, strenuous crack. Both variations are only one pitch in length.

Route 9. The Great Book. V, 5.9. The upper part of this intimidating route lies in the large dihedral which rises above the upper part of the Washboard. Begin climbing several hundred yards to the right of the obvious Route 10 and climb many difficult pitches to the top of the Washboard. Move into the Great Book and climb it to the summit blocks.

Route 10. Direct East Face. IV, 5.7, A3. To the left of the east face area a long, prominent chimney splits the huge, true eastern escarpment. The steep, direct entrance into this chimney (5.8) can be avoided by starting near the base of the chimney and making a left-diagonaling traverse up to a short chimney which ends on a huge terrace. Traverse right from this to the main chimney and follow it (or the walls on either side) for many pitches. Eventually, the Fresh-Air Traverse of Route 8 is reached.

Route 11. Southeast Buttress. Class 4 or 5. This route lies on the wall to the right of the Keeler Needle–Whitney couloir. A prominent tower will be seen near the top of the buttress. Climb easy class 4 rock to a point where it is possible to traverse right and cross a steep chimney. The tower is soon passed on its right side and many class 4 pitches lead to the summit slopes.

Keeler Needle

South of Mt. Whitney is a series of peaklets, very striking from the east, very dull and inconspicuous from the west. All are short walk-ups from the nearby trail. Although in no way could these formations be called separate mountains, their east faces contain some of the finest big-wall climbs in the range. The face of Keeler Needle is rated V, 5.10, A3. The route lies in the obvious crack system just right of the Day-Keeler couloir. Most of the route goes free, and the climb has been done in a day.

Another technical route has been done; this one lies to the right of the preceding route. Start near the right side of the face and climb six pitches (almost all free) into a huge, reddish dihedral. From the top of this feature work left out onto the center of the face. Steep aid climbing up discontinuous cracks leads to a good ledge. Higher, the other route is joined for its final pitches. V, 5.9, A2.

"Day Needle"

The east face route on this needle begins just right of the base of the Third Needle–Day Needle couloir. Stay near the prow all the way up. IV, 5.7, A2.

"Third Needle"

This needle, not so distinguished as its two northern neighbors, has several summits. It can be further recognized by the fact that Pinnacle Ridge, the long fin which divides the north and south forks of Lone Pine Creek, hits the main Sierra crest at the northern part of Third Needle. All three technical routes begin from just above the saddle which lies at the Pinnacle Ridge–Third Needle junction.

Route 1. East Buttress. Class 5, with a short bit of aid. From the Pinnacle Ridge saddle follow the talus-covered ridge upward to the buttress. Climb this for about 500 feet; then move a short distance left and climb a chimney. Above, move up and right into a rotten chimney which leads onto the main buttress. Soon the difficulties ease and one hits the summit ridge near the Third Needle–Day Needle notch.

Route 2. East Face, Right Side. Class 5. From the Pinnacle Ridge saddle scramble up and left into the first shallow gully left of the ridgecrest. After about 500 feet one is faced with a very steep wall; move right and climb many class 4 pitches up to the summit ridge.

Route 3. East Face, Left Side. III, 5.3. Follow Route 2 until faced with the steep wall; then head left to a thin buttress and climb a narrow, chockstone-filled chimney. When the angle eases climb up and left to a wide ledge which cuts across the upper part of the east face. This leads to a conspicuous, curving chimney. A few easy class 5 pitches up this lead to the notch separating the north and south summits.

The east faces of the Mt. Whitney massif. At the lower left, Pinnacle Ridge abuts Third Needle. The two prominent summits between Third and Whitney are Day and Keeler needles, respectively. The long, right-slanting chimney of the true east face route of Whitney lies above a thin, horizontal snowfield. Route 6 lies to the right of the big, shadowed face.

"Aiguille Extra"

Left of the Third Needle complex is a higher, more monolithic tower. The upper part of the east face has a long, prominent open book. The route begins directly below this book. Rope up on the left side of a small platform 40 feet above the talus and climb four long pitches of mixed free and aid to a series of excellent ledges. From here climb up into the prominent open book and follow it to the summit. V, 5.8, A3.

Mt. Muir (14,015)

The Sierra's most insignificant 14,000-footer lies a mile south of Mt. Whitney. One can't help but feel that a more worthy mountain could have been chosen to carry the name of one of the Sierra's greatest figures.

Route 1. West Side. Class 3. From Trail Crest walk about 600 yards up the Mt. Whitney Trail. Leave the trail at a large cairn and climb a chute to the summit rocks, some 350 feet above.

Route 2. East Buttress. Class 4. A well-defined buttress will be seen on the east face. Climb upward either on or just right of the ridgecrest until about halfway up. Move into a fractured chute on the left and head up to a point behind two gendarmes. From here work up large blocks to the top.

Route 3. East Face. Class 4. Climb the ridgecrest of Route 2 for a few pitches to difficult slab problems. A sloping traverse left leads to a chute which can be followed easily to a divided chimney. Above this climb up to a 70-foot squeeze chimney. One more pitch leads to an arete; from here climb up and right to large blocks and the summit.

Pinnacle Ridge (13,040+)

This is the sharp, mile-long fin which divides the north and south forks of Lone Pine Creek. A traverse of the ridge involves class 4 climbing. A pinnacle at the east end of the ridge, near Pinnacle Pass, is class 4 or 5 via a crack on the northwest side.

Wotan's Throne (12,720+)

Class 2 via a chute on the south side. The peak is also class 2 via the northwest ridge or the northernmost of three chutes on the southeast face.

Thor Peak (12,300)

Rising above Bighorn Park on the Mt. Whitney Trail is a great granite wall—the southeast face of Thor.

Route 1, West Arête. Class 2

Route 2. Southwest Side. Class 2. From Mirror Lake ascend talus to the gentle southwest plateau. Walk up to a notch just south of the top; then circle around to the northeast and scramble to the top.

Route 3. South Crack. III, 5.9. From the top of the switchbacks above Bighorn Park, ascend a broad, brush-covered talus slope up and to the right. Climb into the crack which separates Thor's face from a subsidiary peaklet called Mirror Point. After two class 4 pitches, move right across a series of ledges. Looking upward now, one will see several cracks to the right of the left skyline. Climb the very difficult second-from-the-left crack to the summit area.

Route 4. Satan's Delight. Class 5. Follow Route 3 out onto the series of ledges, continue on these ledges, and climb a crack to the reddish ledge known as the Pink Perch. From here drop down eastward for about 100 feet; then move out onto the face a few steps. Climb a crack for two rope-lengths to a shelf behind a gendarme. Move right a bit and climb a delicate face which leads to easier climbing. Next, a pitch of steep blocks is followed by a traverse to the left. Ledges lead upward to the short summit cap. One emerges on the summit ridge about 100 feet east of the top.

A variation has been made on the lower part of the route. Ascend the broad, brush-covered talus slope mentioned in Route 3; then, instead of beginning the climb, walk up and right on talus. After a while one will notice a steep, narrow gully which leads up to the Pink Perch. This variation is class 4.

Route 5. Truncated Buttress. II, 5.7, A1. This route lies a few hundred feet to the right of the preceding route. Start at the highest pine tree in the immediate area and climb cracks just left of an incomplete buttress or rib.

Route 6. Principal Dihedral. III, 5.8, A2. About 200 feet to the right of the preceding route is a long, shallow dihedral which is very conspicuous from Bighorn Park. The climbing route lies mainly in this dihedral. At one point, several pitches up, bat-hooks must be placed in pre-drilled holes to overcome a blank slab. The zigzag route above here is rather obvious. A pitch up the left side of a headwall high up is the crux and involves sustained jamming. The route ends quite a way east of the summit, and the best descent is by a gully to the east.

Route 7. Southeast Crack. Class 4 or 5. A few hundred feet to the right of the prominent dihedral of Route 6 is a line of trees extending out onto the naked face. From near the highest trees traverse out left on a ledge. Climb a crack up to a ledge, move right, and climb to a detached, reddish pinnacle. From the notch behind it move right to a gully. Ascend this; then exit left on a classic ledge. The summit ridge is just above.

Route 8. East Slopes. Class 2. Leave the Whitney Trail where it first crosses the 10,000-foot contour and walk up to the summit.

Route 9. Mirror Point. This is the small, somewhat detached pinnacle on the west side of the lower southeast face of Thor. It is easily seen in profile from Bighorn Park. The Point is an easy climb from the west, but a technical route has been done on the southeast face. Climb the left side of an apron and follow a series of cracks which lies above. The crux is a steep, 20-foot, class 5 crack.

"Wrinkled Lady"

From the end of the road at Whitney Portal one will see, high on the ridge to the north, a prominent pyramidal rock laced with cracks and dihedrals. Fifteen hundred feet of class 3 and 4 climbing up gullies and slabs brings one to the pyramid. Five pitches straight up the central dihedral (a pine is passed at the end of the second lead) take one to the top. III, 5.7, A2.

"Whitney Portal Buttress"

From the loop at the end of the Whitney Portal road this buttress will be seen as the smooth, high formation to the north. Climb a sandy gully to a fork; then take the left branch and follow it to the obvious cracks on the lower part of the buttress. Rope up and climb a hard, 60-foot crack left of a pillar. Next, a long aid pitch passes a roof on the right. The third pitch, a low-angle slab, brings one to a single crack system which leads upward for hundreds of feet. Mixed free and aid climbing is encountered in the remaining eight pitches. From the top the best method of descent is to rappel east to a notch; then head down slabs and gullies leading first east, then south. IV, 5.8, A3.

"El Segundo Buttress"

Near the top of the Whitney Portal road the highway makes a single switchback. Above the east end of the switchback are two inconspicuous buttresses covered with bushes. Between these two buttresses is a gully filled with large firs. The left buttress is called El Segundo, the right is Premiere Buttress. The route on El Segundo begins to the right of a giant tree which is itself right of a large, dead tree. A ledge leads left to the first pitch, a left-facing open book. Mixed free and aid climbing leads up five or six pitches to the top. III, 5.7, A2.

"Premiere Buttress"

See the preceding climb for location. This six pitch route follows the rounded spur of the buttress. III, 5.8, A1.

South of the John Muir Trail

Discovery Pinnacle (13,760+)

This insignificant peaklet lies just south of Trail Crest and is class 2.

Mt. Hitchcock (13,184)

The spectacular northeast face, deeply incised with avalanche chutes, is a familiar sight to all Whitney climbers. The easiest couloir on this face is apparently class 3 or 4. The ascent from Crabtree Lakes is considerably easier.

Mt. Chamberlain (13,169)

The south and west slopes are quite easy. The ridge coming over from Mt. Newcomb is class 2 or 3.

Mt. Newcomb (13,410)

This peak has been climbed from the southwest, from the northeast, and from the north via chutes which lead up between Newcomb and Chamberlain. All routes are class 2 or 3.

Mt. McAdie (13,760+)

The highest summit can be reached from Arc Pass by climbing up easy talus until nearly at the top of the middle summit and then working over right to the main peak. Class 3. The west face of this highest peak has been climbed and is class 3–4. The lower two summits are easily climbed from Arc Pass.

Mt. Mallory (13,850)

This peak and its lower neighbor to the north were named in 1925 by Norman Clyde in honor of the climbers who had vanished on Everest the year before. The plateau southeast of the summit rocks can be reached by at least four routes: from Meysan Lake, from the north fork of Tuttle Creek, from Mt. Irvine, and from the small lake northeast of Sky Blue Lake. All these routes are class 2, as is the summit from the plateau. The northwest ridge, from the Arc Pass area, is class 3 and involves passing over the lower north summit.

Mt. Irvine (13,770)

Class 2 from Arc Pass and from Mirror Lake. A class 2–3 route has been done on the west side and ascends the fourth chute south of

Consultation Lake. A technical route, rated III, 5.7, has been done on the east buttress and is easily seen from Meysan Lake. Begin climbing in a chimney just left of the toe of the buttress and proceed upward over easy rock. Higher, towers on the prow of the buttress are turned, sometimes on the left, sometimes on the right. High on the buttress a wall is encountered which would require aid; at this spot drop down to the right a few feet and move (5.7) into a crack. Easier climbing leads up to the last tower; turn this on the right and scramble to the summit. III, 5.7. A prominent couloir just left of this route has been climbed.

"Candlelight Peak" (Pk. 12,000+, 1.5 NE of Mt. Irvine)

This peak, actually a 2.5-mile-long spur extending northeast from Mt. Irvine, has a plethora of exposed, climbable granite. Two routes have been done on the face above Little Meysan Lake. One, class 3, begins in a chimney, and the other, the standard walk-up route, ascends the slopes left of the face. Only two technical routes have been reported. The northeast buttress is III, 5.6(?). The north face, easily seen from the campground at Whitney Portal, has been climbed. Begin on a huge ledge on the left side of the face. At its end climb into a cleft and follow it upward to a saddle. Follow the ridge to the top. III, 5.6, A2.

Lone Pine Peak (12,944)

This enormous, complex mountain, very striking from Lone Pine, has attracted the attention of many rockclimbers in the past five years. Routes 4–11 have basically the same approach, which begins from the end of the Tuttle Creek road. From this point a good trail leads, in a mile and a half, to the Stone House, an abandoned building at the base of the ridge which separates the two forks of Tuttle Creek.

Route 1. North Ridge. III, 5.4. This is the long and spectacular right-hand skyline ridge as viewed from the Owens Valley. The lower part of the ridge can be reached in many ways, but a fairly standard class 3–4 route is from near the 9,600-foot level of the

Meysan Lakes trail. Once the ridgecrest is gained, stay on it, turning towers above notches usually on the right. This is a classic, adventurous route; most parties will take a day and a half round trip from Whitney Portal. Variations exist by the score; by staying always to the left when the towers are reached, the route becomes largely class 4. The tower above the first major notch is still passed on the right. The normal descent route is via Route 12.

Route 2. Bastille Buttress. V, 5.8, A3. This classic, polished buttress, easily visible from the Whitney Portal road, lies on the curving north ridge of the peak, 1.5 miles east-southeast of the loop at the end of the road. From the summer cabins a mile east of the end of the road, contour around into the Inyo Creek drainage and climb a gully to the buttress. A long, easy pitch up cracks and a ramp leads to a big ledge. Climb up left of an arch for two pitches to a hanging belay. Move right on slabs to a long bolt ladder and proceed to another sling belay. Move up and left, mostly on aid, for two pitches; then climb a chimney. Pitches 8 and 9 use much aid and lead to a belay on a smooth ridge. Using aid, climb up, and then down and left, and then up again to a slab belay. The next lead goes generally up and left, although at one point a short traverse to the right is made. Pitch 12 is a deep, easy groove. Next, climb to bolts; then ascend friction grooves to a belay block. Climb up and right from here to a belay platform and ascend to a false summit. Two more pitches lead to scrambling and the top. Descend a system of gullies one-quarter mile left of the top.

Route 3. Northeast Side. Class 4. No one seems to know much about this route except that one climbs the "second chute south of the north ridge." There is an enormous number of possible lines on this side of the peak, and many are obviously more difficult than class 4.

Route 4. East Slopes. Class 2. This is by far the easiest route from the east. From the end of the Tuttle Creek road the route is quite clear; a barrier at about 10,500 feet would be a major problem, but at least two class 2 gullies can be found leading through the cliffs.

Route 5. Stonehouse Buttress, Southeast Face. IV, 5.8, A2.

Across the valley from the Stone House is a large outcropping. The main wall, which faces southeast, has several distinct crack systems. Most striking of these is a narrow chimney, the lower part of which curves gently to the right. A few hundred feet right of this chimney is a shallow and sometimes ill-defined, right-facing corner. Begin climbing just left of an obvious, triangular flake. Work upward past bushes and mixed free and aid pitches to the top.

Route 6. Stonehouse Buttress, Chimney Route. IV, 5.8. Follow the curving chimney mentioned in the preceding route. Shortly after passing the chockstones in the upper chimney, move out onto the face at the left and climb orange chickenheads to the summit.

Route 7. Stonehouse Buttress, Milky Way Chimney. IV, 5.9, A3. Climb the preceding route until the base of the curving chimney; then move up and left a pitch to a cavernous chimney. Climb this and the walls above.

Route 8. C.A.F. Route. IV, 5.9, A1. This is the first, and easternmost, of the three routes which have been established on the wide, gigantic southern escarpment of Lone Pine Peak. As seen from the Stone House, the main part of the wall lies nearly a mile up canyon. On the right side of this wall, and about one-half mile up canyon from the house, one will pick out easily a wide, fairly low-angle gully which heads up and slightly left for over 1,000 feet. This is the beginning of Route 9. Just right of the gully, and about halfway up the wall, is a huge, ledge-covered area with many bushes. Route 8 climbs up to the left side of these ledges (mostly class 2) and then drops down into a couloir on the left. Climb this for about 300 feet; then enter and follow a long cleft (fourteen pitches) to the summit plateau. Two overhangs in the cleft require small amounts of direct aid.

Route 9. Winter Route. IV, 5.7. From the Stone House one looks directly at the lower half of this mountaineering route. Follow an obvious, wide gully which heads up and left. After about 1,000 vertical feet have been gained, turn left and enter a narrower, slabby gully which shoots upward. As seen from the Stone House, this gully lies behind a serrated ridge. From the top of the gully climb about 800 feet of class 4 and 5 rock to the summit talus.

Route 10. Direct South Face. V, 5.7, A2. A mile or so up from the Stone House is the most monolithic section of the wide south face. Wander up ledges and cracks for about 1,000 feet to a very prominent tower. Climb a large, right-facing open book above this; then climb up and right, following a line of bushes, for another 1,000 feet to join Route 9 on its final headwall.

Route 11. South Gully. Class 4. To the left of the monolithic wall of the preceding route is a noticeable break in the wall. The gully is picked out easily on the map as the westward-trending, low-angle break in the cliffs some three-quarters of a mile south-southeast of the summit. The gully is a feasible descent route for climbs on the south face.

Route 12. West Side. Class 2. This is probably the most popular route. Leave the Meysan trail at the 10,900-foot level (halfway between the two Meysan Lakes) and climb very loose talus and scree to any of several chutes. Once the ridge is reached, easy walking northeast across the plateau brings one to the top.

Peak 12,960+ (1.2 SW of Lone Pine Pk.)

This peak, shown on some maps as Peak 13,016, lies just southeast of Meysan Lake. The summit can be reached from Lone Pine Peak by a class 2 or 3 traverse. Two technical routes have been established and both lie on a face 0.8 mile due south of Lone Pine Peak. According to the map, the face appears to be on Lone Pine Peak, but the watershed division between that peak and Peak 12,960+ lies quite close to the former. The impressive, high-angle wall is visible from the Stone House as the left skyline of the long massif. The climb known as the South Face Route lies close to this skyline. Start on a big transverse ledge system. V, 5.8, A2. The second route, Red Baron Tower, lies a bit farther to the left. Its reddish summit is seen as a very flat platform part way up the skyline when viewed from the Stone House. After two continuous, exposed aid pitches, the remainder of the route turns out to be interesting free climbing. Rappel the route. III, 5.7, A2.

Peak 12,880+ (1.5 SSW of Lone Pine Pk.)

Easy from the southwest. Class 4 via the west arete. Two small towers on the long east ridge have been climbed. The Tuttle Obelisk is a prominent spire near the head of the south fork of Tuttle Creek and is easily approached from the Stone House (see Lone Pine Peak). The route begins in a left-facing dihedral on the left side of the face. The obvious crack in the summit block presents the major problem. III, 5.9. A mile down canyon, near Point 10,607, is the Keystone. A chimney system provides a III, 5.8 route.

Mt. LeConte (13,960)

Route 1. Northwest Ridge. Class 3. Follow the gentle ridge to the final summit tower; then turn it on the right via a shelf. A short drop-off is downclimbed to a chimney or chute which is followed to the top.

Route 2. North Face. Class 4. A large cairn has been built under the north side of the final summit mass. Climb cracks above the cairn to a notch north of the summit.

Route 3. Northeast Face. Class 3. From the above-mentioned cairn, traverse southeast for about 200 yards. Halt before reaching the east arete and climb directly to the top.

Route 4. East Arete. Class 3. From the cairn traverse southeast, past the northeast face route, to the east arete. Climb a chimney nearly to the top; then follow the actual arete to the top.

Route 5. Southwest Ridge. This is a medium class 5 traverse from nearby Mt. Corcoran.

Route 6. West Side. Class 3. From a point about 200 yards north of the east side of Iridescent Lake climb up into a long couloir. When just below the crest, traverse left. It is possible to climb to the top from several points on this traverse; one can reach the final chute of Route 1 if desired.

Mt. Corcoran (13,760+)

Southeast of Mt. LeConte is a confusing jumble of summits. There has been some discussion about the location of the actual summit; the consensus seems to be that it is the tower with the very prominent east face, some 0.3 mile southeast of LeConte. Thus, working south from LeConte, one finds the following geography: a few small bumps, a bigger bump, and then a fairly significant notch. Above this notch are the steep ramparts of Corcoran's summit tower. This is followed by a smaller tower shaped like a shark tooth. Finally, one finds two massive, pyramidal humps.

The traverse of the four main Corcoran summits has been done. The southern summits are relatively easy, and the shark tooth can be climbed on its west side (5.3) or its east side (5.7). From the notch between the shark tooth and the main tower drop down a few hundred feet to the west; then traverse around onto the west face via class 4 rock. Easy going brings one quickly to the top. The main tower is also reached from the notch north of it and is class 2–3.

The Miter (12,770)

Climb easily to a small saddle just south of the summit; then wander up ledges to the top. Class 3. A chute on the northwest side of the mountain is also class 3.

Mt. Pickering (13,485)

Class 2 from most directions, but class 3–4 from nearby Mt. Newcomb.

Joe Devel Peak (13,325)

This peak, climbed very early, is the southernmost 13,000-footer in the Sierra. Class 2 from almost anywhere.

Mt. Guyot (12,300)

This isolated mountain is an easy stroll from all directions.

The Major General (12,400+)

This peaklet, at the end of the southwest spur of Mt. Langley, has a class 3 summit pinnacle.

Mt. Langley (14,027)

This peak represents the southern end of the climber's Sierra. Easy routes can be found on the south and west sides. The easy east plateau can be reached either from Diaz Creek (class 2) or from the Cottonwood Lakes (class 3 via the saddle just west of Point 12,722). The north face is class 3. A route has been done on the northeast side: from Tuttle Creek ascend slopes just east of Point 11,940. Class 2 or 3.

List of First Ascents

The following list shows the known first ascents for many Sierra peaks. The information is given in the same order in which it is found in the text. Peaks with unknown first ascents, or "first recorded ascents" (i.e. a cairn with no register was found) are omitted. Three abbreviations are used: FA: first ascent. FFA: first free ascent. FWA: first winter ascent.

Northern Yosemite

Bigelow Peak. Allan Starr, Ralph Minor, and Sherman Chickering. 1927.

Keyes Peak. A.J. Reyman. Sept. 1, 1942.

Forsyth Peak. South side: Rene Kast, Don Hersey, Paul Hersey, Al Teakle, Harry Tenney, Jr., Arthur Evans, and Leon Casou. July 10, 1937. North ridge: LeRoy Johnson, Fred Schaub, and Ken Hondsinger. Aug. 23, 1953.

Saurian Crest. John Dyer. Sept. 7, 1938.

Tower Peak. Standard route: Charles Hoffmann, W.A. Goodyear, and Alfred Craven. 1870. West face: Raffi Bedayan and Barbara Norris. July 15, 1941. Southeast face: Descended by Dave Brower, Dorothy Markwad, Pat Goldsworthy, Ted Grubb, and Bruce Meyer. July 1941.

Snow Peak. John Dyer. 1938.

Wells Peak. A.J. Reyman. July 27, 1945.

Ehrnbeck Peak. A.J. Reyman. July 27, 1945.

Grouse Mountain. Northwest side: A.J. Reyman. Aug. 3, 1949. East face: LeRoy Johnson, Fred Schaub, and Ken Hondsinger. Aug. 1953.

Center Mountain. Survey party. 1905.

Eagle Peak. George Davis, A.H. Sylvester, and Pearson Chapman. Sept. 1905.

Acker Peak. A.J. Reyman. July 28, 1945.

Price Peak. A.J. Reyman. July 28, 1945.

Piute Mountain. From Bear Valley: Francis Farquhar, James Rennie, and Frank Bumstead. July 27, 1911. North chute: FA unknown.

Bath Mountain. Ridge: Glen Dawson and John Cahill. July 30, 1934. Technical route: Vern Clevenger and Bill Dougherty. Sept. 1974.

Cirque Mountain. A.J. Reyman. Aug. 16, 1948.

Crown Point. Class 2 route: George Davis, A.H. Sylvester, and Pearson Chapman. 1905. Peeler Pillar: Greg Donaldson, Larry Johnson, and Geert Dijkhuis. Sept. 1971.

The Juggernaut. Open book: Galen Rowell, Vern Clevenger, Mike Farrell, and Bill Dougherty. Sept. 1974. Other route: Fred Beckey, Jack Roberts, and Dave Black. Sept. 1973.

Slide Mountain. Norman Clyde. 1921.

Suicide Ridge. Glen Dawson and John Cahill. May 31, 1934.

Kettle Peak. Easy route: Bill Dunmire and Bob Swift. Aug. 1948. Outguard Spire, original route: Bob Grow, Joe Kiskis, and John York. Sept. 1968. East face: Mike Warburton and Roger Gocking. July 1973. The Turret: Joe Kiskis. 1970. FFA: Bob Grow and Margaret Quick. July 1972. Regge Pole, original route: Greg Donaldson and Joe Kiskis. July 1970. Regge Pole, other route: Mike Warburton and Roger Gocking. Aug. 1973. The Duck: Greg Donaldson and Joe Kiskis. July 1970.

The Incredible Hulk. Easiest route: Bob Grow and Joe Kiskis. May 1971. Grade V route: Greg Donaldson, Joe Kiskis, and Bob Grow. 1970. Third route: Mike Warburton, Dave Warburton, Roger Gocking, and Darien Hopkins. 1973.

Eocene Peak. Richard Leonard and Herbert Blanks. July 16, 1932.

Blacksmith Peak. Route 1: Richard Leonard and Bestor Robinson. July 3, 1933. Route 2: Lito Tejada-Flores and Chris Jones. July 1973. Route 3: Doug Robinson and friend. July 1973. Route 4: Bestor Robinson and Carl Jensen. Sept. 8, 1936.

Cleaver Peak. Route 1: Oliver Kehrlein and Henry Beers. July 3, 1933. Route 2: Glen Dawson and Jack Riegelhuth. July 27, 1934. Route 3: M.L. Wade and F. Chrisholm. Aug. 6, 1950.

The Cleaver. FA unknown. Goldfinger: Fred Beckey and Joe Brown. Oct. 27, 1968.

The Sawblade. Hervey Voge and Dave Brower. July 25, 1934.

The Three Teeth. Route 1: Henry Beers, Richard Leonard, and Bestor Robinson. July 2, 1933. Route 2: Glen Dawson and Jack Riegelhuth. July 25, 1934. Route 3: Dave Brower, Art Argiewicz, and Bruce Meyer. July 23, 1941. Route 4: Oscar Cook, Joe Firey, Larry Taylor, and Jack Hansen. 1949. Route 5: Lewis Clark, Richard Johnson, Oliver Kehrlein, and Randolph May. July 2, 1933. Route 6: Mike Heath and Bill Sumner. Aug. 1972. Route 7: Galen Rowell, Jim Jones, and Fred Beckey. June 1969.

The Doodad. South side: Kenneth May and Howard Twining. July 7, 1934. Glacier face: James Derby, Peter Lipman, and Tom Vaughan. July 1956.

The Dragtooth. Route 1: Walter Brem, Glen Dawson, and Jules Eichorn. July 20, 1931. Route 2: Joe Firey, Norm Goldstein, Chuck Wharton, and John Ohrenschall. 1952. Route 3: Hervey Voge and J.C. Southard. July 16, 1941. Route 4: Jack Miller and Reed Cundiff. June 1971. Route 5: K. Boche and M. Bomba. July 1970.

Matterhorn Peak. Route 1: James Hutchinson, Lincoln Hutchinson, M.R. Dempster, and Charles Noble. 1899. Route 2: FA unknown. Route 3: FA unknown. Route 4: Jerry Gallwas, Wally Kodis, and Don Wilson. Sept. 1954. Lower 5.8 variation: Rupert Kammerlander and Bruce McCubbrey. July 1974. Direct arete: Mike Hane and Frank Uher. July 1970. Route 5: Rich Gnagy, Burt Turney, Gen Turney, and Rick Brosch. July 1965. Route 6: Walter Brem, Glen Dawson, and Jules Eichorn. July 20, 1931.

Petite Capucin. Gene Drake, Rich Stevenson, and Jim Orey. July 1972.

Horse Creek Tower. Fred Beckey, Mike McGoey, and Leland Davis. May 1973.

Finger Peaks. Jules Eichorn, Glen Dawson, and Walter Brem. July 19, 1931.

Whorl Mountain. Middle summit: Herbert Blanks, Kenneth May, and Elliot Sawyer. July 9, 1933. South summit: J.W. Combs, R.W. Messer, and William Goldsborough. July 23, 1911. North summit: Ralph Chase and Sierra Club party. July 17, 1921.

Horse Creek Peak. Jim Orey and Gene Drake. July 1972.

Wapama Rock. Galen Rowell and Joe Faint. April 1969.

Hetch Hetchy Dome. Galen Rowell and Chris Jones. 1970.

Kolana Rock. Galen Rowell and Warren Harding. June 1971.

West Peak. Kenneth May and Gus Smith. July 17, 1931.

Regulation Peak. R.A. Chase. 1921.

Volunteer Peak. H.C. Benson and Lt. McBride. 1895.

Doghead Peak. H.C. Bradley. Prior to 1911.

Quarry Peak. George Davis, A.H. Sylvester, and Pearson Chapman. 1905.

Virginia Peak. Kenneth May and Howard Twining. July 3, 1934.

Stanton Peak. Richard Johnson, Kenneth May, and Howard Twining. May 31, 1934.

Grey Butte. Howard Twining. Aug. 1934.

Camiaca Peak. Walter Huber. 1917.

Epidote Peak. Sierra Club party. 1917.

Dunderberg Peak. Lt. Macomb and other Wheeler Survey members. 1878.

Black Mountain. George Davis, A.H. Sylvester, and Pearson Chapman. 1905.

Excelsior Mountain. Howard Sloan. June 13, 1931.

Shepherd Crest. South side: Herbert Blanks, Kenneth May, and Elliot Sawyer. July 13, 1933. Northeast ridge: W. Ryland Hill and Charles Chesterman. July 5, 1941.

Sheep Peak. Kenneth May and Howard Twining. July 1, 1934.

North Peak. Class 2 route: Smoke Blanchard, Gary Leech, and Hubert North. June 26, 1937. Snow couloir: FA unknown. Long, deep chimney: Bob Summers and John Gibbins. Aug. 1969. Northeast face, right side: Galen Rowell and Barry Hagen. July 1969.

Mt. Conness. Route 1: Clarence King and James Gardiner. Sept. 1, 1866. Route 2: FA unknown. Route 3: FA unknown. Route 4: George Harr, Lynn Grey, and Ray Van Aken. July 1958. Route 5: Galen Rowell and Barry Hagen. July 1969. Route 6: Dick Long and friends. 1957? Route 7: Warren Harding, Herb Swedlund, and Glen Denny. Sept. 1959. Route 8: Gary Colliver and Chris Vandiver. July 1974.

White Mountain. Walter Huber. 1917.

Ragged Peak. Easiest route: William Brewer and Charles Hoffmann. July 6, 1863. Northwest face: Boynton Kaiser and Sierra Club group. Aug. 25, 1939. Northeast face: Adrian Rosenthal and Jeff Genest. July 1971. East face: Warren Harding, Norah Straley, and Ray Alcott. Aug. 16, 1953.

Peak 12,002. Daniel Zucker. June 24, 1969.

Mt. Warren. Mr. Wackenreyder. Prior to 1868.

Tuolumne Peak. Route 1: FA unknown, but prior to 1932. Route 2: Bruce

Kinnison and Ken Gobalet. July 1968. Route 3: Bruce Kinnison, Ken Gobalet, and George Gray. Sept. 10, 1974. Route 4: Bob Ashworth and Bruce Kinnison. July 1972.

Mt. Hoffmann. Route 1: Josiah Whitney, William Brewer, and Charles Hoffmann. June 24, 1863. Route 2: FA unknown. Route 3: George Sessions and Bob Summers. Aug. 1969. Route 4: Merle Alley and George Sessions. July 1957. Route 5: Vern Clevenger and Virginia Wallblom. Aug. 1974. Route 6: Steve Williams and Richard Doleman. Sept. 1970. Route 7: Jules Eichorn. Oct. 16, 1932. Route 8: Jerry Gray, George Ewing, and Les Overstreet. Aug. 1968.

Wildcat Point. FA unknown. South buttress: Galen Rowell and Dale Bard. Aug. 1972.

Cold Mountain. FA unknown, but prior to 1929. Buttress: Joe Kelsey, Galen Rowell, and TM Herbert. Sept. 1972.

Tuolumne Domes

Stately Pleasure Dome. Route 1: Bob Summers, John Gibbins, and Sue German. 1969. Route 2: Bob Summers and John Fischer. July 1969. Major variation: Bob Summers and Steve Williams. 1970. Route 3: Tom Naylor, Mary Naylor, and Earl Olsen. 1965. Route 4: Eric Beck and Bob Kamps. July 1971. Route 5: Hope Morehouse, Jim Baldwin, and Jeff Foott. 1962. Route 6: Vern Clevenger and Rob Frick. Nov. 1973. Route 7: Vern Clevenger and Bill Nickell. May 1974. Route 8: Gordon Webster and Frank deSaussure. 1965. Route 9: Vern Clevenger, Eric Schoen, and Rob Frick. Nov. 1973. Route 10: Tom Higgins and Bob Kamps. July 1974.

Harlequin Dome. Route 1: Jim Bridwell and Roger Breedlove. July 1972. Route 2: Loyd Price. Aug. 1970.

Mountaineer's Dome. Route 1: Vern Clevenger and Mike Munger. Aug. 1971. Route 2: Tom Gerughty, Chris Vandiver, Dick Dorworth, and Jim Speck. July 1971. Route 3: Vern Clevenger, Rick Accomazzo, Tom McCabe, and Daryle Teske. July 1974. Route 4: Vern Clevenger and Jon Ross. July 1972. Route 5: Vern Clevenger and companion. July 1972.

Polly Dome. Route 1: Mark Klemens and Jerry Anderson. Aug. 1967. Route 2: Dick Erb and Tom Gerughty. Aug. 1966. Route 3: Tom Higgins and Tom Gerughty. Aug. 1970. Route 4: Loyd Price and Bob Marsh. 1969.

Pywiack Dome. Route 1: Greg Donaldson. 1970. Route 2: FA unknown. Route 3: Tom Gerughty, Dave Meeks, and Roger Evja. 1966. Route 4: Jeff Foott and Gary Colliver. 1966.

Pennyroyal Arches. Route 1: Tom Higgins and Tom Gerughty. Aug. 1970. Route 2: Tom Gerughty, Don Lauria, Mike Cohen, and Jack Miller. 1970. Route 3: Wayne Merry, Jack Miller, and Tom Gerughty. 1969.

Medlicott Dome. Route 1: FA unknown. Route 2: Wayne Merry and Jerry Mernin. 1962. Route 3: FA unknown. Route 4: Dave Calfee and TM Herbert. June 1967. Route 5: TM Herbert and Gordon Webster. 1966. FFA: Phil Bircheff. 1969. Route 6: Tom Higgins and Bob Kamps. 1968. Route 7: Tom Higgins and Bob Kamps. June 1968. Route 8: Bob Kamps and Tom Higgins. June 1968. Route 9: Bob Kamps and Tom Higgins. June 1968. Route 10: Tom Higgins and Chris Vandiver. June 1972.

Mariuolumne Dome. Route 1: Charlie Raymond and Gordon Webster. 1965. Route 2: Dick Erb and Steve Roper. 1968.

The Lamb. Route 1: FA unknown. Route 2: TM Herbert, Jim Bridwell, and Royal Robbins. 1970? Route 3: Eric Furman and Earl Furman. Sept. 1970. Route 4: Dick Erb and Tom Gerughty. 1966. Route 5: Steve Williams and Bob Summers. Aug. 1970. Route 6: Tom Higgins and TM Herbert. 1968. Route 7: Mike Graham, Rick Accomazzo, and Vern Clevenger. July 1974 Route 8: Chris Vandiver, Pat Ament, and Tom Higgins. June 1971.

South Whizz Dome. Route 1: George Sessions, Dave Harvey, and Buddy Huff. Aug. 1969. Route 2: Mark Powell, Bev Powell, and Bob Kamps. 1969.

North Whizz Dome. Route 1: Steve Thompson and Tom Higgins. June 1968. Route 2: Tom Higgins. 1970. Route 3: Ellen Wilts and Janet Wilts. Sept. 1961. Route 4: Steve Thompson and Mary Thompson. June 1968. Route 5: Art Beckman and John Shervais. July 1974.

Fairview Dome. Route 1: Dick Irvin, Bob Summers, and Howell Helmke. 1964. Route 2: Tom Higgins and Bob Kamps. July 1967. Route 3: Glen Denny and Wally Reed. July 1962. Route 4: Bob Kamps and Mark Powell. 1964. Route 5: Chuck Pratt and Wally Reed. Aug. 1958. Route 6: Tom Higgins, Bob Kamps, and Mike Irwin. Sept. 1973. Route 7: Tom Higgins and Vern Clevenger. Aug. 1974. Route 8: Bob Kamps and Tom Higgins. July 1967. Route 9: Bob Harrington, Dale Bard, and Vern Clevenger. June 1974.

Daff Dome. Route 1: Frank Sacherer and Wally Reed. 1963. Route 2: Layton Kor and Fred Beckey. June 1965. FFA: Bob Kamps and TM Herbert. Route 3: Wayne Merry and Dick Dorworth. July 1971. Route 4: Bob Kamps and Tom Higgins. July 1967. Route 5: Mark Powell, Bev Powell, and Bob Kamps. 1968?

Lembert Dome. Route 1: Dorothy Dern, Richard Leonard, H. Stewart Kimball, Philip Dern, and Alfred Dole. 1951. Route 2: Warren Harding and Frank deSaussure. 1954. Route 3: Lance Poulson, Royal Robbins, and Dick Dorworth. July 1970. Route 4: Russ Warne and friends. Late 1950s. FFA: Mark Powell, Bev Powell, and Bob Kamps. 1964? Route 5: Frank Tarver and Gordon Petrequin. 1953. Route 6: FA unknown. Route 7: Warren Harding and friends. Mid–1950s. Route 8: Dick Dorworth and Chris Vandiver. 1971. Route 9: Tom Higgins and Bob Kamps. 1970. Route 10: Mike Cohen, Ken Boche, and Russ McLean. 1970. Route 11: Werner Braun. Aug. 1969. Route 12: Jim Speck, Bruce Brossman, Dick Dorworth, and Chris Vandiver. July 1971. Route 13: Patsy Batchelder, Alan Bard, Micky Caldwell, Paul Wehr, and Vern Clevenger. June 1974. Route 14: Bob Summers and Steve Williams. Aug. 1971. Route 15: Chris Vandiver and Dick Dorworth. 1971. Route 16: Vern Clevenger and Doug Clyde. Aug. 1971.

Dog Dome. Route 1: Dick Erb, Larry Malliett, and Steve Roper. June 1968. Route 2: Jack Miller and Bill Worthington. Aug. 1970. Route 3: Bob Ashworth and Craig Patterson. Aug. 1974.

Southern Yosemite

Mt. Dana. From Tioga Pass: William Brewer and Charles Hoffmann. June 28, 1863. Via glacier: FA unknown. Pillar: Phil Bircheff and Bill Bonebrake. July 1969. Buttress: Phil Bircheff and Gary Ogg. July 1971.

Mt. Gibbs. William Brewer, F.L. Olmsted, and a horse. Aug. 31, 1864.

Mt. Lewis. FA unknown. Technical route: Art Buck and Allen Fletcher. Oct. 1972.

Mammoth Peak. Walter Huber. 1902.

Kuna Crest. Walter Huber. 1909.

Kuna Peak. Walter Huber. 1919.

Koip Peak. Chester Versteeg. 1912.

Parker Peak. Norman Clyde. 1914.

Koip Crest. Traverse: Milton Hildebrand and George Templeton. Aug. 9, 1939. Prominent chimney: Richard Leonard and Jim Koontz. Aug. 1950. Grade II route: Art Buck and Allen Fletcher. July 1973.

Donohue Peak. Sgt. Donohue and a horse. 1895.

Mt. Lyell. Route 1: John Tileston. Aug. 29, 1871. FWA: Dave Brower, Lewis Clark, Boynton Kaiser, Einar Nilsson, and Bestor Robinson. Mar. 2, 1936. Routes 2 and 3: FA unknown. Route 4: George Whitmore. July 1955. Route 5: Les Wilson, Dennis Schmitt, Tim Gerson, and Peter Haan. Aug. 1963. Route 6: FA unknown.

Mt. Maclure. Normal route: Willard Johnson. 1883. Class 4 ridge: Allen Steck and George Steck. Mid–1950s. Southwest face: Ted Waller and a Sierra Club group. 1934.

Peak 12,358. Julie Mortimer and May Pridham. July 1934.

Peak 12,720+. George Whitmore. July 1955.

Peak 12,132. George Whitmore. July 1955.

Rodgers Peak. John Muir (probably). 1870s.

Peak 12,560+. Ansel Adams, Cedric Wright, and Willard Grinnell. July 10, 1924.

Electra Peak. Norman Clyde. 1914.

Mt. Ansel Adams. Glen Dawson, Jack Riegelhuth, and Neil Ruge. July 11, 1934.

Foerster Peak. Norman Clyde. 1914. North ridge: George Whitmore. July 1954.

Long Mountain. Ansel Adams. 1922.

Tenaya Peak. FA unknown. 5.6 route: Wayne Merry and John Ward. July 1961. 5.7 route: George Sessions and Dave Harvey. Aug. 23, 1971.

Columbia Finger. William Staniels, Donald Tripp, and B.H. Bochmer. July 22, 1921. Grade II route: Richard Hechtel and Jan Mostowski. Sept. 1970.

Tresidder Peak. FA unknown, but prior to 1948. North arete: Bruce Kinnison, Alan Zetterberg, and Pierre Zetterberg. July 4, 1966.

Cathedral Peak. Route 1. John Muir. Sept. 1869. Route 2: Wally Reed and Cathy Warne. July 1961. Route 3: Frank Tarver and Gordon Petrequin. July 1953. Route 4: Chuck Wilts and Spencer Austin. 1940s. Route 5: Wally Reed and Don Harmon. July 1962. Route 6: Glen Dawson and Jules Eichorn. July 24, 1931. Route 7: Wally Reed and Gary Colliver. June 1966. Route 8: Gary Colliver and Mike Cohen. July 1972. Route 9: Larry Corona and Jim Mitchell. July 1972.

Echo Peaks. Peak 1: Owen Williams. Aug. 4, 1936. Direct west face: Jerry Anderson and Ron Cagle. July 1972. North arete: Bruce Kinnison and Ken Gobalet. June 1967. Peak 2: FA unknown. Peak 3: Norman Clyde and Carl Sharsmith. July 7, 1931. Peak 4: Owen Williams and Ethyl Mae Hill. Aug. 6, 1936. Peaks 5–8: FA unknown. Peak 9: Chuck Wilts and Spencer Austin.

Echo Ridge. FA unknown. North face: Joe Firey, Peter Hoessly, Ron Hahn, and Ed Robbins. 1949.

Cockscomb. Lipman and Chamberlain. 1914.

Matthes Crest. Jules Eichorn, Glen Dawson, and Walter Brem. July 26, 1931. South arete: Chuck Wilts and Ellen Wilts. 1947. 5.9 route: Roger Gocking, Mike Warburton, and Ken Dekleva. July 1973. Grade III route: Same team as preceding route.

Unicorn Peak. Regular route: FA unknown. Northeast face: Francis Farquhar and James Rennie. 1911. 5.8 route: Alex Bertulis and Half Zantop. Sept. 1965.

Johnson Peak. Herbert Blanks. 1933.

Rafferty Peak. Edward Hernden. Date unknown.

Peak 11,282. Julie Mortimer, Alice Carter, and Eleanor Smith. 1931. Buttress: Chuck Pratt and Doug Robinson. July 1968. 5.9 route: Fred Beckey and Pete Metcalf. Sept. 22, 1974.

Fletcher Peak. FA unknown. Class 4 route: Ronald Smith and Bob Happle. Aug. 1959.

Vogelsang Peak. François Matthes. Prior to 1923.

Amelia Earhart Peak. FA unknown. Class 4 route: Allen Steck and Lee Steck. July 1973.

Parsons Peak. Marion Randall Parsons. Prior to 1931.

Simmons Peak. Sierra Club group. 1931.

Mt. Florence. Theodore Solomons and F.W. Reed. Aug. 1897.

Mt. Clark. Route 1: Clarence King and James Gardiner. July 12, 1866. FWA: Dave Brower, Ken Adam, Hervey Voge, and Ken Davis. Feb. 1937. Route 2: Ken Boche and Joe McKeown. Aug. 1970. Route 3: Neil Ruge and Douglas Olds. Oct. 1934. Route 4: Henry Kendall, Herb Swedlund, Hobey DeStaebler, and Tom Frost. Sept. 1958. Route 5: Francis Farquhar. 1916.

Gray Peak. Ansel Adams. 1920.

Red Peak. California Geological Survey (probably). 1870.

Merced Peak. California Geological Survey (probably). 1870. Grade III route: Ken Boche and Mary Bomba. July 1971.

Triple Divide Peak. Norman Clyde. 1920.

The Ritter Range

Mt. Davis. Route 1: Milton Davis. Aug. 28, 1891. Route 2: Jim Koontz and Sarah Haynes. Aug. 20, 1950. Route 3: Hervey Voge and Virginia Romain. Aug. 20, 1950. Route 4: Dave Rossum, Ann Gibson, and Rich Clough. July 1966.

Banner Peak. Route 1: FA unknown. Route 2: Chuck Wilts and Harry Sutherland. July 6, 1946. Route 3: Jules Eichorn and Robert L.M. Underhill. Aug. 3, 1931. Route 4: Allen Steck and Floyd Burnette. Aug. 1961. Route 5: Kim Grandfield and Arne Myrabo. Aug. 9–10, 1975. Route 6: Kevin Sutter and Dave Harden. Aug. 1973. Route 7: Jim Koontz and Sarah Haynes. Aug. 1950. Route 8: Willard Johnson and John Miller. Aug. 26, 1883. FWA: Chester Errett, Bob Brinton, and Lloyd Warner. Mar. 1, 1939.

Mt. Ritter. Route 1: John Muir. Oct. 1872. Route 2: Art Argiewicz and Lorin Trubschenk. Aug. 7, 1941. Route 3: Nick Clinch and Tom Hornbein. Sept. 1961. Route 4: Descended by John Muir. Oct. 1872. Harder route: Norman Clyde. June 28, 1928. Route 5: Theodore Solomons. Aug. 20, 1892. FWA: George Bloom, Bob Swift, and Floyd Burnette. Feb. 1952.

Peak 12,344. Mike Loughman and Steve Arnon. 1964.

Volcanic Ridge. Craig Barbash and Howard Gates. Aug. 13, 1933.

Starr Minaret. From South Notch: Walter Starr, Sr., Ansel Adams, and Rondal Partridge. July 14, 1937. East face: Chuck Wilts and Ray Van Aken. Sept. 1960. Sleeping Beauty Chimney: Rupert Kammerlander and John Schaffert. Aug. 1974.

Watchtower. Rupert Kammerlander and John Schaffert. Aug. 1974.

Riegelhuth Minaret. From col: Jack Reigelhuth, Charlotte Mauk, Josephine

Allen, and Bill Leovey. July 13, 1938. North face: Lito Tejada-Flores and David Tonkin. Aug. 6, 1955. East face: Gilles Corcos and Steve Roper. Aug. 1973.

Pridham Minaret. May Pridham and Mary Van Velsen. July 4, 1938.

Kehrlein Minaret. From South Notch: Norman Clyde. Aug. 23, 1933. North face: Fred Hudson and R. Olson. Aug. 1941. East ridge: Chuck Wilts and Ray Van Aken. Sept. 3, 1961.

Ken Minaret. Northeast face: W. Kenneth Davis and Ken Adam. Sept. 5, 1938. Southeast ridge: Chuck Wilts, Ellen Wilts, and Ray Van Aken. Labor Day, 1958. West face: Descended by Northeast-face team.

Clyde Minaret. Route 1: Walter Starr, Jr. Aug. 8, 1932. Route 2: Glen Dawson, John Nixon, and William Horsfall. July 26, 1929. Route 3: Norman Clyde. June 27, 1928. Route 4: FA unknown: probably in the early 1930s. Route 5: FA unknown. FWA: Allen Steck, Bill Long, and Jim Wilson. Jan. 2, 1948. Route 6: Allen Steck, John Evans, Chuck Wilts, and Dick Long. June 22, 1963.

Eichorn Minaret. Jules Eichorn, Glen Dawson, and Walter Brem. July 31, 1931. Northeast face: Jim Gorin and friends. 1955.

Michael Minaret. Route 1: Charles Michael. Sept. 6, 1923. Route 2: Glen Dawson, Jules Eichorn, and Richard Jones. Aug. 16, 1933. Route 3: Walter Starr, Jr. Aug. 3, 1933. FWA: Dick Long, Jim Wilson, George Bloom, and George Marks. Route 4: FA unknown. Route 5: Mike Sherrick and Wally Tinsley. Aug. 31, 1958. Route 6: Allen Steck, George Steck, and John Dorsey. Aug. 13, 1962. Route 7: Norman Clyde. Aug. 25, 1933.

Adams Minaret. Ansel Adams and Rondal Partridge. July 15, 1937.

Rice Minaret. Via Starr's Chute: William Rice and Torcom Bedayan. Aug. 11, 1936. Other chute: Hervey Voge and L. Bruce Meyer. Aug. 25, 1950. East side: Rich Gnagy and Barbara Lilley. Sept. 1965.

Bedayan Minaret. Route 1: Torcom Bedayan and William Rice. Aug. 11, 1936. Route 2: Hervey Voge and L. Bruce Meyer. Aug. 25, 1950. Route 3:

FA unknown. Route 4: Rich Gnagy and Barbara Lilley. July 6, 1963.

Dawson Minaret. From the Bedayan-Dawson notch: FA unknown. From North Notch: Glen Dawson, Jules Eichorn, and Richard Jones. Aug. 16, 1933.

Dyer Minaret. William Horsfall and John Dyer. 1940. Other route: Allen Steck and John Dorsey. Aug. 1962.

North Notch Minaret. FA unknown.

Jensen Minaret. From North Notch: Carl Jensen and Howard Gates. June 1937. Chimney route: Spencer Austin, Chuck Wilts, and Dan Bannerman. July 27, 1943.

Turner Minaret. Ed Turner and two others. July 14, 1938. Other route: Rupert Kammerlander. Sept. 1972.

Leonard Minaret. Route 1: Richard Leonard and Herbert Blanks. Aug. 4, 1932. Route 2: Norman Clyde. Aug. 19, 1933. Route 3: Don Wilson and Bob Weyman. Sept. 3, 1964.

Waller Minaret. Route 1: Ted Waller and Jules Eichorn. Aug. 1934. FWA: Dick Long, Jim Wilson, Dave Beck, and George Bloom. Dec. 29, 1963. Route 2: Bob Hill and Dick Long. July 1961. Direct route: Rupert Kammerlander and Craig Mackay. Aug. 1971.

Carson Peak. FA unknown. Grade III route: Pete Kilbourne and Loring Young. June 11, 1974. Grade IV route: Pete Kilbourne, Vern Clevenger, and Bill Dougherty. Sept. 6, 1974.

The Mono Recesses

Crystal Crag. FA unknown, but probably before 1900. North buttress: Alvin McLane, John Houghton, and Reggie Donatelli. Mar. 3, 1968. Northeast face: Owen Williams. Aug. 11, 1936. East face: Galen Rowell and Vern Clevenger. Jan. 1973.

Peak 12,052. E.S. Wallace, E.E. Wix, and Bill Dye. Aug. 18, 1924.

Peak 11,760+. Andy Smatko, Ellen Siegal, Bill Schuler, and Bob Herlihy. Sept. 4, 1966.

Peak 11,894. Andy Smatko, Bill Schuler, and Bob Herlihy. Sept. 5, 1966.

Bloody Mountain. Norman Clyde. July 3, 1928.

Laurel Mountain. Norman Clyde. Sept. 25, 1926. Trough: John Mendenhall 1925. Class 4 route. John Mendenhall and James Van Patten. Sept. 7, 1930.

Mt. Morrison. Route 1: John Mendenhall. 1928. Route 2: Chuck Wilts and Harry Sutherland. Sept. 1946. FWA: Reggie Donatelli, Alvin McLane, and Brian Bartlett. Jan. 22, 1968. Route 3: Ron Hayes, Allen Steck, and Jim Wilson. July 4–5, 1960. Route 4: Tom Higgins and Charlie Raymond. May 1967. Route 5: John Mendenhall. 1931. Route 6: Norman Clyde. June 22, 1928.

Mt. Aggie. A.J. Reyman. Sept. 1, 1952.

Peak 12,240+. Galen Rowell, Pat Callis, and Charlie Raymond. Apr. 1968.

Mt. Baldwin. Norman Clyde. July 2, 1928.

Peak 12,227. Dave Brower. July 17, 1934.

Peak 12,160+. Bill Schuler, Andy Smatko, and Ed Treacy. July 7, 1971.

Red Slate Mountain. James Gardiner (possibly). 1864.

Peak 12,400+. A.J. Reyman. Aug. 29, 1952.

Peak 12,320+. Dave Brower and Hervey Voge. July 17, 1934.

Graveyard Peak. William Stewart and David Parish. Sept. 8, 1935.

Peak 11,840+. Norman Clyde and Jim Harkins. July 20, 1938.

Mt. Izaak Walton. Andy Smatko, Bill Schuler, and Ed Treacy. July 5, 1971.

Peak 12,238. G.A. Daum, G.F. Hurley, and J.M. Schnitzler. Aug. 14, 1952. Class 5 route: Tom Flynn and Ken Cardwell. Aug. 1972.

Red and White Mountain. James Hutchinson, Lincoln Hutchinson, and C.A. Noble. 1902.

Mt. Crocker. Nazario Sparrea. Aug. 25, 1929.

Peak 12,408. T.H. Hasheim, Elly Hinreiner, and Jean Campbell. July 5, 1950.

Mt. Hopkins. Dave Brower, Norman Clyde, and Hervey Voge. July 16, 1934.

Peak 12,178. A.J. Reyman. Aug. 26, 1958.

Mt. Morgan (north). Dave Brower and Norman Clyde. July 9, 1934.

Mt. Stanford. George Davis, C.F. Urquhart, R.B. Marshall, and L.F. Biggs. 1907?

Peak 12,318. Dave Brower, Norman Clyde, and Hervey Voge. July 14, 1934.

Mt. Huntington. Dave Brower, Norman Clyde, and Hervey Voge. July 14, 1934.

Mt. Morgan (south). Wheeler Survey party. About 1870.

Peak 13,265. Chester Versteeg. Sept. 25, 1944.

Broken Finger Peak. Frank Yates, Andy Smatko, and Bill Schuler. Oct. 28, 1967.

Mono Rock. Norman Clyde and friend. July 18, 1934. East face: Bill Wallace. Aug. 17, 1953. North face: Lester LaVelle, Paul Hunter, Joe Sharp, Willard Dean, Dan Sharp, and Homer Wellman. Aug. 6, 1946.

Mt. Starr. Walter Starr, Sr. and Allen Chickering. July 16, 1896.

Peak 13,198. First route: Fritz Gerstacher and Virginia Whitacre. July 25, 1946. Second route: Jim Koontz, Ralph Perry, and Fred Peters. Aug. 17, 1953. East buttress: Lester LaVelle and Malcolm Smith. Aug. 1, 1946. Gendarmes: Mike Loughman and Jay Waller. 1963.

Mt. Mills. Route 1: James Hutchinson, Joseph N. LeConte, and Duncan McDuffie. July 10, 1908. Route 2: FA unknown. FWA: Dick Beach, Barnard Hallet, Dave MacCoard, Charles Morfin, Frank Risely, and Mike Risely. Feb. 14, 1971. Route 3: Rich Gnagy, Barbara Lilley, and Sy Ossofsky. July 1960. Route 4: Jim Koontz, Marian Steineke, Louis Christian, and Jim Carl. July 23, 1953.

Mt. Abbot. Route 1: M. Yeatman and M.L. Huggins. Aug. 30, 1927. Route 2: C.N. LaVene and Hervey Voge. July 22, 1953. Route 3: Jame Hutchinson, Joseph N. LeConte, and Duncan McDuffie. July 13, 1908. Route 4: S.W. French. Aug. 19, 1932. Route 5: Descended by S.W. French. Aug. 19. 1932. Route 6: FA unknown. FWA: George Barnes, Lowell Smith, Margaret Young, Pat Buchanan, Bob Summers, and Dave Duff. Dec. 30, 1967.

Mt. Dade. Route 1: Liston and McKeen. Aug. 19, 1911. Route 2: FA unknown. Route 3: Lloyd Chorley and Don Chorley. Aug. 24, 1951. Route 4: Arold Green, Dave Brown, and Bill Stronge. 1972. Route 5: Ray Van Aken and Kim Malville. Sept. 1956. Route 6: Fredrick Roy Suppe. Aug. 20, 1960.

Mt. Gabb. Route 1: H.H. Bliss and A.L. Jordan. June 17, 1917. Route 2: FA unknown. Route 3: Jim Koontz, Al Schmitz, Ralph Perry, Fred Peters, and George Wallerstein. Aug. 13, 1953. Route 4: FA unknown. Route 5: FA unknown.

Mt. Hilgard. Easy route: Charles Urquhart. July 10, 1905. Northeast ridge: Arkel Erb, Ed Lane, and Barbara Lilley. Sept. 8, 1963.

Peak 12,720+. Class 4 route: Jim Koontz, Al Schmitz, George Wallerstein, and Fred Peters. Aug. 11, 1953. South side: Descent by same group.

Volcanic Knob. Owen Williams. Aug. 14, 1937.

Bear Creek Spire. Route 1: H.F. Ulrichs. Aug. 16, 1923. Route 2: Galen Rowell and Jeanne Neale. Aug. 1971. Route 3: Norman Clyde. May 27, 1932. Route 4: Norman Clyde. Oct. 6, 1931. Route 5: FA unknown. Route 6: Galen Rowell. Aug. 1971. Route 7: FA unknown.

Peak 13,120+. Jim Koontz, Mike Loughman, Dan Popper, and Roger Popper. July 8, 1954.

Peak 12,866. Norman Clyde. 1927.

Mt. Julius Caesar. A.H. Prater and Myrtle Prater. Aug. 12, 1928. From lake: Jim Koontz, Pete Murphy, Al Wolf, and Ed Toby. Aug. 9, 1953. A winter ascent, by an unknown route, was made by Tom Ross and Pete Lewis. Mar. 18, 1965.

Peak 12,756. Dave Brower and George Rockwood. July 13, 1933.

Peak 12,563. Norman Clyde. 1938. First 5.7 route: Gary Colliver, Andy Lichtman, and Mark Waller. Aug. 1966. Other technical route: Andy Lichtman and Mike Cohen. Aug. 1966.

Feather Peak. Southwest ridge: Dave Brower. July 13, 1933. East-northeast face: Gary Colliver, Edward Keller, Mark Waller, and Andy Lichtman. Aug. 1966.

Royce Peak. Nathan Clark and Roy Crites. June 23, 1931.

Merriam Peak. Lewis Clark, Julie Mortimer, and Ted Waller. July 14, 1933. East side: A. Bryant and B. Helliwell. 1939.

Seven Gables. From west: Theodore Solomons and Leigh Bierce. Sept. 20, 1894. Class 4 route: Steve Roper and Jani Roper. Aug. 1, 1970.

Peak 12,287. W.J. Losh. July 1947.

Gemini. Jim Koontz and Rosemary Lenel. July 30, 1953.

The Pinnacles. Highest point: Glen Dawson, Neil Ruge, and Alfred Weiler.

July 14, 1933. Two southern pinnacles: Bruce Meyer and Jim Harkins. July 5, 1939.

Mt. Hooper. Glen Dawson, William Horsfall, and John Nixon. 1929.

Mt. Senger. George Davis, T.G. Gerdine, C.F. Urquhart, and L.F. Biggs. 1907?

Four Gables. Norman Clyde. 1931. Grade III route: Galen Rowell and Jeanne Neale. June 1971. Grade II route: Fred Beckey and Mike Levine. June 15, 1974.

Mt. Tom. Tom Clark (possibly). 1860.

Basin Mountain. Norman Clyde. Sept. 15, 1937.

Peak 12,160+. Smoke Blanchard. 1940s. Northeast face: Galen Rowell, Jay Jensen, Gordon Wiltsie, and Helmut Kiene. Aug. 1975.

Mt. Humphreys. Route 1. G.R. Bunn and others. Aug. 3, 1919. FWA: Dick Long, Jim Wilson, Gary Hemming, Steve Roper, Fred Martin, and Terry Tarver. Dec. 28, 1956. Route 2: Jack Reigelhuth, Dick Cahill, George Wilkins, Bill Leovy, and Bruce Meyer. July 28, 1938. Route 3: James Hutchinson and E.C. Hutchinson. July 18, 1904. Route 4: Hervey Voge. July 7, 1933. Route 5: Norman Clyde. June 29, 1935. Route 6: Galen Rowell and Joe Faint. May 1970. Route 7: FA unknown. Route 8: C.H. Rhudy, L.C. Bogue, and J.L. Findlay. July 18, 1920.

Peak 13,112. FA unknown. Snow couloir: Doug Robinson and friend. 1970.

Mt. Emerson. Route 1: Norman Clyde. July 1, 1926. Route 2: FA unknown. Route 3: FA unknown. Route 4: G. Ledyard Stebbins and Robert Stebbins. Aug. 1955.

Piute Crags. High point: Norman Clyde. 1927. Other climbs were done in 1949, 1950, and 1951 by George Harr, Chuck Wilts, Ray Van Aken, and a few others.

Balloon Dome. Route 1: Alex LaPralty and Mel Lamberson. July 22, 1942.

Route 2: Dave Black, Jim Black, and Mike Graber. June 1974. Route 3: Fred Beckey, Reed Cundiff, and Bill Hackett. June 2, 1971. Route 4: Dave Black, Jim Black, and Mike Graber. June 1974. Route 5: Dave Black and Mike Graber. June 1974.

East Fuller Butte. Route 1: Fred Beckey, Greg Donaldson, Jim Stuart, and Walt Vennum. May 1972. Route 2: Galen Rowell and Jerry Coe. Apr. 1971.

The Balls. Most routes were put up by guides and members of the Rockcraft Climbing School in 1973 and 1974.

Fresno Dome. The first route done on this dome was the right side of the alcove: Fred Beckey and Jim Stuart. Nov. 5, 1971. Many other routes were done later by guides and members of the Rockcraft Climbing School.

The Evolution Region

Peak 12,498. Glen Dawson and Neil Ruge. July 11, 1933.

Peak 12,971. R.S. Fink. July 25, 1942.

Mt. Goethe. Dave Brower and George Rockwood. July 6, 1933.

Muriel Peak. Hervey Voge. July 8, 1933.

Mt. Lamarck. Norman Clyde. 1925. Ice gully: John Fischer and Jay Jensen. 1974.

Peak 13,385. R.G. Dunn. Aug. 23, 1964.

Mt. Mendel. Route 1: FA unknown, but prior to 1930. Route 2: Mike Waddell and Steve Roper. Aug. 1966. Route 3: Felix Knauth and John Whitmer. June 21, 1958. Route 4: Mike Cohen and Roy Bishop. July 1967. Route 5: Bud Bingham and Don Clarke. 1956. Route 6: FA unknown.

Mt. Darwin. Route 1: E.C. Andrews and Willard Johnson. Aug. 12, 1908. Route 2: Robert Price and Peter Frandsen. Aug. 21, 1921. Route 3: Dave Brower and Hervey Voge. July 5, 1934. Route 4: Chuck Wilts, Spencer

Austin, and William Pabst. 1945. Route 5: Sierra Club party. 1960. Route 6: Craig Lehman and Bruce Kinnison. Sept. 1973. Route 7: Dick Leigh and Morrough O'Brien. Sept. 9, 1955. Route 8: Fred Martin, George Wallerstein, Herbert Weidner, Don Wilson, and Robert Wyman.

Peak 13,280+. Glen Dawson, Neil Ruge, and Bahlah Ballantine. July 19, 1933.

Mt. Spencer. Robert Price, George Young, H.W. Hill, and Peter Frandsen. Aug. 20, 1921.

Mt. Haeckel. Route 1: Walter Huber and friends. July 14, 1920. Route 2: Jack Riegelhuth. 1933. Route 3: Mike Loughman and Jay Holliday. 1958. Route 4: O.H. Taylor, Angus Taylor, and Merton Brown. 1935. Route 5: Edward Allen, Francis Crofts, and Olcutt Haskell. July 14, 1920.

Picture Peak. Route 1: Norman Clyde. 1931. Route 2: Sierra Club group. 1960. Route 3: Gary Colliver and Steve Thompson. July 1967. Route 4: Mike Loughman, Dick Grunebaum, Bob Orser, and Rick Polsdorfer. 1958.

Mt. Wallace. Theodore Solomons and E. Bonner. July 16, 1895.

Clyde Spires. Norman Clyde, Jules Eichorn, Ted Waller, Helen LeConte, Julie Mortimer, Dorothy Baird, and John Forbes. July 22, 1933. South spire: Clyde, Eichorn, and Waller of above group.

Mt. Fiske. Charles N. Fiske, John Fiske, Stephen Fiske, and Frederick Kellet. Aug. 10, 1922. From saddle: Jack Sturgeon. Aug. 18, 1939. Class 2–3 route: Andy Smatko, Peter Hunt, and John Robinson. Aug. 20, 1958.

Mt. Warlow. Nathaniel Goodrich and Marjory Hurd. 1926. Class 4 ridge: Mike Waddell. Aug. 1966.

Mt. Huxley. Route 1: Norman Clyde. July 15, 1920. Route 2: A.J. Reyman. Aug. 9, 1942. Route 3: Steve Rogero and Wally Henry. May 30, 1970. Route 4: Arkel Erb. Aug. 22, 1963.

Emerald Peak. Norman Clyde, Julie Mortimer, and Eleanor Bartlett. Aug. 25, 1925.

Peter Peak. Peter Grubb and Richard Johnson. July 11, 1936.

Mt. McGee. Route 1: Glen Dawson, Charles Dodge, Jules Eichorn, and John Olmsted. July 16, 1930. Route 2: Glen Dawson, Neil Ruge, and Bahlah Balantine. July 17, 1933.

The Hermit. Route 1: L. Keeler, R. Brandt, and others. July 28, 1924. Route 2: FA unknown. Route 3: Richard Johnson and Peter Grubb. July 9, 1936. Route 4: Harriet Parsons, Madi Bacon, and Maxine Cushing. July 9, 1939.

Mt. Powell. Route 1: Walter Huber and James Rennie. Aug. 1, 1925. Route 2: Norman Clyde. June 29, 1931. Route 3: Galen Rowell, Dan McHale, and Fred Beckey. June 1969. Route 4: Sierra Club group. June 1961. Route 5: Norman Clyde.

Peak 12,960+. Norman Clyde. East face: Jay Holliday and Mike Loughman. 1958.

Mt. Thompson. Clarence Rhudy and H.F. Katzenbach. 1909. From Sunset Lake: Norman Clyde. June 30, 1931. Via Thompson Ridge: Charlie Bell, Stu Ferguson, and Henry Mandolf. Sept. 1959.

Peak 13,323. Norman Clyde. Sept. 6, 1931.

Peak 12,993. Norman Clyde. Nov. 7, 1931.

Mt. Gilbert. Southeast slopes: Jack Sturgeon. Aug. 14, 1939. East ridge: Norman Clyde. Sept. 15, 1928. Ice couloir: Al Fowler, Ron Cale, and Dan Eaton. Sept. 1972.

Mt. Johnson. Norman Clyde (probably). Before 1939.

Mt. Goode. FA unknown. Grade II route: TM Herbert, Jay Jensen, Dennis Hennek, and John Fischer. 1974. Other route: Mark Fielding and Bill Nicolai. Aug. 1972.

Hurd Peak. H.C. Hurd. 1906.

Peak 12,913. R.S. Fink. July 27, 1941.

Mt. Goddard. Route 1: Lil Winchell and Louis Davis. Sept. 23, 1879. Route 2: FA unknown. Route 3: FA unknown.

Peak 13,081. Jack Sturgeon. Aug. 16, 1939.

Mt. Solomons. M.H. Pramme and T.F. Harms. Aug. 12, 1929.

Scylla. Dave Brower and Hervey Voge. July 3, 1934.

The Three Sirens. George Wallerstein, Don Wilson, and Mike Raudenbush. Aug. 1963. East Siren: FA unknown.

Charybdis. Anna Dempster and John Dempster. July 7, 1931.

Black Giant. George Davis. 1905. Other route: Steve Roper. Aug. 1966.

Peak 13,046. Carl Miller. Oct. 1952. Chute: Frank Orme and Robin McKeown. Aug. 13, 1954.

Peak 12,320+. Glen Warner and Suzanne Burgess. Aug. 5, 1941.

Mt. McDuffie. Route 1: Charles Bays Locker, Karl Hufbauer, and Alfred Elkin. July 23, 1951. Route 2: Charles Bays Locker, Karl Hufbauer, Gary Hufbauer, and Don Albright. July 15, 1952.

Langille Peak. Nathaniel Goodrich, Marjory Hurd, and Dean Peabody, Jr. Aug. 1926. Technical route: Fred Beckey and Chris Jones. July 1970.

The Citadel. Route 1: Richard Searle and William Wirt. June 24, 1951. Route 2: Charles Bays Locker, R.J. McKenna, S. Hall, D.E. Albright, and Karl Hufbauer. July 1952. Route 3: TM Herbert, Dennis Hennek, and Don Lauria. 1968. Route 4: Don Goodrich and Bob Means. June 24, 1951.

Peak 12,425. Herbert Blanks and Boynton Kaiser. Aug. 9, 1934.

Wheel Mountain. First route: Marjory Bridge, Lewis Clark, John Poindexter, and John Cahill. July 26, 1933. Other route: Andy Smatko, Tom Ross, Jess Logan, and Phil Clayton. Aug. 1963.

Rambaud Peak. Albert Tachet and Ruth Prager. 1925.

The Devil's Crags. Crag 1, first route: Charles Michael. July 21, 1913. Second route: Jules Eichorn, Helen LeConte, and Alfred Weiler, July 25, 1933. Third route: Raffi Bedayan, Kenneth Davis, and Jack Riegelhuth. Aug. 5, 1938. Crag 2: Jules Eichorn, Glen Dawson, and Ted Waller. July 26, 1933. Crag 3, first route: Dave Brower, Hervey Voge, and Norman Clyde. June 24, 1934. Other routes: FA unknown. Crag 4: Dave Brower, Hervey Voge, and Norman Clyde. June 24, 1934. Crag 5: Same party as Crag 4, but next day. Crags 6, 7, and 8: Same as Crag 5. Crag 9: Glen Dawson and Jules Eichorn. Aug. 1, 1933. Crags 10 and 11: Dave Brower, Norman Clyde, and Hervey Voge. June 23, 1934.

Mt. Woodworth. Bolton Coit Brown. Aug. 1, 1895.

The Palisades

Cloudripper. Norman Clyde (probably). June 15, 1926.

Gendarme Peak. Andy Smatko and Bill Schuler. Aug. 13, 1967.

Aperture Peak. Dave Brower and Hervey Voge. 1934.

Two Eagle Peak. Norman Clyde. July 6, 1929. Grade II route: Don Jensen and Grant Hoag. July 1972.

Mt. Robinson. Route 1: Don Jensen, D. Kennedy, and R. Davis. Aug. 1969. Route 2: Norman Clyde. July 4, 1930. Route 3: Descended by party of Route 5. Route 4: Steve Roper, Jon Lonne, John Clark, and Dick James. July 1968. Route 5: Dave Brower and Hervey Voge. June 14, 1934.

Mt. Agassiz. Route 1: Norman Clyde. Aug. 30, 1925. FWA: Rich Gregersen and Gary Vogt. Mar. 20, 1967. Route 2: Norman Clyde. Sept. 11, 1927. Route 3: FA unknown. Route 4: Norman Clyde. June 13, 1927.

Mt. Winchell. Route 1: Don Harmon and Bob Dohrmann. June 21, 1959. Route 2: H.C. Mansfield, J.N. Newell, and W.B. Putnam. June 10, 1923. FWA: Dave Brower, Norman Clyde and Morgan Harris. Jan 10, 1938.

Route 3: Robert Stebbins, Bill Rogers, and G. Ledyard Stebbins. Aug. 14, 1955. Route 4: Chris Fredericks and Tim Harrison. Aug. 1971. Route 5: Jules Eichorn, Glen Dawson, and John Olmsted. July 29, 1930. Route 6: W.K. Davis and Jack Reigelhuth. Aug. 11, 1938.

Thunderbolt Peak. Route 1: Robert L.M. Underhill, Jules Eichorn, Lewis Clark, Norman Clyde, Glen Dawson, Francis Farquhar, and Bestor Robinson. Aug. 13, 1931. Route 2: Charles Ray and Ulrich Brosch. Aug. 1965. Route 3: Brad Fowler and Robert Lindgren. Aug. 1968. Route 4: Rich Gnagy and Ellen Wilts. July 1959. Route 5: W. Katra and D. Sommers. Aug. 1970. Route 6: Norman Clyde. 1930s. Route 7: W.K. Davis and Jack Riegelhuth. Aug. 11, 1938. Route 8: Oscar Cook, Sylvia Kershaw, Mildred Jentsch, Hunter Morrison, and Isabella Morrison. Sept. 3, 1949. Route 9: Kim Tucker, Stan Hedberg, and Allen Jedlicka. Aug. 1964. Route 10: Descended by party of Route 8. Route 11: Norman Clyde, John Poindexter, and Philip Von Lubkin. Aug. 3, 1933.

North Palisade. Route 1: Norman Clyde. June 1928. FWA: Dave Brower and Fred Kelley. Mar. 17, 1940. Route 2: Larry Williams, John Sharsmith, Burt Turney, and Gen Turney, July 1961. Route 3: Allen Steck and Doug Robinson. July 1970. Route 4: Ken Boche and Lee Panza. July 1970. Route 5: Norman Clyde. July 1929. Route 6: FA unknown. Route 7: Lower part by Doug Robinson and Carl Dreisbach. July 1968. Upper part by W. Katra and D. Sommers. Aug. 1970. Route 8: Steve Roper, Jon Lonne, Dick James, and John Clark. July 1968. Route 9: Norman Clyde, Hervey Voge, and Dave Brower. June 29, 1934. Route 10: James Wright. July 13, 1933. Route 11: Richard Jones and Mary Jane Edwards. Aug. 1936. Route 12: James Hutchinson, Joseph N. LeConte, and J.K. Moffitt. July 25, 1903.

Polemonium Peak. FA unknown. V-Notch Couloir: John Mathias and John Ohrenschall. Sept. 1957.

Mt. Sill. Route 1: Descended by Dave Brower, Hervey Voge, and Norman Clyde. June 16, 1934. Route 2: Tom Condon and Fred Kepfelsbeger. 1959? Route 3: Spencer Austin, Ruth Dyar, Ray Ingwersen, Richard Jones, and Joe Momyer. July 3, 1938. Route 4: Walter Starr, Jr. Sept. 25, 1931. Route 5: Norman Clyde. June 10, 1927. Route 6: Jules Eichorn, Glen Dawson, John Olmsted, and Charles Dodge. July 27, 1930. Route 7: James Hutchinson, Joseph N. LeConte, James Moffitt, and Robert Pike. July 24, 1903. A winter ascent, via an unknown route, was made in 1960 by John Mendenhall and Tom Condon.

Mt. Gayley. Route 1: Norman Clyde. June 10, 1927. Route 2: Descended by Walter Starr, Jr. Sept. 28, 1931. Route 3: Bob Cogburn and Ed Robbins. June 1950. Route 4: Smoke Blanchard and friends. 1950s?

Temple Crag. Route 1: USGS. 1909. Route 2: Norman Clyde. Nov. 1926. Route 3: Bob Swift, Pete Kennedy, and Tom Thayer. 1970. Route 4: Don Jensen, S. Petroff, A. Walker. Aug. 1969. Route 5: Lower part by Don Jensen and J. Conners. July 1969. Upper part by Carl Dreisbach and P. Armstrong. Sept. 1969. Route 6: Lower part by Don Jensen, W. Miller, and R. Schwartz. July 1969. Upper part by Don Jensen and John Fischer. Sept. 1969. Route 7: Mike Heath, K. Kinsley, R. Rosenburger, D. Sharp, and R. Stafford. Oct. 1970. Route 8: John and Ruth Mendenhall. July 1940. Route 9: Don Jensen and Chuck Kroger. July 1970. Route 10: Tom Higgins and Bud Couch. 1966. Route 11: Lower part by Don Jensen and John Fischer. Sept. 1970. Upper part by Don Jensen and Keith Brueckner. July 1971. Route 12: Doug Robinson and Chuck Kroger. Sept. 1970. Route 13: John Mendenhall, Vivian Mendenhall, Roy Coates, and Ed Lane. Aug. 1963. Route 14: Les Roberts and Joe Herbst. 1970. Route 15: Norman Clyde, Robert L.M. Underhill, Glen Dawson, and Jules Eichorn. Aug. 11, 1931. Route 16: Norman Clyde. 1930. Route 17: Don and Joan Jensen. 1969. Route 18: Chuck Pratt, Bob Swift, and friends. 1968. Route 19: Don Jensen and Chuck Kroger. Aug. 1970. Route 20: Don Jensen and friend. 1969.

Isosceles Peak. Wear and Morse. July 1938.

Giraud Peak. Norman Clyde. Sept. 1925.

Peak 13,920+. Walter Starr, Sr. and A.M. Starr. July 1925.

Mt. Jepson. Don McGeein, Chet and Evelyn Errett. July 3, 1939. Grade III route: Doug Robinson and Don Jensen. Aug. 1970.

Palisade Crest. Southeastern three pinnacles: John and Ruth Mendenhall. July 4, 1954. Central pinnacles: Stu Dole and Don Jensen. 1967. Northwestern pinnacles: Don Jensen, Rex Post, and Joan Jensen. 1969.

Clyde Peak. Route 1: Glen Dawson and Jules Eichorn. July 1933. Route 2:

Hank Abrons and Pete Carmen. June 1965. Route 3: Don Jensen and Frank Sarnquist. July 1966. Route 4: Allen Steck, Larry Williams, and John Sharsmith. Aug. 1961. Route 5: Arkel Erb and M. McNicholas. July 1961. 5.9 variation: Fred Beckey and Mike Graber. 1974. Route 6: Norman Clyde. June 9, 1930. Route 7: Norman Clyde. June 19, 1930.

Middle Palisade. Route 1: Dave Brower, Bruce Meyer, and Keith Taylor. July 20, 1939. Route 2: FA unknown. FWA: John Mendenhall and Tom Condon. Jan. 5, 1960. Route 3: Norman Clyde. June 7, 1930. Route 4: Jules Eichorn and Glen Dawson. July 30, 1933. Route 5: Francis Farquhar and Ansel Hall. Aug. 26, 1921.

Disappointment Peak. Route 1: FA unknown. Route 2: Norman Clyde. June 20, 1930. Route 3: J.M. Davies, A.L. Jordan, and H.H. Bliss. July 20, 1919.

The Thumb. Route 1: W.B. Putnam. Dec. 12, 1921. Route 2: Leigh and Irene Ortenburger. Sept. 12, 1957. Route 3: Norman Clyde. June 5, 1930. Route 4: Hank Abrons, Pete Carmen, and C. Bickel. June 1965.

Peak 13,520+. Norman Clyde. June 1930.

Birch Mountain. J.W. Bledsoe. 1887.

Mt. Bolton Brown. Northwest ridge: Chester Versteeg and Rudolph Berls. Aug. 14, 1922. North slopes: Fred Jones. Oct. 6, 1948. Southwest side: Descended by Versteeg and Berls.

Mt. Prater. Southeast ridge: FA unknown. North ridge: Fred Jones. Oct. 6, 1948.

Peak 13,040+. Chester Versteeg. Aug. 1922.

Split Mountain. Route 1: Descended by Norman Clyde. Route 2: Norman Clyde. Route 3: Frank Saulque and others. July 1887. Routes 4 and 5: FA unknown.

Cardinal Mountain. George Downing, Jr. Aug. 11, 1922.

Peak 12,851. A.J. Reyman. Aug. 5, 1945.

The Kings River Region

Mt. Henry. North ridge: Art Reyman. July 10, 1951. Northeast ridge: Dave Brower and others. July 7, 1939. West slope: Bob Helliwell and Alden Bryant. Aug. 29, 1940.

Red Mountain. Joseph N. LeConte and C.L. Cory. July 12, 1898.

Peak 11,998. A.J. Reyman. July 12, 1951. Grade II route: Walt Vennum, Rick Boyce, and Curt Chadwick. Aug. 1973.

Peak 12,265. A.J. Reyman. July 13, 1951.

Peak 12,479. George Wallerstein and Gordon Oates. Aug. 1958.

Peak 12,209. George Wallerstein and Gordon Oates. Aug. 1958.

Peak 12,309. George Wallerstein and Gordon Oates. Aug. 1958.

Finger Peak. Government survey party. Date unknown.

Blue Canyon Peak. Robin McKeown and Frank Orme. Aug. 1959.

Peak 11,969. Martial Thiebaux and George Wallerstein. Aug. 1960.

Kettle Dome. Hermann Ulrichs. July 20, 1920. Grade II route: Walt Vennum, Fred Beckey, and Phil Warrender. Oct. 20, 1974.

Tehipite Dome. Easy route: Walter Starr, Sr. and Allan Chickering. July 31, 1896. Route 1: Fred Beckey, Herb Swedlund, Ken Weeks, and John Ahern. June 1963. Route 2: Chuck Kroger, Curt Chadwick, and Norm Weeden. July 1970.

Obelisk. Route 1: Allen Steck and Jim Wilson. 1948. Route 2: John Salathé, Anton Nelson, Dave Hammack, and Alice Ann Dayton. June 1951. Route 3: Fred Beckey and Hooman Aprin. Apr. 1971. Route 4: Chuck Kroger and Ben Dewell. Mar. 1972.

Spanish Mountain. Hermann Ulrichs. 1921.

Silver Turret. Class 4 route: Dave Hammack and Anton Nelson. July 27, 1951. Harder route: Mort Hempel and Mike Cohen. July 1972.

Fang Turret. Dave Hammack and Anton Nelson. July 27, 1951 FFA John Ohrenschall and Russ Hoopes. Sept. 1955.

The Python. Fred Martin, Kim Malville, and Robert Tambling. June 1955.

Friday's Folly. Felix Knauth, Harold Sipperly, and John Whitmer. July 8 1955.

Silver Maiden. Bruce Edwards, Howard Lewis, Bob Smith, Jim Smith, and Ed Sutton. Aug. 3, 1962.

Tenderfoot Peak. Fred Martin, Kim Malville, and Robert Tambling. June 1955. Grade II route: Steve Devoto and others. Aug. 1971.

Crystal Turret. Window route: Anton Nelson and Dave Hammack. July 25, 1951. Second route: Steve Devoto and Bill Oldfield. Aug. 1971. Southwest face: Tom Gerughty and Steve Roper. July 1972.

Cobra Turret. Dave Hammack and Anton Nelson. July 26, 1951.

El Comandante Turret. Original route: Dave Hammack and Anton Nelson. July 26, 1951. Easier route: Sierra Club group. July 19, 1952. Third route: George Sessions, Mort Hempel, and Steve Roper. July 1972.

El Corporale Turret. Dave Hammack and Anton Nelson. July 25, 1951.

Frustration Turret. Dave Hammack, Jules Eichorn, Bob Smith, and Clinton Kelley. June 18, 1952.

Fascination Point. Kim Malville, Fred Martin, and Robert Tambling. June 16, 1955. Pinnacle: Same team.

The Grand Dike. Tower ½, first route: Kim Malville, John Ohrenschall, and Richard Smyth. Nov. 26, 1954. East face: John Ohrenschall and Russ Hoopes. Aug. 11, 1956. Tower 1: Dave Hammack and Anton Nelson. July

28, 1951. Tower 2, first route: Same as Tower 1. Other route: John Ohrenschall and Russ Hoopes. Aug. 12, 1956. Tower 3: Dave Hammack and Anton Nelson. July 28, 1951. Tower 4: Dave Hammack, Bob Smith, George Larimore, and Bob Purington. June 15, 1952. Towers 5, 6, 7, and 8: Same party as Tower 1.

Kings Tower. Richard Sessions, George Sessions, Larry Hawley, Chris Jessen, and Wayne Kincheloe. May 16, 1954. FFA: George Sessions and Rich Calderwood. Aug. 1954.

Windy Bluff. Merle Alley and George Sessions. July 20, 1954.

Boyden Rock. Mark Powell, Merle Alley, and George Sessions. June 30, 1954.

Bulldog Rock. Merle Alley and George Sessions. June 13, 1957.

Hathaway's Delight. Merle Alley and George Sessions. June 13, 1957.

Spook Spire. Merle Alley, Jerry Dixon, and George Sessions. May 17, 1958.

Roaring River Falls. All three routes by Dick Blankenbecler and J. Botke. 1970–73.

North Dome. Back side: Neil Ruge and Florence Rata. June 1940. Grade IV route: TM Herbert and Tom Frost. 1968. Grade III route: Dick Blankenbecler and J. Botke. June 1971.

Grand Sentinel. Back side: Joseph N. LeConte, Helen Gompertz, Mr. and Mrs. W.S. Gould, and others. 1896. Y-shaped gully: Dick Blankenbecler, W. Thompson, and G. Nelson. 1967 or 1968. Class 5 route: Roy Gorin and Jerry Ganapole. July 7, 1951. Grade V route: Royal Robbins and Yvon Chouinard. June 1967.

The Sphinx. Art Argiewicz and Bob Jacobs. July 26, 1940. Grade II route: Fred Beckey, Greg Donaldson, and Walt Vennum. Oct. 1970.

Mt. Harrington. North ridge: Dave Hammack and Anton Nelson. July 27, 1951. South ridge: Arkel Erb and friend.

Hogback Peak. James Carl and John Ohrenschall. Sept. 10, 1955.

Slide Peak. George Whitmore. May 29, 1960.

Kennedy Mountain. Government survey party.

Comb Spur. Robert Owen. July 1931.

Mt. Hutchings. Norman Clyde and friend. Apr. 1, 1933.

Goat Mountain. James Gardiner and Charles Hoffmann. July 22, 1864.

Kid Peak. Dave Brower, Norman Clyde, and others. July 2, 1940.

Dougherty Peak. Sierra Club group. 1935.

Slate Peak. Sierra Club group (probably). 1935.

Marion Peak. Joseph N. LeConte and Curtis Lindley. July 22, 1902.
Northwest ridge: A.J. Reyman. Aug. 11, 1945.

Red Point. A.J. Reyman. Aug. 11, 1945.

Windy Cliff. Douglas Dooley. Aug. 29, 1970.

Mt. Shakspere. Francis Furquhar, Mary Lou Michaels, Doris Drust, Lorna
Kilgariff, and Robert Lipman. July 20, 1930.

Observation Peak. Joseph N. LeConte and Curtis Lindley. July 25, 1902.
Northwest ridge: Marjory Hurd. 1926.

Peak 12,860+. A.J. Reyman. Aug. 12, 1945.

Saddlehorn. Bruce Meyer, Dave Brower, and Charlotte Mauk. July 22,
1939. 5.8 route: Galen Rowell and Steve Roper. May 1972.

Mt. Perkins. FA unknown, but prior to 1910. From the east: Bill Brown.
Oct. 1974.

Colosseum Mountain. Chester Versteeg. Aug. 5, 1922.

Mt. Cedric Wright. Norman Clyde. Aug. 25, 1935.

Mt. Baxter. Route 1: FA unknown. Route 2: FA unknown. Route 3: Descended by Fred Jones. Aug. 5, 1948. Route 4: FA unknown. Route 5: FA unknown. Route 6: George Davis (probably). 1905.

Acrodectes Peak. Norman Clyde and others. July 1935.

Peak 12,852. Norman Clyde and others. July 1935.

Peak 12,804. Vance Hopkins, Tom Bundy, R.L. Worden, W.F. Angbauer, Bill Widney, Earl Wallace, and Toni Freeman. July 6, 1929. Route unknown. Southeast ridge: Norman Clyde and others. July 1935. From Woods Lake: Fred Jones. July 21, 1948.

Peak 12,160+. FA unknown. Two northern summits: Jim Harkins. Art Argiewicz, Bob Jacobs, and Bruce Meyer. July 6, 1940.

Mt. Clarence King. Route 1: Bolton Coit Brown. Aug. 1896. Route 2: Galen Rowell and Greg Henzie. Aug. 1970. Route 3: Fred Davenport and Standish Mitchell. Aug. 1948. Route 4: Gilles Corcos and Graeme Wilson. Sept. 1971.

Mt. Cotter. Bob Fitzsimmons. Aug. 6, 1922. North peak, north ridge: Dave Brower and others. July 8, 1940. Grade IV route: Tony Qamar and Galen Rowell. June 1972.

Mt. Gardiner. South side: Bolton Coit Brown, Joseph N. LeConte, and others. July 1896. Southeast ridge: Paul Estes and Jack Pointeki. July 7, 1940. Glacier route: Norman Clyde and others. July 9, 1940.

Glacier Monument. Andy Smatko, Tom Ross, and Bill Schuler. Sept. 1972.

Charlotte Dome. Class 3 route: Ed Lane. Aug. 1966. South face: Galen Rowell, Chris Jones, and Fred Beckey. Oct. 1970. Southwest arete: Galen Rowell and Dave Lomba. May 1973.

Mt. Bago. Either Joseph N. LeConte and W.S. Gould on July 11, 1896, or

Bolton Coit Brown and Lucy Brown, July 1896. Grade IV route: David Boyd and Paul Hurd. Sept. 1, 1974.

Peak 11,360+. Bolton Coit Brown, Lucy Brown, Dr. Wood, and Dr. Little. July 1896.

Fin Dome. Regular route: James Rennie. 1910. South side: Dave Brower and others. July 7, 1940. East face: Galen Rowell and Marek Glogoczowski. 1972.

Castle Domes. High point: USGS survey party. Second dome: Art Argiewicz and Bob Jacobs. July 5, 1940.

Peak 12,285. Andy Smatko, Bill Schuler, and Tom Ross. Sept. 18, 1970.

Goodale Mountain. FA unknown, but prior to 1939. From west: Fred Jones. Aug. 1, 1948.

Striped Mountain. George Davis. July 1905. West ridge: Fred Jones. Aug. 1, 1948.

Peak 12,720+. Madi Bacon and Tom Noble. July 23, 1939. Northwest ridge: Ed Lane. 1960s. Southeast ridge: Andy Smatko, Bill Schuler, and Tom Ross. 1971.

Peak 13,259. FA unknown. South slopes: Andy Smatko, Bill Schuler, Ellen Siegal, and Tom Ross. June 9, 1968. North face. Ed Lane and Gary Lewis. Sept. 26, 1965.

Mt. Pinchot. USGS members. 1905.

Mt. Wynne. Sierra Club group. 1935.

Crater Mountain. W.H. Ink, Meyers Butte, Frank Baxter, and Capt. Wallace. July 19, 1922.

Mt. Ruskin. Bolton Coit Brown. Aug. 7, 1895. Southwest slope: A.J. Reyman. Aug. 13, 1945. East ridge: Andy Smatko, Tom Ross, and Arkel Erb. 1961.

The Kearsarge Pass Area

Arrow Peak. Northeast spur: Bolton Coit Brown. Aug. 8, 1895. Southeast slope: Joseph N. LeConte, Tracey Kelley, and Robert Pike. June 1902. From Bench Lake: Walter Starr, Jr. (probably). Aug. 20, 1930.

Peak 12,000+. W. Sloane and J. Sloane. Aug. 12, 1922. Grade III route: Vern Clevenger and Jon Ross. July 1973.

Pyramid Peak. A.J. Reyman. July 21, 1942.

Peak 12,350. Jed Garthwaite, Jim Quick, and Howard Leach. June 27, 1940.

Window Peak. Art Argiewicz and Bob Jacobs. July 5, 1940. North ridge: Descended by A.J. Reyman.

Peak 13,070. From Baxter Pass: Fred Jones. Aug. 6, 1948. Route unknown: Norman Clyde. 1925.

Diamond Peak. FA unknown. Snow couloir: Descended by Henry Mandolf, Charlie Bell, and Rowland Radcliffe. May 30, 1960. Ascended by Fred Beckey and Mike Heath. May 1971.

Mt. Mary Austin. Andy Smatko, Tom Ross, Ellen Siegal, and Eric Schumacher. May 3, 1965. FWA: Tom Ross.

Black Mountain. George Davis. 1905.

Dragon Peak. Either Norman Clyde or Fred Parker and J.E. Rother. 1920.

Mt. Gould. Joseph N. LeConte, Hubert Dyer, Fred Phelby, and C.B. Lakeman. 1890.

Mt. Rixford. Dr. Emmet Rixford and friends. 1897.

Kearsarge Pinnacles. Pinnacle 1: May Pridham, Niles Werner, and Pam Coffin. July 28, 1935. Pinnacle 2: Same as Pinnacle 1. Pinnacle 3: Ted Waller, Don Woods, Dave Nelson, and Edward Koskinen. Pinnacles 4, 5,

6, and 7: FA unknown, but west face of Pinnacle 6 was climbed by Richard Hechtel and Liesl Day. July 1970. Pinnacle 8: Glen Dawson, Owen Ward, and Hans Leschke. 1932. Pinnacle 9: R. Howard (probably). July 25, 1924. Pinnacles 10, 11, and 12: Same as Pinnacle 8 (probably).

Nameless Pyramid. Class 3 route: Phil Berry, Frank Tarver, and Ted Matthes. July 1952. Technical route: Burt Turney and Chuck Ray. May 1968.

Peak 12,160 +. Andy Smatko, Bill Schuler, and Arkel Erb. Apr. 1972.

University Peak. Route 1: Joseph N. LeConte, Helen Gompertz, Estelle Miller, and Belle Miller. July 12, 1896. Routes 2, 3, and 4: FA unknown. Route 5: FA unknown, but probably in 1947. Route 6: Fred Beckey, Joe Brown, and Dan Clements. July 1968. Route 7: Norman Clyde. Before 1928.

Independence Peak. Norman Clyde. 1926.

Center Basin Crags. Crag 1: Phil Berry and friends. Aug. 29, 1953. Crags 2, 3, and 4: Dave Brower and Bruce Meyer. July 1940. Crag 5: FA unknown.

Mt. Bradley. From Center Basin: R.M. Price, J.E. Price, J.C. Shinn, and C.B. Bradley. July 6, 1898. East slopes: Fred Jones. Oct. 27, 1948. From Center Basin Crags: Fred Jones. Aug. 31, 1948.

East Vidette. Sierra Club group. 1910.

East Spur. Jim Harkins and Pat Goldsworthy. July 14, 1940.

West Vidette. Norman Clyde. 1926.

West Spur. William Morrison and friends. Aug. 8, 1940.

The Minster. Ted Waller, Don Woods, and Edward Koskinen. Aug. 3, 1939.

Deerhorn Mountain. Route 1: Norman Clyde (probably). July 8, 1927. Route 2: Norman Clyde, Jules Eichorn, Robert Breckenfield, and others. July 1946. Route 3: Norman Clyde, Hervey Voge, and Ted Waller. Aug. 5,

1939. Route 4: Norman Clyde. Route 5: Arkel Erb, Andy Smatko, Frede Jensen, Tom Ross, David Oyler, and Mike McNicholas.

Center Peak. C.G. Bradley. July 5, 1898. North side: Dave Brower and Hervey Voge. May 22, 1934. Third route: Phil Berry and Frank Tarver. July 26, 1952.

Peak 13,280+. Sy Ossofsky and Arkel Erb. Aug. 1963.

Mt. Keith. Northwest side: C.G. Bradley, R.M. Price, J.C. Shinn, and J.E. Price. July 6, 1898. Class 3 route: Sierra Club group. 1916.

Junction Peak. Route 1: E.B. Copeland and E.N. Henderson. Aug. 8, 1899. Route 2: FA unknown. Variation: Gary Lane and Jack Chamberlain. Sept. 1973. Route 3: Fred Beckey and John Rupley. June 1973. Route 4: Descended by Carl Heller, Bob Stein, and Hermit Ross. 1956. Route 5: A.R. Ellingwood. Aug. 21, 1929.

Peak 13,760+. Dave Brower and Hervey Voge. June 3, 1934.

Mt. Stanford. Route 1: Bolton Coit Brown. Aug. 1, 1896. Route 2: Descended by Brown. Route 3: Art Argiewicz and friends. Aug. 1940. Route 4: Descended by Dave Brower and Norman Clyde. Aug. 4, 1939. Route 5: Jim Harkins and others. Aug. 1947.

Peak 13,414. Boynton and Edith Kaiser. Aug. 7, 1948.

Caltech Peak. Norman Clyde. June 22, 1926. East ridge: Andy Smatko, Arkel Erb, Tom Ross, and Gordon MacCleod. June 8, 1963.

Peak 13,030. Jack Sturgeon. July 10, 1939.

Mt. Ericsson. Route 1: Lewis Clark and Carl Jensen. 1936. Route 2: Bolton Coit Brown and Lucy Brown. Aug. 1, 1896. Route 3: Norman Clyde, Robert Breckenfield, Jules Eichorn, Joe Brower, and Danny Kaplan. July 1946. Route 4: Descended by party of Route 1.

Ericsson Crags. Crag 1A: Hervey Voge, Ted Waller, and Don Woods. 1939. Crag 1: Don Woods, Edward Koskinen, and DeWitt Allen. Aug. 4,

1939. Crag 2: Hervey Voge and Dave Brower. Aug. 3, 1939. Crag 3: FA unknown, but prior to 1939. North face: Fred Beckey and Reed Cundiff. May 1972.

Mt. Genevra. Norman Clyde. July 15, 1925. Route unknown. From the east: Dave Nelson, Earl Jessen, and Hal Leich. Aug. 6, 1939. From Milly's Foot Pass: Robert Schonborn and others. Aug. 3, 1940. Class 3 snow chute: Bill Bade, Barbara Lilley, and Franklin Barnett. July 19, 1951. From the southwest: Andy Smatko, Bill Sanders, Frede Jensen, and Peter Hunt. Snow chute on south: Descended by preceding party.

Mt. Jordan. Norman Clyde (lower summit, apparently). July 15, 1925. From the east: Lewis Clark, Carl Jensen, and others. 1936. North face: Art Argiewicz and friends. Aug. 3, 1940. From the west: Descended by preceding party.

Peak 12,070. M. Roth and Calkins Fletcher. Prior to 1952.

Peak 12,513. Fritz Lippmann, Dave Nelson, Don Woods, and Ed Koskinen. Aug. 1939.

Peak 13,090. Norman Clyde. July 1931.

The Great Western Divide

Cross Mountain. Walter Huber. 1929.

Peak 12,893. Norman Clyde, Thomas Rawles, Lincoln O'Brien, and others. July 17, 1932. Grade IV route: Galen Rowell and Jeanne Neale. Sept. 1971.

Peak 12,600. Andy Smatko and Bill Schuler. Sept. 1973.

North Guard. Norman Clyde. July 12, 1925. Northeast side: Dave Brower and Hervey Voge. May 28, 1934.

Mt. Brewer. Route 1: William Brewer and Charles Hoffmann. July 2, 1864. Route 2: FA unknown. Route 3: Oliver Kehrlein, August and Grete Fruge, E. Hanson, L. West, R. Leggett, and A. Mulay. Aug. 4, 1940. Route 4: Ken

Boche and Russ McLean. Sept. 1963. Route 5: Bolton Coit Brown and A.B. Clark. 1895.

Peak 12,960+. Walter Huber, Florence Burrell, Inezetta Holt, and James Rennie. July 26, 1916.

Peak 11,520+. Dave Brower and Hervey Voge. May 28, 1934. North face: Alan MacRae and Oliver Kehrlein. Aug. 3, 1940.

South Guard. Clarence King and Richard Cotter (probably). July 4, 1864.

Thunder Mountain. George Davis. Aug. 1905.

Peak 12,560+. Class 2 route: Sierra Club party. 1940. Class 3–4 route: Phil Arnot and others. July 1958.

Table Mountain. Route 1: Norman Clyde and party. July 26, 1927. Route 2: Norman Clyde and friends. July 1932. Route 3: Norman Clyde. July 29, 1927. Route 4: Paul Shoup, Fred Shoup, and Gilbert Hassel. Aug. 25, 1908.

Midway Mountain. Francis Farquhar, William Colby, Robert Price, and four others. 1912.

Milestone Mountain. Route 1: FA unknown. Route 2: Walter Starr, Jr. Sept. 19, 1931. Route 3: Francis Farquhar, William Colby, and Robert Price. July 14, 1912. Route 4: Steve Thompson and Jeff Dozier. 1964.

Peak 13,255. Francis Farquhar, William Colby, and Robert Price. 1912.

Peak 13,520+. W.F. Dean, Otis Wright, Harry Dudley, and W.R. Dudley. Aug. 3, 1897.

Kern Point. William Horsfall and C. Laughlin. July 25, 1924.

Peak 12,600. Class 3 route: Jules Eichorn, Kenneth May, and A. Tagliapietra. 1936. Class 2 route: Carl Jensen and Howard Gates. 1936.

Whaleback. May Pridham and Adel Von Lobensels. Aug. 5, 1936.

Peak 12,237. E. Grubb, May Pridham, and D. Von Lobensels. July 1936.

Peak 12,416. Grade II route: Galen Rowell and Jeanne Neale. Sept. 1971. Easy route: Descended by same team.

Peak 12,640+. George Bunn and R.C. Lewis. July 21, 1926.

Triple Divide Peak West ridge: John Wedberg, Bill Engs, and friends 1963. South ridge: Don Clarke. East ridge: James Hutchinson and Charles Noble. 1920.

Lion Rock. Dave Winkley, William Curlett, and Earl Wallace. July 7, 1927.

Mt. Stewart. Norman Clyde. Aug. 14, 1932. Grade II route: Mike Graber, Jack Roberts, and Hooman Aprin. Aug. 1973.

Angel Wings. Route 1: Descended by Galen Rowell and Chris Jones. June 1971. Route 2: Allen Steck, Dick Long, Les Wilson, and Jim Wilson. July 1967. Route 3: Same team as Route 1.

Peak 11,598. Grade III route: Galen Rowell, Chris Jones, and Greg Henzie. Sept. 1970.

Peak 11,830. Chris Jones, Greg Henzie, and Galen Rowell. Sept. 1970.

Peak 13,140. G.A. Gaines, C.A. Gaines, and H.H. Bliss. July 11, 1924.

Kaweah Queen. G.A. Gaines, C.A. Gaines, and H.H. Bliss. July 11, 1924.

Peak 13,232. Andy Smatko, Bill Schuler, and Ellen Siegal. July 2, 1967.

Black Kaweah. Route 1: James Hutchinson, Onis Imis Brown, and Duncan McDuffie. Aug. 11, 1920. Route 2: Philip Smith. July 26, 1921. Route 3: A.R. Ellingwood and Carl Blaurock. Aug. 1928. Route 4: David Beck, Nick Hartzell, and Gary Kirk. Route 5: Neil Ruge and James Smith. June 1935.

Pyramidal Pinnacle. Glen Dawson and Jules Eichorn. Aug. 1, 1932.

Koontz Pinnacle. Jim Koontz, Fred Peters, and Pete Murphy. Aug. 26, 1953.

Red Kaweah. Charles Michael. 1912.

Michael's Pinnacle. Charles Michael. 1912.

Squaretop. Jim Smith and Neil Ruge. June 26, 1935.

Bilko Pinnacle. Jim Koontz, Fred Peters, and Pete Murphy. Aug. 27, 1953.

Second Kaweah. Norman Clyde. 1922. Three pinnacles: Jim Koontz, Fred Peters, and Pete Murphy. Aug. 29, 1953.

Mt. Kaweah. William Wallace, James Wright, and F.H. Wales. Sept. 1881. North ridge: Eduardo Garcia and Carlos Puente. Sept. 1964.

Peak 13,285. Jules Eichorn, Virginia Adams, Jane Younger, and Carl Jensen. July 1936.

Red Spur. Jules Eichorn, Virginia Adams, Jane Younger, and Carl Jensen. July 1936.

Picket Guard Peak. C. Dohlman, H. Manheim, and B. Breeding. Aug. 1, 1936.

Hamilton Dome. Chuck Kroger and Curt Chadwick. 1969. Grade II route: TM Herbert and Don Lauria. 1971.

Hamilton Towers. Some by Sierra Club group. 1953. Third tower: Galen Rowell, Chris Jones, and Greg Henzie. Sept. 1970.

Eagle Scout Peak. Francis Farquhar, Frederick Armstrong, Eugene Howell, and Coe Swift. July 15, 1926.

Lippincott Mountain. Norman Clyde. 1922.

Peak 11,760+. Andy Smatko and Bill Schuler. Aug. 30, 1969.

Mt. Eisen. Howard Parker, Mildred Jentsch, Ralph Youngberg, and Martha Ann McDuffie. July 15, 1949.

Peak 11,440+. Easy route: FA unknown. Grade IV route: Galen Rowell and Vern Clevenger. Sept. 1975. Grade III route: Fred Beckey, Rob Dellinger, and Debbie Winters. July 14, 1974.

Sawtooth Peak. Joseph Lovelace. 1871. Grade III route: Ben Dewell, Dale Kruse, and Gary Goodson. June 1970.

Mineral Peak. Chester Errett and Don McGeein. Aug. 3, 1937.

Needham Mountain. From the southeast: A.J. Reyman. 1951. Class 3 couloir: Howard Parker and Helen Parker. July 1949. From Lost Canyon: R.R. Breckenfield, Emily Frazer, and Don Scanlon. July 1949. Another route on same face: Mildred Jentsch. July 1949. South slopes: M.R. Parsons, Agnes Vaile, H.C. Graham, and Edmund Chamberlain. July 1916. Grade IV route: Gary Kirk and Bernard Hallet. Nov. 1968.

Peak 11,861. W.K. Jennings and friend. 1966.

Peak 12,320+. A.J. Reyman. Aug. 8, 1951. Grade III route: Vern Clevenger and Jon Ross. June 1973.

Rainbow Mountain. Oliver Kehrlein, Jack Allen, and Black Bart Evans.

Florence Peak. Routes 1 and 2: FA unknown. Route 3: Gary Kirk and Craig Thorn. Aug. 1972. Route 4: Jack Delk and Bill Sorenson. Sept. 1968. Route 5: Bruce Rogers and Carl Boro. Aug. 1972.

Vandever Mountain. FA unknown. Northwest couloir: Bruce Rogers. Sept. 1971.

The Watchtower. FA unknown. Grade V route: Galen Rowell and Greg Henzie. Labor Day, 1970.

Moro Rock. Route 1: FA unknown, but probably in 1939. Route 2: Roy Gorin, George Harr, Harry Sutherland, and Bob Cosgrove. Oct. 1948.

Route 3: Jerry Dixon, George Sessions, Merle Alley, and George Whitmore. Sept. 28, 1958.

Castle Rock Spire. Route 1: Bill Long, Allen Steck, Jim Wilson, Phil Bettler, and Will Siri. Apr. 27, 1950. Route 2: Tom Frost and TM Herbert. Sept. 1967. Route 3: Galen Rowell, Fred Beckey, Mort Hempel, and Ben Borson. May 1969.

Amphitheater Dome. Southeast side: Anton Nelson, DeWitt Allen, and Ted Knowles. 1947. Grade II route: Fred Beckey, Roger Briggs, Jim Jones, and Dave Leen. June 23, 1968.

The Needles. Sorcerer Needle, southwest-face route: Fred Beckey and Jim Stoddard. May 9, 1970. Northwest face: Fred Beckey and Greg Thomsen. Apr. 21, 1973. East face: Mike Heath and D. Johnson. May 15, 1972. First ascent of Sorcerer: Mike and B.J. Heath via traverse from Wizard (the upper part is now the upper section of Route 1). Apr. 11, 1970. Wizard Needle: Mike and B.J. Heath. Apr. 11, 1970. Witch Needle, 5.5 route: FA unknown. West face: Mike Heath and friend. Warlock Needle, south face: Fred Beckey, Mike Heath, and Dan McHale. Apr. 1970. East face: Mike and B.J. Heath. Apr. 1970. Traverse: FA unknown. Voodoo Dome, 5.9 route: Fred Beckey and Dan McHale. Oct. 1970. Second route: Charles Haas and Gregory Cloutier. 1974.

The Mt. Whitney Area

Mt. Tyndall. Route 1: Descended by Clarence King and Richard Cotter. July 6, 1864. Route 2: FA unknown. Route 3: Clarence King and Richard Cotter. July 6, 1864. Route 4: William Loomis and Marjory Farquhar. Aug. 13, 1935. Route 5: Bill Sumner and Mike Heath. Aug. 1972. Route 6: Fred Beckey and Charlie Raymond. May 1970.

Mt. Williamson. Route 1: Bolton Coit Brown and Lucy Brown. July 1896. Route 2: Galen Rowell. Oct. 1970. Route 3: John and Ruth Mendenhall. July 6, 1957. Route 4: Lito Tejada-Flores and Edgar Boyles. July 1972. Route 5: Homer Erwin. 1925. FWA: Warren Harding and John Ohrenschall. Dec. 28–31, 1954. Route 6: W.L. Hunter and C. Mulholland. 1884. FWA: Leigh Ortenburger and Bill Buckingham. Dec. 22, 1954. Route 7: Leroy

Jeffers. Route 8: Homer Erwin. 1925. Northern side: George Wallerstein, Andy Smatko, Barbara Lilley, Bill Schuler, and Ed Treacy. Oct. 11, 1970.

Trojan Peak. Norman Clyde. June 26, 1926.

Mt. Barnard. John Hunter, William Hunter, and C. Mulholland. Sept. 25, 1892.

Peak 13,680 I. FA unknown. Grade IV route: Galen Rowell, and Tim Auger. Apr. 1972. Shaw Spire: Galen Rowell and Jerry Gregg. Mar. 1972.

Peak 12,723. FA unknown. Class 4 route: Arkel Erb and Sy Ossofsky. July 1963.

Tawny Point. A.J. Reyman. July 12, 1946.

Peak 13,211. FA unknown, but probably in 1940. East-northeast ridge: Harvey Hickman and friend. Before 1966. Class 4 route: Andy Smatko, Bill Schuler, Tom Ross, and Ellen Siegal. Aug. 14, 1966.

Tulainyo Tower. Original route: Galen Rowell and Marek Glogoczowski. Oct. 1972. Direct finish: Bill Stronge and Arold Green. Sept. 1973.

Tunnabora Peak. George Davis. Aug. 1905. Northwest side: B. Bingham, Barbara Lilley, and F. Bressel. 1958.

Peak 13,355. FA unknown. Southwest ridge: Galen Rowell, Dennis Hennek, and Dave Lomba. July 1973.

Mt. Carillon. Route 1: FA unknown. Route 2: Norman Clyde. 1925. Route 3: FA unknown. Route 4: Fred Beckey and Chuck Haas. July 1968. Route 5: Chuck Ray and Brad Fowler. June 1968. Route 6: Fred Beckey and Charlie Raymond. Nov. 1968. Route 7: Fred Beckey, Joe Brown, and Dan McHale. Nov. 1969.

Peak 12,960+. Andy Smatko, Tom Ross, and Ellen Siegal. June 5, 1965.

Mt. Russell. Route 1: Norman Clyde. June 24, 1926. Route 2: Fred Beckey and friend. 1970s. Route 3: A.E. Gunther. 1928. Route 4: Jules Eichorn, Glen Dawson, Walter Brem, and Hans Leschke. July 1932. Route 5: Gary Colliver and John Cleare. June 1974. Route 6: Gary Colliver, TM Herbert, and Don Lauria. Sept. 1974. Route 7: Galen Rowell and Chris Jones. June 1972. FFA: Mark Moore and Julie X. 1974. Route 8: Descent by team of Route 4. Route 9: Descent by Norman Clyde. July 1927. Route 10: Descent by Norman Clyde. June 24, 1926. Route 11: Fred Beckey and Reed Cundiff. June 1971.

Peak 13,920+. Norman Clyde. June 1926.

Mt. Hale. Mildred and J.H. Czock. July 24, 1934. Grade V route: Galen Rowell and Dennis Hennek. July 1973. Pinnacles: Galen Rowell. June 1973.

Mt. Young. Frederick Wales, William Wallace, and James Wright. Sept. 7, 1881.

Mt. Whitney. Route 1: FA unknown. Route 2: A.H. Johnson, C.P. Begole, and John Lucas. Aug. 18, 1873. Route 3: FA unknown. Route 4: Vern Clevenger and Keith Bell. Sept. 1973. Route 5: Vern Clevenger, Mark Moore, and Julie X. 1973. Route 6: John Muir. Oct. 21, 1873. Route 7: Glen Dawson, Bob Brinton, Richard Jones, Howard Koster, and Muir Dawson. Sept. 5, 1937. Route 8: Glen Dawson, Norman Clyde, Jules Eichorn, and Robert L.M. Underhill. Aug. 16, 1931. Route 9: Gary Colliver and Chris Vandiver. July 1974. Route 10: Denis Rutovitz and Andrzej Ehrenfeucht. July 4–6, 1959. Route 11: John and Ruth Mendenhall. Oct. 11, 1941.

Keeler Needle. FA unknown, but prior to 1890. First Grade V route: Warren Harding, Glen Denny, Rob McKnight, and Desert Frank. July 1960. Other Grade V route: Jeff Lowe and John Weiland. Sept. 1973.

Day Needle. FA unknown, but prior to 1903. Grade IV route: Fred Beckey and Rick Reese. Sept. 1963.

Third Needle. FA unknown. Route 1: John Mendenhall, Ruby Wacker, and John Altseimer. Sept. 5, 1948. Route 2: John and Ruth Mendenhall. Sept. 3, 1939. Route 3: Mike Heath. Aug. 1966.

Aiguille Extra. FA unknown. Grade V route: Mike Heath and Bill Sumner. June 1971.

Mt. Muir. Route 1: FA unknown. Route 2: John Mendenhall and Nelson Nies. July 11, 1935. Route 3: William Rice and Arthur Johnson. Sept. 1, 1935.

Pinnacle Ridge. Nelson Nies and John Mendenhall. July 10, 1935. Needle: Bob Brinton, Glen Dawson, and William Rice. Sept. 7, 1936.

Wotan's Throne. Norman Clyde. 1933. Chute: Chester Versteeg. July 10, 1937.

Thor Peak. Route 1: Descended by Bob Brinton, Glen Dawson, and William Rice. Sept. 7, 1936. Route 2: Norman Clyde. Route 3: Tom Condon and Ron Dickenson. July 1962. Route 4: Howard Koster, Arthur Johnson, and James Smith. Sept. 4, 1937. Route 5: Bill Putnam, Tom Cosgrove, and Fred Beckey. May 1972. Route 6: Fred Beckey, Leland Davis, and Mike McGoey. May 1973. Route 7: Ascent by party of Route 1. Route 8: FA unknown. Route 9: William Rice and Bob Brinton. Sept. 6, 1936.

Wrinkled Lady. Fred Beckey and Joe Brown. May 1969.

Whitney Portal Buttress. Fred Beckey and Pat Callis. May 1967.

El Segundo Buttress. Fred Beckey and Mike Heath. Mar. 1971.

Premiere Buttress. Fred Beckey and Brian Gochoel. Nov. 1968.

Discovery Pinnacle. Clarence King and Frank Knowles. Sept. 1873.

Mt. Hitchcock. Frederick Wales. Sept. 1881. Class 3–4 route: Vern Clevenger. 1970.

Mt. Chamberlain. West slope: J.H. Czock. From Mt. Newcomb: Barbara Lilley, Andy Smatko, Frede Jensen, and Graham Stephenson.

Mt. Newcomb. From the southwest: Max Eckenburg and Bob Rumohr.

Aug. 1936. From Mt. Chamberlain: Descended by Andy Smatko, Frede Jensen, and Graham Stephenson.

Mt. McAdie. High point, from Arc Pass: Norman Clyde. 1922. West face: Jim Koontz, Hervey Voge, Norv LaVene, Mike Loughman, Claire Millikan, Rosemary Lenel, and Bent Graust. July 1954. Middle summit: Norman Clyde. June 1928. South summit: Oliver Kehrlein, Chester Versteeg, and Tyler Van Degrift. June 12, 1936.

Mt. Mallory. From small lake: Oliver Kehrlein, Chester Versteeg, and Tyler Van Degrift. July 18, 1936. From Mt. Irvine: Norman Clyde. June 1925. Class 3 route: Howard Sloan. July 26, 1931.

Mt. Irvine. From Arc Pass: Norman Clyde. June 1925. Class 2–3 route: Charles House. 1957. Grade III route: Bill Stronge and Arold Green. Sept. 1971. Prominent couloir: John Mendenhall and Bill Dixon. 1969.

Candlelight Peak. Standard route: Chester Versteeg. Aug. 31, 1940. Grade III route: Richard Hechtel, Dave and Fran Stevenson, and Dave French. July 1962. North face: Mike Hass and Preston Birdwell. July 1966.

Lone Pine Peak. Route 1: A.C. Lembeck and Ray Van Aken. Sept. 1952. Route 2: Fred Beckey and Eric Bjornstad. Apr. 1969. Route 3: Warren Harding. July 1952. Route 4: Norman Clyde. 1925. Route 5: Dan Hurd and Dave Boyd. Mar. 1972. Route 6: Galen Rowell and Joe Faint. Jan. 1970. Route 7: Fred Beckey, Jack Roberts, and Hooman Aprin. Apr. 1973. Route 8: Henri Agresti and Tom Birtley. July 1973. Route 9: Galen Rowell and Chris Jones. Mar. 1970. Route 10: Fred Beckey and Eric Bjornstad. May 1970. Route 11: Galen Rowell, Joe Faint, and Chris Jones. May 1970. Route 12: Murray Bruch and Fred Johnson. July 1947.

Peak 12,960+. FA unknown. South face: Chris Jones, Galen Rowell, and Joe Faint. May 1970. Grade III route: Fred Beckey and Barry Hagen. May 1972.

Peak 12,880+. Easy route: Ed Lane and Alice Lewis. Sept. 24, 1967. West arete: Galen Rowell. Aug. 1970. Obelisk: Galen Rowell and Chris Jones. Apr. 1970. Keystone: Galen Rowell and Chris Jones. Mar. 1970.

Mt. LeConte. Route 1: Norman Clyde. June 1925. Route 2: Carl Heller and Bill Stronge. 1971. Route 3: Steve Wilkie, Barbara Lilley, Wes Cowan, George Wallerstein, and June Kilbourne. Sept. 7, 1952. Route 4: FA unknown, but prior to 1937. Route 5: Galen Rowell. Aug. 1970. Route 6: Oliver Kehrlein, Tyler Van Degrift, and Chester Versteeg. July 17, 1936.

Mt. Corcoran. High point: Howard Gates. 1933. South summit: R.S. Fink. July 20, 1938. Sharktooth, west side: Sierra Club group. 1960s. Sharktooth, east side: Galen Rowell. Aug. 1970.

The Miter. R.S. Fink. July 18, 1938. Chute: Donald Clarke (probably).

Mt. Pickering. Chester Versteeg, Tyler Van Degrift, and Oliver Kehrlein. July 1936.

Joe Devel Peak. Wheeler Survey party. Sept. 20, 1875. Southeast arete: Owen Williams. 1937.

Mt. Guyot. William Wallace. 1881.

The Major General. Chester and Elizabeth Versteeg. Aug. 1937.

Mt. Langley. FA unknown, but prior to 1871. North face: Howard Gates and Nelson Nies. Aug. 1937.

Index

Notes

Notes